Supporting the Physical Health Needs of People with Learning Disabilities

A handbook for professionals, support staff and families

Edited by Steve Hardy,
Eddie Chaplin and Peter Woodward

Pavilion

Supporting the Physical Health Needs of People with Learning Disabilities
A handbook for professionals, support staff and families

© Pavilion Publishing and Media, on behalf of the authors

The authors have asserted their rights in accordance with the Copyright, Designs and Patents Act (1988) to be identified as the authors of this work.

Published by:
Pavilion Publishing and Media Ltd
Rayford House
School Road
Hove
East Sussex
BN3 5HX
Tel: 01273 434 943
Fax: 01273 227 308
Email: info@pavpub.com

Published 2016

A catalogue record for this book is available from the British Library.

ISBN: 978-1-910366-25-7
EPDF ISBN: 978-1-910366-26-4
EPUB ISBN: 978-1-910366-27-1
MOBI ISBN: 978-1-910366-28-8

Pavilion is the leading training and development provider and publisher in the health, social care and allied fields, providing a range of innovative training solutions underpinned by sound research and professional values. We aim to put our customers first, through excellent customer service and value.

Editors: Steve Hardy, Eddie Chaplin and Peter Woodward
Production editor: Ruth Chalmers, Pavilion Publishing and Media Ltd
Cover design: Tony Pitt, Pavilion Publishing and Media Ltd
Page layout and typesetting: Phil Morash, Pavilion Publishing and Media Ltd
Printing: CMP Digital Print Solutions

Contents

About the authors

Dave Atkinson

Dave currently works as an independent consultant nurse and is also the strategic lead for learning disabilities at Lancashire Care NHS Foundation Trust. Dave has a strong background in developing and delivering services for people with challenging needs, as well as supporting initiatives across the UK which aim to address the health inequalities experienced by people with learning disabilities and to measure the outcomes of effective service delivery.

Jim Blair

Jim is currently a consultant nurse intellectual (learning) disabilities at Great Ormond Street Hospital in London, clinical advisor learning disabilities, NHS Healthy London Partnership and associate professor intellectual (learning) disabilities at Kingston University and St Georges' University of London, as well as clinical advisor learning disabilities, NHS England. He is also the health advisor at the British Institute of Learning Disabilities and the Learning Disability Advisor to the Sates of Jersey.

From 2008-2013 Jim was consultant nurse learning disabilities at St. George's Hospital in London. Between 2006 and 2009 he was president of the Royal Society of Medicine's council for the Forum on Intellectual Disability. From 2011-2013 Jim was vice chairman of Special Olympics Great Britain. Jim is an expert advisor to the Parliamentary Health Service Ombudsman, an advisor for the Down Syndrome Medical Interest Group and is on the editorial board of www. intellectualdisability.info. Jim is also a specialist clinical advisor to the Care Quality Commission.

Mark Bradley

Mark Bradley is the clinical lead for transition, working with Oxleas NHS Foundation Trust across two London boroughs. Mark has previously led on health facilitation, supporting access to primary care, acute hospital and all mainstream NHS services. During this time, he chaired the National Health Facilitation Network. Additionally, Mark has worked with the Valuing People Support Team as project lead for 'promoting equality', supporting the Department of Health's response to the 2006 Disability Rights Commission report: *Equal Treatment: Closing the Gap*. Mark is a learning disability nurse and has worked in community learning disability services for 16 years.

Lesley Brown

Lesley Brown is the professional lead for learning disability speech and language therapy in Oxleas NHS Foundation Trust. She qualified as a speech and language therapist in 1990 and has worked with children and adults with learning disabilities in a wide range of settings. She is an advanced dysphagia practitioner and an advisor on dysphagia for the Royal College of Speech and Language Therapy. She also has extensive experience working with individuals with autistic spectrum disorder and is qualified to use both the DISCO and ADOS. She has a particular interest in the practical application of the Mental Capacity Act and sits on the Oxleas Mental Capacity Act Steering Group.

Phil Boulter

Phil is a consultant nurse at Surrey and Borders Partnership NHS Foundation Trust and an Honorary Lecturer at Kingston University. He has worked in the field of learning disabilities for over 40 years and has been involved in a range of national, regional and local groups advising on learning disabilities. He has a particular interest in physical health issues.

Eddie Chaplin

Dr Eddie Chaplin is a senior lecturer at London South Bank University. He has extensive clinical experience managing and working in a range of local and national mental health services for people with learning disabilities and autism. Eddie is editor for the *Advances in Autism* and *Advances in Mental Health in Intellectual Disabilities* journals, and recently published the first guided self-help manual specifically aimed at people with intellectual disabilities and autism.

Sarah Clayton

Sarah started working with families whose children were using night time positioning in 1998, and this work was published in *Physiotherapy* in 2000. In 2004 she co-wrote the accredited postural care courses using her skills as a fully qualified teacher. Sarah has worked with national charities such as In Control working to support their partners in policymaking and related family leadership courses since 2004. During 2010 she was shortlisted for an Accolade Award for a partnership project with Skills for Health for Most Effective Practice in Workforce Development.

In 2010 she co-wrote *The Patterns of Body Shape Distortion* with John Goldsmith, published within *Tizard Learning Disability Review*.

In September 2007 Sarah's oldest daughter Abigail was diagnosed with a malignant brain tumour aged just six, and she has undergone extensive treatment. Abi is now 15 and continues to do well with great support at school.

Sarah currently leads a fantastic team at Simple Stuff Works to develop and deliver their nationally accredited courses in postural care alongside their multi award winning equipment range.

Hayley Goleniowska

Hayley's ignorance of Down's syndrome came to the fore when her daughter was born, motivating her to create world-renowned blog Downs Side Up. It challenges fear and stigma and celebrates the narratives of those with the condition.

The award-winning website is part of the greater work Hayley does toward inclusion of those with a learning disability. Her daughter Natty was the first UK model with a disability to feature in a national Back to School campaign as she believes we all need to see ourselves represented in the media.

Publishing a beautiful book for children and support material for new families, writing for various publications, taking part in a BBC documentary, giving countless interviews and working alongside the NHS to ensure medical professionals value everyone's worth equally, Hayley ensures diversity in a gentle, heartfelt way.

Mark Gray

Mark is an independent consultant learning disability nurse specialising in dual sensory loss.

He was formerly the RNIB Multiple Disability Service training research and development officer from 1990 to 2005. He is a visiting tutor in Rehabilitation Studies Visual Impairment at Birmingham City University and runs a health and social care service providing, consultancy, training and personal budget support services. He is widely published and is an editor for several professional journals, a Nursing Times award Judge, and chair of the National Advocacy Charity POhWER.

Renée Francis

Renée Francis has been a registered learning disability nurse since 1997. She is the course director of the BSc (Hons) Learning Disability Nursing at London South Bank University. Her special interests are palliative care of people with intellectual disabilities, participatory research with people with intellectual disabilities and supporting families of people with intellectual disabilities. She is also interested in interprofessional learning and ensuring key messages about the health of people with intellectual disabilities are delivered across the nursing and midwifery curriculum.

Steve Hardy

Steve Hardy qualified as a learning disability nurse in 1994 and has worked in both clinical and educational settings. He is currently a nurse consultant in learning disabilities at Oxleas NHS Foundation Trust. Sharing news, information and developing resources is his keen passion. He is widely published in the mental health needs of people with learning disabilities, capacity and facilitating a platform for people with learning disabilities to be heard.

Jane Hart

Jane Hart has 21 years' experience as a registered learning disability nurse; 15 of which were spent as a nurse manager in residential services supporting people with learning disabilities, their families and carers, which has continued over the past six years in her role as community learning disability nurse with Oxleas NHS Foundation trust. Her professional interests focus on facilitating access to primary health care helping to prevent hospital admissions and supporting people when admitted to hospital by working with wards for better outcomes and safe discharge planning.

Crispin Hebron

Crispin is currently seconded to NHS England where he leads on health inequalities for people with learning disabilities and also works as a consultant nurse in a Mental Health and Learning Disability Foundation Trust in Gloucestershire. He has previously worked in the NHS and third sector in a range of nursing, project and leadership roles. He contributed as an investigator to the confidential inquiry into premature deaths in people with learning disability published in 2013, run by the Norah Fry research centre at Bristol University. He is part of the current National NHS IT review team and has published various articles and book chapters focusing on health issues, inequalities and the delivery of effective services for people with learning disabilities.

Tony Hollands

Tony Hollands, epilepsy nurse specialist, is currently employed in the Adult Learning Disability Epilepsy Service in Bromley, South East London, part of Oxleas NHS Foundation Trust. His background is in learning disability care since 1982. Then in 2003 he completed the MSc in Epileptology at Kings College and focused increasingly on epilepsy care for people with learning disabilities. He then gained experience as an epilepsy nurse in a neurology team at a district general hospital in Kent, before moving into his current post.

Daniel Marsden

Daniel Marsden (Twitter @dmarsden49) is a practice development nurse for people with learning disabilities in East Kent Hospitals NHS Foundation Trust. Having studied at the University of Brighton and Canterbury Christchurch University, Daniel has recently undertaken a participatory action research study relating to My Healthcare Passport, and is currently writing up the results for publication. He also has an article pertaining to EKHUFT 4C Framework for making reasonable adjustments in press. Daniel has spoken internationally on harnessing technology to support the delivery of person centred care for vulnerable adults, which resulted in short listings for Nurse of the Year and the Patient Safety Improvement Nursing Times Award 2013. Daniel regularly lectures at Canterbury Christchurch University and the University of Kent on a variety of subjects, and over the last three years has established a regional community of practice which has successfully generated income.

Daniel recently featured in Health Education England's #inspiringleadersinld campaign and is a founder of @WeLDNurses a two weekly twitter chat for learning disabilities nurses. Daniel is particularly interested in clinical systems leadership and digital facilitation and remains enthusiastic for being a critical companion or offering mentorship to anyone in the clinical leadership programme and the aspiring consultant practitioner programme.

Karina Marshall-Tate

Karina Marshall-Tate is a learning disability nurse who has led and managed national specialist inpatient and community services for people with learning disabilities with additional mental illness or behaviours that challenge. She currently leads an education and training project for healthcare staff who do not usually work in the field with the aim of increasing clinician confidence and capability and improving health outcomes for people with a learning disability.

Karina qualified as an RNLD from the University of Southampton in 2000. She has a BSc in Mental Health Work (University of Greenwich, 2003), using adapted psychosocial interventions for psychosis for people with learning disabilities and she is currently studying for an MSc in Advanced Clinical Practice at King's College London. Karina is a national steering committee member of the Royal College of Nursing Learning Disability Forum.

Marian Marsham

Marian Marsham is clinical lead for health access with Oxleas NHS Foundation Trust. She has 25 years' experience working with adults and children with learning disabilities, across a range of settings and roles. Marian has a passion for promoting excellent practice and cites her professional interest as 'making things better by enabling people to be their best'. In addition to writing about nurse education and accessing healthcare she has published research into the therapeutic role of community learning disability nurses.

Gwen Moulster

Gwen Moulster OBE (MA, Cert Ed, RNLD) is an independent consultant nurse and honorary senior fellow with the Faculty of Health, Social Care & Education, Kingston University and St George's, University of London. She is co-chair of the UK Learning Disability Consultant Nurse Network and a member of the UK steering group for modernising learning disabilities nursing.

Gwen has extensive experience of working closely with people who have learning disabilities, families, advocates and others to improve the quality of health experiences and outcomes. She is part of the team who developed the Health Equalities Framework (HEF), including presenting this with colleagues at conferences across the UK and in Australia and Finland.

Gwen has also been instrumental in the development and implementation of the Moulster & Griffiths model for learning disabilities nursing and pain profiles for people with profound and multiple learning disabilities.

Laurence Taggart

Laurence Taggart is a registered nurse for people with intellectual disability and a research psychologist. He works in the Institute of Nursing & Health Research, Ulster University, where he leads the Centre of Intellectual & Developmental Disabilities. Laurence is the 2013-2016 president of the Royal Society of

Medicine Intellectual Disability Forum and current chair of the Health SIRG of IASSIDD (International Association for the Scientific Study of Intellectual and Developmental Disabilities). Laurence's main interests focus on the health of people with intellectual disabilities.

Maria Truesdale

Dr Maria Truesdale is a lecturer in learning disabilities within the School of Health and Social Care at Edinburgh Napier University, Scotland. Having spent over a decade as a research psychologist in the field of learning disability her interests lie within the health of people with learning disabilities. She is an associate member of the Centre for Intellectual and Developmental Disabilities at Ulster University and is a member of the Health Special Interest Research Group of IASSIDD (International Association for the Scientific Study of Intellectual and Developmental Disabilities).

Sue Turner

Sue Turner trained as a nurse for people with learning disabilities in Bristol, and has worked within and managed a variety of services for people with learning disabilities. Sue was the Valuing People Lead in the South West Region for four and a half years. When she joined the National Development Team for Inclusion (NDTi) she led on the Improving Health and Lives (IHaL) Learning Disabilities Health Observatory project for three years. She now leads on learning disabilities for the NDTi, and is a co-director of IHaL.

Sally Wilson

Sally is an experienced RNLD working in an acute hospital as matron for older adults and safeguarding lead. Prior to taking this post she worked in an acute liaison role for five years. Her previous experience includes residential and nursing homes, managing respite, assessment and treatment unit and she has worked with all age groups from children to older adults.

Twenty years after first working with people with learning disabilities Sally is still passionate about all things to do with learning disability care.

She is a founder member of Team @WeLDNurses, which runs a fortnightly twitter chat for LD professionals, and there are other platforms including use of a Facebook page to support the sharing and dissemination of innovation and best practice examples within the field of LD nursing. Through this work, undertaken as a volunteer, Sally remains committed to improving networking opportunities and the use of social media for people in LD care. Sally is currently studying for her Masters in advanced nursing studies.

Peter Woodward

Peter Woodward is a senior lecturer in learning disabilities at the University of Greenwich. His background is in challenging behaviour, mental health and forensic behaviours as well as the physical health of people with learning disabilities.

Introduction

People with learning disabilities are more likely to suffer from poor physical and mental health compared with the general population. They are likely to face health inequalities and live shorter lives. They are also two and a half times more likely to have multiple health needs than other people. The reasons for this are complex. People with learning disabilities are more likely to be affected by genetic conditions and syndromes, as well as neurological conditions such as epilepsy and developmental disorders such as autism. In addition to physical illness, people with learning disabilities have higher rates of physical disabilities (particularly those with severe and profound learning disabilities). As a result, they may need additional support for a variety of physical and psychological impairments including poor mobility or restricted movement, or sensory impairments such as poor hearing or sight. A number of people may also have physical health issues that have arisen due to lifestyle choices or having a routine imposed upon them. An example would be obesity, which increases the risk of conditions such as heart disease and diabetes.

Social disadvantage experienced by people with learning disabilities compared with the general population may also contribute to increased rates of physical and mental ill health. This can include increased levels of hardship, deprivation and abuse from others (for example hate crime, physical and sexual abuse and neglect). People with learning disabilities are also less likely to engage outside of familiar circles. This may affect quality of life because integration and inclusion are then limited and opportunities often missed. A lack of support may mean that people are unaware of and therefore less likely to access health services.

Reasonable adjustments are often required to improve access to services and the patient experience. This is necessary if we are to achieve equality in healthcare. Often clinicians, by their own admission, lack awareness of how illness may present in people with learning disabilities. They may also lack the skills necessary to capture the person's experience and health concerns accurately. This is required to build a picture of their health needs and any health risks they may be vulnerable to. A lack of awareness of the health needs of people with learning disabilities on the part of healthcare workers will often lead to a negative experience of healthcare. Often people with learning disabilities will have difficulty reporting their health needs or describing their experiences. They may also get frustrated in trying to express and articulate their feelings. This makes assessment more difficult for healthcare workers to complete, and often symptoms may be missed. This can be worsened if the person is non-verbal or if symptoms are expressed through changes in behaviour e.g. a person might injure themself if they are in pain. The difficulty in accessing healthcare extends to health prevention and health education programmes, as well regular general health checks, which are also seen at lower rates than the general population. However, there is evidence that in areas where reasonable adjustments are made, people with learning disabilities may access services (such as screening) at higher rates than the general population. Collaboration and co-ordination between health agencies for people with learning disabilities is generally poor, although this situation can vary greatly within different health trusts.

Our aim is to simplify what can be a complex area in order to improve understanding of how to meet an individual's physical health needs. This book provides a practical guide to a range of physical illnesses and health needs and how to support people with these conditions. Physical ill health can have a negative effect on general well-being and may lead to poor mental health. The book also covers mental health and mental well-being, as often people can miss the psychological issues that may arise in tandem with physical ill-health and may be missed.

We hope you enjoy this book, which explores these issues from a number of perspectives, including the point of view of people with learning disabilities and their carers, who bear the brunt of these inequalities.

Eddie Chaplin, Steve Hardy and Peter Woodward

Part I
Health inequalities

Chapter 1: Reasonable adjustments

Sue Turner

Introduction

People with learning disabilities experience poorer health than the general population, and die younger. As there are things that can be done to improve the health of this group, these differences in health status are called health inequalities (Emerson *et al*, 2012). Health inequalities can be due to a number of different factors, including where people live, unemployment, social isolation and problems with accessing services, including health services. Under The Equality Act (2010), health services have a duty to address inequalities by making reasonable adjustments so that disabled people, including people with learning disabilities, are not disadvantaged when using them.

What are reasonable adjustments?

Reasonable adjustments are the changes or adjustments services should make so that they are easier for disabled people to access. Making buildings more accessible by installing ramps, lifts and wide doorways are obvious physical examples. Services may also make changes to procedures, such as routinely sending out easy read appointment letters, so that their services are generally more accessible. However, for many people with learning disabilities, reasonable adjustments need to be individually tailored to meet their needs, for example, ensuring people have the first appointment so they do not have to wait in a crowded waiting room. Tools such as hospital or communication passports can be helpful as they include detailed information about individuals, including the reasonable adjustments they need in order to be able to access services. The duty to make reasonable adjustments is anticipatory, so services should consider in advance the adjustments needed and plan to put these in place (Hatton *et al*, 2011). This chapter will look at some of the reasonable adjustments that can be made across health services, along with the potential they have to improve the health and well-being of people with learning disabilities.

Being aware of people with learning disabilities

Unless people with learning disabilities are identified by health systems, it is difficult to plan ahead for the support they may need. The Confidential Inquiry into Premature Deaths of People with Learning Disabilities (CIPOLD) found that GP referrals did not always state whether a person had learning disabilities or include information on their needs (Heslop *et al*, 2013). Hospital flagging systems to identify people with learning disabilities are also far from comprehensive, so hospital staff may not know when someone with learning disabilities is being admitted and therefore cannot plan for reasonable adjustments to be put in place.

Making appointments

Without reasonable adjustments, people with learning disabilities can find it hard to book appointments and navigate their way through health systems. Phone systems can be difficult to use, as can computerised booking systems like 'Choose and Book'. CIPOLD found that appointment letters were often difficult for people with learning disabilities to read, as were instructions regarding what to do before an appointment. Failure to follow instructions often meant that appointments had to be rebooked, resulting in wasted time and money, as well as seriously disadvantaging the individuals with learning disabilities. People with learning disabilities may not understand the reason for their appointment, and may be afraid of health professionals and health procedures. Once people arrive for their appointment, waiting rooms can be busy and confusing and people with learning disabilities can find it difficult to wait. However, some simple adjustments can improve the outcomes for people with learning disabilities, as illustrated by this example from Public Health England:

> *'The primary care liaison nurses were advised about an individual with learning disabilities who repeatedly did not attend GP appointments …*
> *The individual lived in a supported living environment with intermittent carers and he was unable to read his mail. The liaison nurse arranged for easy read letters to be used in place of the standard GP letters. They also ensured a copy of the letter was sent to the individual's keyworker who took on the role of co-ordinating health appointments for the person. The person has since attended all health appointments and as a result his health needs have been diagnosed and better managed.'*
> (Public Health England, 2014)

Going to the doctor

The first place most people go with a health problem is to their GP, who also acts as a gateway to other health services. However, people with learning disabilities may not know that they are unwell, or may find it difficult to tell people that they are in pain or do not feel 'right'. As a result, people with learning disabilities often have unmet health needs, ranging from life-threatening illnesses to conditions such as constipation and excess ear wax (Robertson *et al*, 2010). In England, Wales and Northern Ireland, a system for the provision of annual health checks has been put in place. The health check should include height, weight and blood pressure checks, what vaccinations the person has had, a record of screening, checks for common illnesses, a review of any medication the person may be taking and a note of any changes in their behaviour. *A Step by Step Guide for GP Practices* (Hoghton & RCGP Learning Disabilities Group, 2010) provides guidance about health checks along with a template of what to include. The guide also includes templates for syndrome-specific checks. Health checks are designed to identify unmet health needs, and are an important reasonable adjustment that primary care services can make to reduce health inequalities.

Providing health checks can also help increase understanding among primary care professionals of the health needs of people with learning disabilities, and improve awareness of the role of community learning disabilities teams (Public Health England, 2014). Some learning disabilities nurses work mainly with primary care services to improve access for people with learning disabilities. They are often called health facilitators or primary care liaison nurses and can help GP practices improve identification of people with learning disabilities as well as supporting them with making appropriate reasonable adjustments.

Health screening

People with learning disabilities access health screening at a lower rate than people in the general population. This is in part due to a failure to implement reasonable adjustments, including a failure to identify people with learning disabilities within screening programmes. As a result, health problems like early-stage cancers may not be picked up until they become difficult to treat. Education and support for professionals, family carers and people with learning disabilities can improve participation, along with partnership working between community learning disabilities teams, primary care and screening services (Turner *et al*, 2013). In Cornwall, screening liaison nurses have been employed, and they facilitate the implementation of reasonable adjustments, as the following case study about breast screening illustrates:

'The screening nurse contacts the woman's GP and then directly contacts the woman. She talks to them about whether they are happy to attend the screening and if there is any practical or emotional support they need. For a first invitation she will always visit the woman to talk about the process, take pictorial information and can offer support with a pre-visit. She will liaise with the Breast Screening Service about any arrangements required. She also supports GP practices to provide good information and has provided learning disability awareness training to the breast screening staff.'
(Turner *et al*, 2013, p19)

Going to hospital

Where possible, hospital care should be planned in advance. This means that any reasonable adjustments the individual needs can be put in place, increasing the likelihood of a successful admission and treatment. One important reasonable adjustment for hospitals is employing a learning disability acute liaison nurse. These nurses now work in many hospitals and support ward staff to understand individuals' needs and facilitate pathways into and out of hospital. Hospitals that employ acute liaison nurses have been found to be better able to provide safe, good quality care to people with learning disabilities, than those that do not (Tuffrey Wijne *et al*, 2013).

The following case study is taken from the *Working Together* guide. It demonstrates the difference a liaison nurse can make to the quality of care and eventual outcome:

'Edana complained of stomach aches and was referred to a hospital specialist. They tried to do a scan, but she was afraid of the machine and would not lie still, so it was abandoned. Edana lost a lot of weight; she was anaemic and very unwell. She was referred to another specialist and this time the learning disability liaison nurse was asked to help support Edana to have the scan she required. The nurse showed Edana and her family some easy read materials about having a scan and took her into the scanner to have a look round, test out the bed and meet the staff. Edana was much more relaxed when she came for the actual scan; the scan was successful and her illness was diagnosed. She required surgery, so a similar process took place to prepare her: she visited the anaesthetic room and the recovery ward, understood why people wore particular clothing and masks and became familiar with what would happen. Edna's surgery and hospital stay were subsequently a positive experience for her and her family.'
(Public Health England, 2015, p22)

Many people with learning disabilities are afraid of health services and health professionals, perhaps because of past experiences (Heslop *et al*, 2013). The *Working Together* guide (Public Health England, 2015) suggests creating a hospital passport or similar document setting out how the person needs to be supported prior to admission, and ensuring that hospital staff know about the document and understand how to use it. Visiting the hospital and meeting key staff before admission can also be helpful. When in hospital, staff should continue to work with family members and support staff who know the individual well, as they can provide crucial information and support to enable a good outcome. However, it is important that carers' needs are also considered when planning a hospital stay. Hospitals should have a protocol for carers, including information on facilities for washing, eating, sleeping, parking and other support (Turner & Robinson, 2011). Planning for discharge is also important, particularly if the person's needs will have changed.

How can families and health and social care staff help ensure the right reasonable adjustments are in place?

Families and health and social care staff need to know that reasonable adjustments are not an optional extra but a legal requirement that people with learning disabilities have a right to, so they can advocate for them if necessary. It is important to check that the person is flagged on health systems so that staff can plan in advance to make the reasonable adjustments the person needs. Having detailed records of the support people need in the form of hospital passports or similar documents is really helpful when planning for health appointments/admissions. Families, support staff, specialist and mainstream health staff all have important roles to play in ensuring people receive the best possible healthcare, so working in partnership and listening to those that know the person best are crucial. There are many websites that provide examples of reasonable adjustments that can be used or adapted, such as:

- Public Health England's reasonable adjustments database: www.improvinghealthandlives.org.uk/adjustments

- Easyhealth: www.easyhealth.org.uk

- NHS A Picture of Health: www.apictureofhealth.southwest.nhs.uk

Conclusion

There are numerous examples of reasonable adjustments being implemented across health services to improve access for people with learning disabilities. Some of these can be implemented at a service level and others need to be individually tailored. Sharing good practice can help health staff understand what is possible, but there is not yet a widespread culture of making reasonable adjustments (Mencap, 2012). The implementation of reasonable adjustments could potentially benefit not just people with learning disabilities, but others who find it hard to access services, including people with autism and people with dementia.

Summary points

- Reasonable adjustments are a legal requirement.

- Identifying people with learning disabilities in health systems can help services implement the right reasonable adjustments.

- Individual documentation such as hospital passports can help health staff provide the right support for people with learning disabilities.

- It is helpful if people with learning disabilities, family members, and health and social care staff work in partnership so that the right reasonable adjustments are implemented.

- It is often possible to use or adapt reasonable adjustments that have already been implemented elsewhere, including easy read information that has already been published.

References

Emerson E, Baines S, Allerton L & Welsh V (2012) *Health Inequalities and People with Learning Disabilities in the UK: 2012* [online]. London: Improving Health and Lives & Department of Health. Available at: www.ihal.org.uk/publications/1165/Health_Inequalities_&_People_with_Learning_Disabilities_in_the_UK:_2012 (accessed October 2016).

Hatton C, Roberts H & Baines S (2011) *Reasonable Adjustments for People with Learning Ddisabilities in England: A national survey of NHS Trusts* [online]. London: Improving Health and Lives. Available at: www.ihal.org.uk/publications/947/Reasonable_Adjustments (accessed October 2016).

Heslop P, Blair P, Fleming P, Hoghton M, Marriott A & Russ L (2013) *Confidential Inquiry into Premature Deaths of People with Learning Disabilities (CIPOLD): Final report* [online]. Bristol: Norah Fry. Available at: www.bris.ac.uk/media-library/sites/cipold/migrated/documents/fullfinalreport.pdf (accessed October 2016).

Hoghton M & RCGP Learning Disabilities Group (2010) *A Step by Step Guide for GP Practices: Annual health checks for people with a learning disability* [online]. London: Royal College of General Practitioners. Available at: http://www.rcgp.org.uk/learningdisabilities (accessed October 2016).

Mencap (2012) *Death by Indifference: 74 deaths and counting – a progress report 5 years on* [online]. London: Mencap. Available at: https://www.mencap.org.uk/sites/default/files/2016-08/Death%20by%20 Indifference%20-%2074%20deaths%20and%20counting.pdf (accessed October 2016).

Public Health England (2014) *Learning Disabilities Self-assessment Framework 2013: Personal experiences – staying healthy* [online]. Available at: www.ihal.org.uk/publications/1232/Joint_Health_ and_Social_Care_Self-Assessment_Framework_2013:_Personal_Experiences_-_Staying_healthy (accessed October 2016).

Public Health England (2015) *Working Together 2: Easy steps to improve support for people with learning disabilities in hospital* [online]. Available at: www.ihal.org.uk/publications/1247/Working_ together_2:_Easy_steps_to_improve_support_for_people_with_learning_disabilities_in_hospital (accessed October 2016).

Robertson J, Roberts H & Emerson E (2010) *Health Checks for People with Learning Disabilities: A systematic review of the evidence* [online]. Available at: http://www.improvinghealthandlives.org.uk/ uploads/doc/vid_7646_IHAL2010-04HealthChecksSystemticReview.pdf (accessed October 2016).

Tuffrey Wijne I, Giatras N, Goulding L & Abraham E (2013) Identifying the factors affecting the implementation of strategies to promote a safer environment for patients with learning disabilities in NHS hospitals: a mixed-methods study. *Health Services and Delivery Research* **1** (13).

Turner S, Giraud-Saunders A & Marriott A (2013) *Improving the Uptake of Screening Services by People with Learning Disabilities across the South West Peninsula: A strategy and toolkit* [online]. Bath: National Development Team for Inclusion & Norah Fry Research Centre. Available at: http:// www.ndti.org.uk/publications/ndti-publications/screening-services-strategy-and-toolkit (accessed October 2016).

Turner S & Robinson R (2011) *Reasonable Adjustments for People with Learning Disabilities: Implications and actions for commissioners and providers of healthcare. Evidence into practice report no. 3* [online]. London: Improving Health and. Available at: www.ihal.org.uk/publications/964/ Reasonable_Adjustments_for_People_with_Learning_Disabilities:_Implications_and_Actions_for_ Commissioners_and_Providers_of_Health_Care (accessed October 2016).

Chapter 2: Promoting health equality: health inequalities and people with learning disabilities

Gwen Moulster, Crispin Hebron,
Phil Boulter and Dave Atkinson

Health inequalities are preventable and unjust differences in health status experienced by certain population groups. It has long been known that people with learning disabilities have poorer health than the general population, but the extent of these differences becomes strikingly obvious when one considers the evidence of reduced life expectancy. In 2013 the Confidential Inquiry into the Premature Deaths of People with Learning Disabilities (Heslop *et al*, 2013) reported that men typically die 13 years younger and women 20 years younger than the general population. In 42% of cases the death was considered premature, meaning that if things had been done differently the person would likely have lived for at least another year.

There is also clear evidence of increased rates of many serious health problems among people with learning disabilities (Emerson *et al*, 2012):

- Regular health screenings typically reveal high levels of unmet needs.
- There is high prevalence of *Helicobacter pylori*, a bacterial infection associated with a range of gastrointestinal cancers.
- Almost half of all people with Down's syndrome have congenital heart defects.
- Respiratory disease accounts for almost three times as many deaths of people with learning disabilities as in the general population.
- There is evidence of increased rates of diabetes.
- People with learning disabilities are 14 times more likely to have musculoskeletal impairments.

- Sensory impairments are significantly more prevalent.

- People with learning disabilities are at increased risk of chronic pain conditions, which can be difficult for carers to recognise.

- Dementia is significantly more common and can occur at younger ages.

- The prevalence of epilepsy is reported to be at least 20 times higher than in the general population.

- There is also evidence that sleep disorders, mental health problems, swallowing difficulties, gastro-oesophageal reflux and constipation are more common.

The wider determinants of health inequality

The specific causes of health inequalities are varied. They include lifestyle factors, such as smoking, poor nutrition, inadequate exercise, and wider social, economic and environmental factors such as poverty, squalid housing, poor education and inaccessible services. Collectively, these are referred to as the determinants of health inequality. In essence, determinants of health inequality are risk factors: exposure to these can have a serious negative impact on health and equality.

Roy's story: part 1

Roy was a 64-year-old man with moderate learning disabilities and dementia. Normally he had a keen interest in public transport, enjoyed listening to music, and liked to visit his local pub for fish and chips.

Roy began experiencing unexplained weight loss and changes in his behaviour. He was living in a small flat where a support worker visited for four hours each day. He was becoming increasingly withdrawn and verbally aggressive towards his support worker. Roy was completely isolated; he had no known family and had lost contact with all of his friends since the changes in his behaviour. He had stopped going out.

Roy had not seen a doctor for several years. He had not had an annual health check, or any other routine health screenings. When Roy eventually saw a doctor, he was diagnosed with terminal prostate cancer.

In this example it is evident that Roy was suffering from the impact of a number of health inequalities. He had become socially isolated, was not accessing healthcare and was not doing any of the activities that he usually enjoyed. The impact of the determinants of health inequality experienced by Roy resulted in late diagnosis of a potentially treatable terminal illness.

In 2010 the Marmot Review reported on evidence of the relationships between health and wider social and economic conditions, and noted the importance of national policy in achieving health improvements:

'The causes of health inequality are complex but they do not arise by chance. The social, economic and environmental conditions in which we live strongly influence health. These conditions are known as the social determinants of health, and are largely the results of public policy.'
Marmot, 2010, p85-91)

Reducing health inequalities has been a major focus of public policy within the UK for many years and is the legitimate focus of public health services. Public health has been defined as:

'The science and art of preventing disease, prolonging life and promoting health through the organised efforts and informed choices of society.'
(Wanless, 2004, p3)

Public health approaches are inherently population-based: they emphasise a collective responsibility for health, its protection and disease prevention; recognise the key role of the state in seeking to address underlying socioeconomic and wider determinants of health, as well as disease; and emphasise partnerships with all who contribute to the health of the population.

Reducing health inequalities for people with learning disabilities

The differing patterns of ill-health and specific challenges experienced by people with learning disabilities clearly require a public health strategy that targets the needs of this vulnerable group. A sustained and growing impetus to improve the health of people with learning disabilities in the UK has been driven by the campaigning of Mencap (2007; 2012), which has highlighted numerous instances where people's health has been compromised and premature deaths have resulted from poor patterns of service delivery and institutional discrimination. In England, in response to these concerns, an independent inquiry as well as parliamentary and health service ombudsman and local government ombudsman investigations have made numerous recommendations, many of which were subsequently incorporated into English health and social care policy (Department of Health, 2009). Key initiatives have included the creation of a learning disabilities public health observatory, the introduction of annual health checks for people with learning disabilities, and a self-assessment framework, whereby all districts provide annual assurances of progress made in terms of improving the quality of healthcare for people with learning disabilities and reducing inequality.

Across the other UK countries, a range of similar initiatives have been developed in response to a recognition of the need to improve the health outcomes experienced by people with learning disabilities (Department of Health, Social Services and Public Safety, 2013; Scottish Government, 2013; Public Health Wales, 2014).

In England, the Improving Health and Lives Learning Disabilities Observatory (IHaL) was set up in 2010. A similar observatory has been commissioned by the Scottish Government. IHaL has produced a series of guides for providers and commissioners of mainstream healthcare services, which advise on making reasonable adjustments to pathways of care for people with learning disabilities. Areas of focus for these guides include epilepsy, end of life care, primary care, dementia, eye care, dentistry and cancer screening.

IHAL has also published a series of systematic reviews that examine the nature, extent and causes of health inequalities experienced by people with learning disabilities (Emerson *et al*, 2011; 2012). These reports suggest that there are five broad determinants of health inequality for people with learning disabilities, which are potentially amenable to intervention (see Box 2.1).

Box 2.1: The five determinants of health inequality for people with learning disabilities

1. Increased risk of exposure (and possibly greater vulnerability when exposed) to well-established 'social determinants' of poorer health

2. Increased risk associated with specific genetic and biological causes of learning disabilities

3. Communication difficulties and reduced health 'literacy'

4. Personal health risks and behaviours

5. Deficiencies in access to and the quality of healthcare and other service provision.

In reviewing these five determinants, a clear message emerges that health inequalities should not be considered an inevitable consequence of having a learning disability. Much can be done to reduce the likelihood of health inequalities and the determinants of health inequality provide a framework from which to consider focused and co-ordinated interventions to reduce risks. Such an approach requires partnership working with all involved, especially those providing direct support.

In 2013 the Health Equalities Framework (HEF) was published by the UK Learning Disability Consultant Nurse Consultant Network (Atkinson *et al*, 2013). The HEF provides a series of graphs that indicate how high or low the likely impact of each of the determinants of health inequality is in various situations. The HEF is heavily based on the IHaL systematic reviews. It draws out 29 discrete indicators of exposure to the determinants of health inequality, thereby identifying a focus for support, intervention and indeed for public health policy. Where these measures can either reduce exposure to the determinants, or mitigate any effects of continuing exposure (where it cannot be reduced further), then people with learning disabilities would likely have a life expectancy and quality of life that would be more akin to people with similar health problems in the general population.

Actions to support people with learning disabilities in tackling health inequalities

The following presents some key considerations when supporting people with learning disabilities along with some questions you can ask yourself in regard to the people you support.

Accessing healthcare

People with learning disabilities should have access to regular health checks. Where they have a long-term condition they should be supported to access the appropriate care pathways. People should have excellent, robust and evidence-based health action plans. Hospital passports should be used to plan for unforeseen health emergencies. Where people take medication, it should be closely monitored and regularly reviewed. There should be provision for access to specialist learning disability healthcare services when required.

Thoughts:
- Do the people you support have regular and effective health checks?
- Do you know all you need to about any long term conditions the people you support may have?
- Based on that knowledge, do they access all the services they need?

- Do you understand the medications prescribed for those you support and do you ensure it is reviewed?

- List three actions you can take to improve someone's health support (such as developing resources, including Easy Read on specific conditions or implementing hospital passports) and reduce exposure to this determinant area.

Communication

People may need to be supported by systems that both maximise their ability to communicate and enable those around them to recognise and respond appropriately to unusual signs or expressions of pain or discomfort. People also need to be empowered to make choices based on information that has been modified/designed in accordance with their specific communication and cognitive needs.

Thoughts:

- What support do you provide to enable the people you support to understand and communicate their health and well-being?

- How well are your support approaches known and shared by others?

- How is pain recognised, acknowledged and responded to?

- Is this known by everyone who needs to?

- List three actions you can take to improve someone's communication (such as developing a pain picture or social stories) and reduce exposure to this determinant area.

Lifestyle

People need support to have healthy nutritious diets which may require modifications taking account of health conditions. They may need support to drink sufficient fluids. People should be helped to engage in physical exercise as a 'lifestyle activity'. Maintaining a healthy weight can have a major impact in terms of reducing health inequalities. People who habitually use hazardous substances (eg. alcohol or tobacco) may need specialist support to remain within safe limits.

Thoughts:

- Think about the behaviour of the people you support and how this might be impacting on their health and well-being.

■ List three actions you can take to help positively minimise the impact of such personal behaviours (such as joining a gym, recording fluid intake, reducing sugar etc.) and reduce exposure to this determinant area.

Reasonable adjustments

Mainstream services need to be well informed about the health implications of learning disabilities as well as how care and support might need to be individually adjusted to meet a person's needs. They should acknowledge their legal duty to make reasonable adjustments to care pathways. Services need to assist people to make important choices about their health and where a person lacks the capacity they need robust systems for lawfully making decisions in their best interests. Wherever a person moves between services, good co-ordination is essential. People need to have access (with support where required) to the usual range of public health screening programmes.

Thoughts:
■ Do the people you support have access to all the services they need, including screening programmes?

■ Do those services make reasonable adjustments to ensure effectiveness?

■ List three actions you can take to improve someone's access to, and outcome from, a service (such as working with services on capacity and best interest decisions) and reduce exposure to this determinant area.

■ You should have a list of 15 actions, based on your answers to the above questions, that you can proactively take forward to reduce an individual's exposure to the known determinants of health inequalities.

■ Use this list to prioritise and address actions over an agreed period of time.

■ Use the list to check back about what has been achieved.

Conclusion

This chapter has presented the evidence base for health inequalities to which people with learning disabilities are exposed. It is clear from this evidence and particularly in light of the findings of the confidential inquiry that this is an important area of focus for anyone interested in promoting the health and well-being of people with learning disabilities. The determinants of such inequalities provide a useful framework to understand risk and identify appropriate action areas. The impact of a lack of attention to these determinants and their consequences is demonstrated through the case study, which provides an example of the difference that can be made by paying due attention to an individual's exposure to health inequalities and its determinants. Finally, key actions are identified with suggestions to get started on addressing some of these important areas.

Summary points

- Public health approaches emphasise a collective responsibility for health, its protection and disease prevention.

- Health inequalities are preventable and unjust differences in health status.

- Men with learning disabilities typically die 13 years younger and women with learning disabilities 20 years younger than the general population.

- Health inequalities should not be considered an inevitable consequence of having a learning disability and much can be done to reduce the likelihood and impact of health inequalities.

References

Atkinson D, Boulter P, Hebron C & Moulster G (2013) *The Health Equalities Framework. An outcomes framework based on the determinants of health inequalities.* Bristol: NDTi & UKLDCNN.

Department of Health (2009) *Valuing People Now.* London: DH.

Department of Health, Social Services and Public Safety (2013) *Learning Disability Service Framework 2013–16.* Belfast: DHSSPS.

Emerson E, Baines S, Allerton L & Welch V (2011) *Health Inequalities and People with Learning Disabilities in the UK: 2011.* Lancaster: IHAL.

Emerson E, Baines S, Allerton L & Welch V (2012) *Health Inequalities and People with Learning Disabilities in the UK: 2012.* London: Improving Health and Lives: Learning Disability Observatory.

Heslop P, Blair P, Fleming P, Hoghton M, Marriott A & Russ L (2013) *Confidential Inquiry into Premature Deaths of People with Learning Disabilities (CIPOLD): Final report* [online]. Bristol: Norah Fry. Available at: www.bris.ac.uk/media-library/sites/cipold/migrated/documents/fullfinalreport.pdf (accessed October 2016).

Marmot M (2010) *Fair Society, Healthy Lives: Strategic review of health inequalities in England post-2010. (The Marmot Review).* London: The Marmot Review.

Mencap (2007) *Death by Indifference: Following up the Treat Me Right! report.* London: Mencap.

Mencap (2012) *Death by Indifference: 74 deaths and counting – a progress report 5 years on.* London: Mencap.

Public Health Wales (2014) *Improving General Hospital Care of Patients Who Have a Learning Disability.* Cardiff: Public Health Wales.

Scottish Government (2013) *The Keys to Life: Improving quality of life for people with learning disabilities.* Edinburgh: Scottish Government.

Wanless D (2004) *Securing Good Health for the Whole Population: Final report.* London: HM Treasury.

Chapter 3: People with learning disabilities, the NHS and primary care

Mark Bradley

Different people with different needs, requiring different services

There are many policies and publications referring to the needs of people with learning disabilities, learning difficulties and/or special educational needs. The interchangeable use of this terminology can be confusing when we want to highlight the unique characteristics of what are very different groups, throughout different stages of life. Emerson and Heslop (2010) provide a useful working definition of learning disabilities for Public Health England, separating learning difficulties and SEN (special educational needs) from people with learning disabilities. However, if we look at published data it can be assumed that even Public Health England struggle to identify children with learning disabilities (Glover *et al*, 2011).

For the NHS and primary care, these distinctions are incredibly important. In England, the Department of Health and NHS England have commissioned investigations into the pattern of ill-health experienced by adults with learning disabilities (Michael, 2008). These investigations have confirmed the reports of poorer health and treatment, recommending improvements to NHS services that start with GPs identifying people with learning disabilities in their practice. NHS England first published changes to the general medical service contract in 2014, introducing annual health checks for people with learning disabilities from the age of 14 and this continues into 2017 (NHS England, 2016). This attempts to address the difficulties experienced by young people in transition from children's to adult services. However, the challenge is identifying the population with learning disabilities. This is confounded by interchangeable terminology. The result of this is often costly, not only in terms of managing scarce public resources, but more importantly in terms of protecting human life (Mencap, 2012).

Adults with learning disabilities requiring health and social care services will have to meet the same eligibility criteria as the rest of the population. For carers and young people preparing for adulthood, transition can be particularly difficult when it is not clear what level of support can be expected beyond education provision. For the NHS, referrals for specialist support for people with learning disabilities are expected from primary care services. Consequently, defining and identifying the population and appropriate services is key to effectively meeting the health needs of this specific group of people.

The British Psychological Society describes three core elements of learning disabilities that must be met for a person to be considered to have a learning disability (BPS, 2000):

- Significant impairment of intellectual functioning.

- Significant impairment of adaptive/social functioning.

- Age of onset before adulthood.

Within the SEN population, the education system identifies children with 'learning difficulties'. This is not a diagnosis, and it incorporates a much wider group of children and young people. According to the SEN Code of Practice, a child of compulsory school age or a young person has a learning difficulty or disability if he or she:

> '... has a significantly greater difficulty in learning than the majority of others of the same age, or has a disability which prevents or hinders him or her from making use of facilities of a kind generally provided for others of the same age in mainstream schools or mainstream post-16 institutions.' (DfE & DoH, 2015)

The SEN definition for learning difficulties does not exclusively focus on children with a measured cognitive impairment. The definition 'includes sensory impairments such as those affecting sight or hearing, and long-term health conditions such as asthma, diabetes, epilepsy, and cancer' (DfE & DoH, 2015).

In education settings, identifying children with learning difficulties (as defined in the SEN code of practice), is an effective way to provide the most inclusive and appropriate education for children and young people.

NHS paediatric services, although heavily involved in the treatment of common conditions in learning disability (for example, epilepsy, hydrocephaly or cerebral palsy) tend to favour the use of the term 'learning difficulties' rather than 'learning disabilities'. Similarly, despite being specialist multidisciplinary services equipped to assess cognitive impairments, child and adolescent mental health services (CAMHS) rarely diagnose or advise primary care services to register learning disabilities. This is because the primary reason for these services working with a child is to address risk rather than cognitive functioning.

IQ measurement and age usually support the identification of children with learning difficulties in education settings. Adaptive functioning assessments are not routinely offered. There is arguably good reason for this in earlier years, as children are less likely to present with adaptive behaviours that could be reliably measured. However, at 16 years of age, it could be argued that adaptive behaviours are possible to identify. As such, they could become a feature of the information available to adult services before the point of transition, and learning disabled children, as a specific group, may not need to remain invisible to the NHS system.

Having explored the differences in terminology and the challenges this creates for the NHS, it is useful to understand more about the NHS and, in particular, primary care and what it can do for people with learning disabilities.

What 'primary care' means for people with learning disabilities

The term 'primary care' applies to the health services people are likely to use first, that is, before they would use a hospital (secondary care) or specialist health service (tertiary care) (see Figure 3.1). The NHS Choices website describes primary care as 'the first point of contact for most people', and it includes the following services in its description:

- GPs
- dentists
- pharmacists
- optometrists
- NHS walk-in centres
- the NHS 111 telephone helpline.

In some cases, services are not directly provided by the NHS, but by private healthcare providers who have a contract with the NHS.

Figure 3.1: Primary, secondary and tertiary care services

The NHS pays for GPs to offer many services that are available to people with learning disabilities as much as anyone else, including consultations, writing prescriptions, health promotion and immunisations.

In 2006 the Disability Rights Commission examined eight million GP health records throughout England and Wales (DRC, 2006). This formal investigation into health inequalities highlighted the fact that just because services are available to people with a learning disability, it does not mean that they will be promoted appropriately or used. The evidence clearly illustrated the poorer health experienced by people with learning disabilities. Furthermore, because much of the information gathered came in electronic form, the value of having good computerised information or data relating to people with learning disabilities was strongly felt throughout the NHS and the Department of Health. The report recommended that the NHS should:

> 'Include incentives in the GP contract for evidence-based regular health checks for people with learning disabilities and / or enduring mental health problems, in line with evidence of need. Their outcomes should be audited in terms of quality and subsequent treatment.'
> (Disability Rights Commission, 2006)

Since 2006 the NHS and the Department of Health have been responding to the growing evidence that primary care services are incredibly important for people with learning disabilities. Part of this response has been the offer of additional payments for GPs to do more for their patients with a learning disability. NHS Employers introduced Learning Disability Registers in GP practices (BMA &

NHS Employers, 2006) and this was followed by further investment in annual health checks from 2009 (NHS Employers, 2011).

Identifying and understanding local health needs

People with a learning disability represent approximately 1.8% of the general population (Emerson & Hatton, 2008) and are one of the minority groups protected by the Equality Act (2010). Having this security as a vulnerable group is essential, and it reinforces the importance attached to primary care services being able to identify which of their patients require this legal protection. To date, only a small fraction of the learning disabled population has been identified by primary care services, with limited uptake for annual health checks. This is evident when looking at the figures published by Public Health England (Emerson *et al,* 2013).

Much of the evidence that highlights health inequalities (Michael, 2008) comes from sophisticated patient information systems in GP practices which electronically record and measure all health activity. As a result, it is possible to compare health outcomes between different populations. These systems record every condition or diagnosis, using a unique 'read code' for each one. There has been a code for people registered with learning disabilities since 2006. Additionally, there are codes for mental illness, heart conditions and even interventions such as health promotion advice, blood tests or referrals to other agencies. The NHS system counts these codes and their consistent use is essential in counting the types of health need and the people who have them. If a code is not recorded, people's needs are invisible to the system. For such a small minority group, the dangers of being overlooked are significant. The system will not necessarily measure the attitudes of healthcare staff but engagement with it, inviting people to be treated appropriately and counted in primary care will help demonstrate that mainstream NHS services are committed to addressing health inequality.

The introduction of annual health checks for people with learning disabilities in primary care supports the NHS system. It provides an opportunity for the needs of people with learning disabilities to be made more visible to the NHS. When seen in primary care, a person's health issues can be coded, counted and shared with local public health departments for analysis. Having enough public health resource for this analysis of data is crucial as it arguably provides the most robust means of comparing the pattern of ill-health in the learning disabled population with those who do not have a learning disability. The Learning Disability Observatory (Emerson *et al*, 2013) reports on the pattern of health need nationally. In many cases, data obtained by the observatory is gathered remotely, without local public health involvement. Whilst this can be useful, it is important for commissioners in health and social care to have a robust understanding of available local evidence, to inform their decision making regarding the use of local resources. Despite relatively recent national evidence (Heslop *et al*, 2013) highlighting health needs and the benefits of health checks in addressing these needs, progress remains slow.

The health check cycle

Exploring opportunities to improve health outcomes requires an understanding of systems beyond primary care. Often this is referred to as a 'whole system approach'. The proposed 'health check cycle' (see Figure 3.2) is an attempt at offering an explanation for the value of each step in the provision of annual health checks, from receiving an invitation from a local GP, to experiencing the development of local services that respond to a greater understanding of local need. Each element of the cycle is linked, and when each element is in place, the chances of benefiting from health checks improve significantly. However, if an element is missing, the meaning and value of health checks can be lost to people with learning disabilities and all of the services employed to support them. Figure 3.2 outlines the stages in the health check cycle.

1. **The GP offers a health check to those registered.**

Who is registered depends on local specialist services appropriately supporting the identification of people with learning disabilities from childhood. This could include providing adaptive functioning assessments within education settings to young people aged 14-16 (one of the three criteria for identifying learning disability). This would support the accuracy of GP registers, ensuring that health check are appropriately offered to those 14 years and above. The offer of a health check must be made in a format understood by the person.

2. **The health check is attended.**

Approaching the right people in the right way, and communicating at the right level prior to, during and after the health check, is vital. This will improve the chances of ensuring a health check appointment is successfully attended. This requires training to be made available to primary care staff, carers and people with learning disabilities, ensuring everyone's expectations, interests or anxieties are addressed. The training needs to include local feedback from previous health checks and health checks need to be consistently comprehensive.

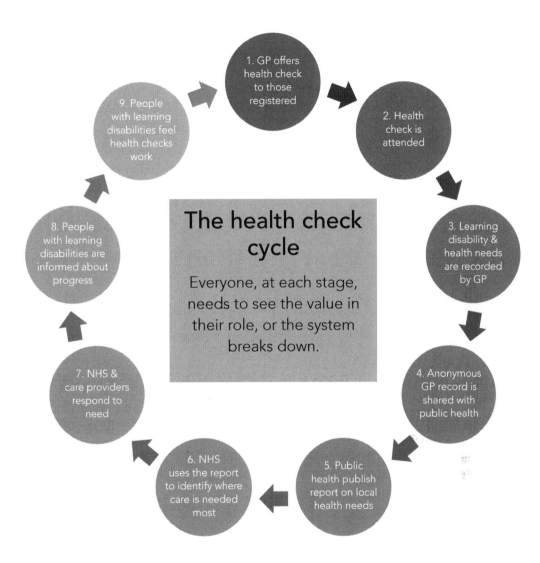

Figure 3.2: The health check cycle

3. **Learning disability and health needs are recorded by the GP.**

Those attending health checks should have a comprehensive health assessment, the results from which should be appropriately recorded on the GP practice information system. There are a variety of electronic guidelines and templates available for the different GP systems, and all of them can consolidate patient group information and produce reports.

4. An anonymous GP record is shared with public health.

Reports from GP records can be focused purely on the computer read codes that exist for every diagnosis, health condition or procedure (for example, blood tests). This information can be anonymously shared with commissioners to demonstrate compliance with an NHS contract. Local or national public health services can access this information too, in order to analyse local or national trends in the prevalence of reported health issues.

5. Public health publishes a report on local health needs.

Public health departments produce strategic reports (Joint Strategic Needs Assessments) that reflect the health needs of the local population originally identified using primary care data or codes. The more accurate the data, the better local areas can understand the health needs of the local population.

6. The NHS uses the report to identify where care is needed most.

Based on reported local evidence, senior commissioners can decide where to allocate resources and think strategically about how any trends in the prevalence of certain health issues can be best addressed. Usually this is through a commissioning plan or strategy.

7. The NHS and care providers respond to need.

Local commissioning plans prompt the NHS and care providers to design their services in a way that satisfies the needs highlighted in the public health reports and related commissioning plans. It is important to maintain the thread, ensuring the information gathered from health checks is not lost in translation – particularly as the evidence travels from the GP to the relevant public health department and then forms part of the NHS commissioning plans that shape what NHS provider services are contracted to do.

8. People with learning disabilities are informed about progress.

Part of the health check cycle involves letting people with learning disabilities know what happens with the information gathered from their health check. Consequently, local public health reports and commissioning plans need to be published in a format that is accessible to people with learning disabilities and their carers (for example, in an Easy Read format).

9. People with learning disabilities feel that health checks work.

With readily available reports, published in an Easy Read format, that explain how information from health checks impacts on local health service design, the meaning and value of health checks will have a better chance of being more successfully communicated to a greater number of people. This is an opportunity to improve the uptake of annual health checks, the quality of local data, the design of local services and ultimately the health outcomes of people with learning disabilities.

Conclusion

In order for services to know that they are getting it right for people with learning disabilities in primary care, the following conditions must be met:

- There needs to be a system in place for making sure that 'learning disabilities' means the same thing for everyone involved. There can be no room for ambiguity. The system needs to include the agencies linked to the annual health check scheme, such as social care, education and specialist health services.

- People with clearly defined 'learning disabilities' should be appropriately and accurately registered with their GP and this registration must be consistent with other care agencies, such as social care or specialist healthcare providers.

- The system needs to be successful in inviting this clearly defined and registered group to have their health checked from the age of 14. Effective and timely communication with people with learning disabilities, which fully incorporates the role of carers, is crucial.

- The health check must be thorough and consistent enough to identify all the health issues that need addressing. Differences in the comprehensiveness of health check models will give different results.

- A good health action plan that meets identified health needs must be implemented.

- There needs to be a clear mechanism by which health action plans are recorded by primary care. The recorded plans need to be produced with people with learning disabilities and their carers. They also need to include other agencies, such as community learning disabilities teams or social care, when these services are involved (having met their eligibility criteria).

- The primary care system needs to be robust enough to follow up on any health action plans, measuring and recording progress as required.

- Primary care records must be appropriately analysed, not just for GP payment purposes but for public health data collection.

- The information gathered from completed health checks should be published and shared. This should include information such as the number of people with certain health conditions – for example, heart disease, diabetes, respiratory disease etc.

■ Any trends in the pattern of ill-health must be effectively addressed by the local NHS and social care commissioners. This can include the publication and sharing of health promotion materials for people with learning disabilities and their carers. It might also include changes to the way local health or social care services are designed or delivered. For example, an increase in the number of people with epilepsy could lead to more specialist nurses in this area or specific epilepsy training being made available for people with learning disabilities and their families or carers.

■ People with learning disabilities, their carers and the services that provide support need to see results from health checks. It is important not to lose sight of the meaning of health checks from a personal, clinical and strategic perspective. It is possible to connect everything together; it just needs the right commitment.

Without a relationship that is meaningful to people with learning disabilities, their families, carers, practitioners and commissioners of services, gaps in service provision will appear. Individuals with learning disabilities need to see the value in visiting their GP practice; primary care staff need to see the value in offering comprehensive health checks; and commissioners of health and social care services need to be able to see the connection between patterns of ill-health and how they invest in services. Only then will people with learning disabilities and their carers see the benefits of their investment in attending annual health checks.

Summary points

■ Specialist support from learning disability services is needed to assist GPs in identifying people with learning disabilities who attend their practice.

■ Annual health checks should be provided for people with learning disabilities from the age of 14.

■ Those seeking health and social care provision have to meet very specific eligibility criteria that can vary by area or service, reinforcing the need for accurate diagnosis and identification of the learning disabled population.

■ It is important not to exclusively focus on cognitive impairment, but also on other needs, for example, sensory impairments such as those affecting sight or hearing, and long-term health conditions such as asthma, diabetes, epilepsy and cancer.

■ NHS paediatric services tend to favour the use of the term 'learning difficulties' rather than learning disabilities.

■ The introduction of annual health checks for people with learning disabilities provides an opportunity for the needs of the learning disabled population to be more visible to the NHS. The health check cycle provides a useful framework for this process to be meaningful at all levels of implementation, from those attending an appointment to those commissioning services for them.

References

British Medical Association & NHS Employers (2006) *Revisions to the GMS contract 2006/7*. BMA & NHS Employers: London.

British Psychological Society (2000) *Learning Disability: Definitions and contexts*. Leicester: The British Psychological Society.

Department for Education & Department of Health (2015) *Special Educational Needs and Disability Code of Practice: 0-25 years*. Department for Education.

Disability Rights Commission (2006) *Equal Treatment: Closing the gap*. Stratford-upon-Avon: DRC.

Emerson & Hatton (2008) *People with Learning Disabilities in England*. Lancaster: Centre for Disability Research.

Emerson E, Hatton C, Robertson J, Baines S, Christie A & Glover G (2013) *People with Learning Disabilities in England 2012*. Lancaster: Improving Health and Lives (Public Health Observatory).

Emerson E & Heslop P (2010) *A Working Definition of Learning Disabilities*. IHAL, Learning Disabilities Observatory/DH.

Glover G, Evison F & Emerson E (2011) *How Rates of Learning Disabilities and Autism in Children Vary between Areas*. London: IHAL/DH.

Heslop P, Blair P, Fleming P, Houghton M, Marriott A & Russ L (2013) *Confidential Inquiry into Premature Deaths of People with Learning Disabilities (CIPOLD): Final report*. Bristol: Norah Fry.

Mencap (2012) *Death by Indifference: 74 deaths and counting – a progress report 5 years on*. London: Mencap.

Michael J (2008) *Healthcare For All – independent inquiry into access to healthcare for people with learning disabilities*. Available at: http://webarchive.nationalarchives.gov.uk/20130107105354/http://www.dh.gov.uk/prod_consum_dh/groups/dh_digitalassets/@dh/@en/documents/digitalasset/dh_106126.pdf (accessed October 2016).

NHS Employers (2011) *Enhanced Services 2008/2009*. Available at: http://www.nhsemployers.org/your-workforce/primary-care-contacts/general-medical-services/enhanced-services/archive-2008-2012/enhanced-services-2008-09 (accessed October 2016).

NHS England (2016) *General Medical Services (GMS) contract*. Leeds: NHS Employers.

Chapter 4: Health promotion for people with learning disabilities

Lisa Hanna-Trainor, Laurence Taggart and Wendy Cousins

Introduction

This chapter aims to raise awareness of health inequalities and the importance of health promotion initiatives for people with learning disabilities.

What is health promotion?

Health promotion has been defined as the 'process of enabling people to increase control over, and to improve their health. It moves beyond a focus on individual behaviour towards a wide range of social and environmental interventions' (WHO, 2016). The key principle of health promotion is empowerment; it is fundamentally concerned with ensuring that individuals and communities can make full use of their capabilities and potential.

This concept of health as a foundation for achieving human potential, enabling and empowering people to become all that they are capable of becoming, has important implications for all those concerned with the care and well-being of people with learning disabilities. Yet there is considerable evidence that people with learning disabilities are not receiving the same level of health promotion opportunities as other members of society despite the widespread recognition that this group of citizens is at particular risk of ill-health.

Causes of poor health

People with learning disabilities will die on average 20 years earlier than their non-disabled peers; however, many of these deaths can be avoided with appropriate care (Heslop *et al*, 2013). People with learning disabilities are more likely to experience a range of secondary or chronic health conditions, such as hearing, vision or dental problems, type 2 diabetes, osteoporosis, and mental health problems. This may result from four main causes:

■ biological/genetic factors

■ lifestyle factors

■ socioeconomic and cultural factors

■ deficiencies in access to health services and health promotion.

Biological/genetic factors

Some people with learning disabilities may have syndrome-related conditions that result in difficulty eating or swallowing, dental problems, reduced mobility, bone demineralisation, gastro-oesophageal reflux, arthritis, decreased muscle tone and progressive cervical spine degeneration. Obesity is more prevalent in people with Down's syndrome, Prader-Willi syndrome, Cohen syndrome and Bardet-Biedl syndrome. There is a strong link between people with Down's syndrome and congenital heart disease and also Alzheimer's disease. Mental health problems and challenging behaviours are more likely to be displayed in people with specific genetic conditions such as Lesch-Nyhan syndrome, autism spectrum disorder (ASD), Rett syndrome, fragile-X syndrome and Williams syndrome.

People with learning disabilities who are frequently prescribed psychotropic and anti-seizure medications on a long-term basis have a higher risk of developing osteoporosis (brittle bone disease), which is compounded by lack of physical activity and diets limited in calcium and vitamin D (Emerson *et al*, 2012).

Lifestyle factors

Few people with learning disabilities eat a balanced diet, and family members and paid carers may lack knowledge about the appropriate recommendations for dietary intake (Hanna *et al*, 2011). Less than 20% of adults and 8% of children with learning disabilities engage in the World Health Organization (WHO) recommendations for physical activity (moderate to vigorous activity). High levels of sedentary behaviour are reported for both children and adults with learning disabilities compared to their non-disabled peers. Women with learning disabilities, people with Down's syndrome, those with a mild disability and those living in less restrictive facilities are at increased risk of obesity (Emerson *et al*, 2012).

More adolescents with learning disabilities are now smoking compared to their non-disabled peers (Taggart & Temple, 2014). Although people with learning disabilities drink less that their non-disabled peers, there is a small but sizeable group of people with disabilities who abuse alcohol and illicit drugs with significant consequences (Taggart & Chaplin, 2014). People with learning disabilities may have limited knowledge about forming appropriate relationships, intimacy and sexual health (for example, the importance of contraception). Family members and paid carers may also have limited knowledge/confidence in supporting the person by promoting sexual health (Lafferty et al, 2013).

Socioeconomic and cultural factors

Emerson and Hatton (2014) reported the negative and discriminatory attitudes that are held by many people across the world about people with learning disabilities. Such discriminatory attitudes and practices can:

- restrict access to good housing, education, employment and timely and effective healthcare services, which can lead to health problems developing and poor management of such health conditions
- lead to people with learning disabilities experiencing harassment, bullying and hate crimes, which can lead to poorer physical and mental health.

People with learning disabilities are more likely to live in low socioeconomic environments and experience poverty compared to the non-disabled population. And because of their cognitive impairment, they will find it more difficult to break out of this poverty trap (Emerson & Hatton, 2014). Many people with mild disabilities live in least restrictive community settings and have been found to have the highest rates of obesity, to have a lower intake of fruits and vegetables, and to be in poorer health. People with learning disabilities have been found to have limited social support when living in the community, and this can result in loneliness, bullying/violence or conflicts with others, which can lead to increased stress (Marks & Sisirak, 2014).

Deficiencies in health access and health promotion

People with learning disabilities are more likely to have communication difficulties that limit how they communicate when ill or unwell; this then leads them to have a greater reliance upon family members and paid carers who may have limited knowledge of the signs and symptoms of ill-health (Hanna et al, 2011). People with learning disabilities face health inequalities from an early age through, for example, a lack of resources, pragmatic barriers such as physical access, a lack of accessible information, untimely appointments, difficulties arranging transport, delays in access to screening, and a lack of early diagnosis and treatment. Recent evidence shows a lack of reasonable adjustments being made within primary healthcare and acute general hospitals (Tuffrey-Wijne *et al*, 2014).

There is a lack of training for primary and secondary healthcare staff, and some hold negative attitudes or carry out discriminatory practices against those with learning disabilities. There is a lack of health promotion literature and educational material – for example, about diet, physical activity, cancer, smoking and mental health – designed specifically for this population. Low uptake of health screening opportunities – for example, vision and hearing tests, dental examinations, and breast/cervical and testicular/prostrate screening – continues today across the world. There is also limited use of health promotion programmes offered to this population, such as weight reduction programmes, exercise/activity programmes, and self-management programmes for chronic illnesses (Taggart & Cousins, 2014). Access to health education/screening/programmes are poorer for people withlearning disabilities from low/middle income countries, people with severe/profound learning disabilities, people with learning disabilities aged over 60 years, people with learning disabilities who are not known to services and also those from ethnic minority communities (Emerson & Hatton, 2014).

Health access and health promotion

In addressing such deficiencies, health checks have recently been introduced in England, Wales and Northern Ireland. There is an increase in the numbers of GP practices that are subscribing to this scheme and that complete annual health checks supported by health facilitators (McConkey *et al*, 2015). There is also growing evidence that health checks can identify many unrecognised health problems.

Using health promotion to improve health

For individuals with learning disabilities, the empowerment of their 'community of carers' – both families and professionals – is of key importance. Multiple opportunities exist for health promotion initiatives.

Health promotion in families

People with learning disabilities have the same health needs as other family members. Therefore, all family members should be aware of small changes in the person's health as well as behavioural changes, and a family member should accompany the person when visiting their GP or practice nurse. Families must support the person with learning disabilities to be involved in a range of local community initiatives and health promotion opportunities, such as well-woman clinics, weight management programmes, sports clubs etc. The application of health promotion to improve the lives of people with learning disabilities is centred on families being able to empower individuals, by helping them to understand the ways in which their behaviour and lifestyles can affect their health (see Box 4.1 for examples). Health promotion must be based upon raising the awareness of the four determinants of health disparity identified above.

Box 4.1: Easyhealth health information guides

In 2011 the Foundation for People with Learning Disabilities funded the production of a range of free Easy Read guides on key medical conditions and concepts, in conjunction with PRODIGY and Easyhealth.

The booklets include guides to:

- acute bronchitis
- ADHD
- breast screening
- contraception
- dental abscesses
- diabetes
- epilepsy
- obesity
- Parkinson's disease
- tooth decay

They are available from www.easyhealth.org.uk

Health promotion in schools

All children and young people with learning disabilities will attend either mainstream or special education. Schools should be aware of the physical and mental health of this population and take an active role in:

- promoting physical activity through sports

- promoting the mental health of pupils through active participation in school activities

- providing a safe and supportive environment for learning

- involving pupils through participation and empowerment

- collaborating with parents and the local community.

Health promotion in communities

People with learning disabilities should, where possible, be supported to participate in their local community health promotion initiatives, including weight management programmes, local sports clubs, leisure centres or gyms etc. Accessing locally based resources and skilled staff will also support the person with learning disabilities and their carers to socialise with their non-disabled peers and may lead to sustainable behaviour change. Some staff may need additional education and/or support to assist individuals with learning disabilities to access different health promotion programmes or activities.

Health promotion and health checks

The poorer health of people with learning disabilities is partly due to deficiencies in health access, health screening and health promotion. Some health conditions may not be recognised, or may be poorly managed, by primary and secondary healthcare professionals. The uptake of health screenings among people with learning disabilities is less than that among the non-disabled population. Annual health checks have been introduced in some parts of the UK and in other countries. A health check involves a GP or practice nurse undertaking a yearly physical examination of the person with learning disabilities. Health checks have been shown to identify a number of unrecognised health problems and also to offer better management of chronic health conditions.

Health promotion and physical activity/sports

Research shows that both young people and adults with learning disabilities do not engage in the appropriate amount of moderate physical activity per day. This is despite physical activity and sports being shown to improve physical health and psychological well-being. People with learning disabilities face barriers to becoming more involved in physical activity. These include a lack of support, having no means of transportation and the fact that these activities may be too expensive. Another barrier is that family members and paid carers perceive that people with learning disabilities do not want to engage in physical activity or sports. However, this is refuted by people with learning disabilities themselves, who have highlighted that, if offered the option and supported to do so, they would be willing to engage in different physical activities and sports (Temple & Walkley, 2003).

Walking interventions have been shown to promote the health of many people. Components of successful walking interventions have included the use of pedometers, physical activity consultations and social support.

Social media as a tool for health promotion

With the increase in the use of digital devices and social media applications such as Facebook and Twitter, health promotion practitioners have been quick to recognise social media's capacity to reach large audiences almost instantaneously, using cost-efficient methods. While the use of social media in health promotion interventions potentially introduces new barriers for people with learning disabilities, there is far greater potential for the internet and communications technologies, if appropriately designed, to make the world a much more accessible and inclusive place (Treveranus *et al*, 2010). Social media messages can also be customised and tailored to the needs and preferences of different audiences (Korda & Itani, 2013), and can help provide a voice for vulnerable groups as well as giving organisations better access to those in need of programmes and services.

While the use of social media for health promotion should be valued for its potential to engage with audiences for enhanced communication and improved capacity to promote programmes, products and services, some caution is needed. Social media should not be viewed as a solution to the complexities of behaviour change and guaranteed improved health outcomes, though there are certainly applications that can support the change process (Neiger *et al*, 2013). Just as health is a multi-factorial issue, health promotion is itself a multidimensional endeavour: not just a single activity, but an approach that may encompass a number of activities aiming to empower individuals and communities to promote health through a range of enabling measures.

Conclusion

The United Nations Convention on the Rights of Persons with Disabilities (2007) has recognised that persons with disabilities have the right to the enjoyment of the highest attainable standard of health without discrimination on the basis of disability. Nevertheless, there is often a lack of appreciation of the range of capabilities of individuals with learning disabilities and low expectations of what they can achieve (Siperstein *et al*, 2003). A clear opportunity exists for health promotion efforts to improve the health prospects and quality of life for people with learning disabilities within their families, schools and local communities.

Summary points

- The poorer health of people with learning disabilities is partly due to deficiencies in health access, health screening and health promotion.

- People with learning disabilities are still not receiving the same level of health promotion opportunities as other members of society.

- People with learning disabilities will die on average 20 years earlier than their non-disabled peers.

- It is only recently that health checks have been introduced in England, Wales and Northern Ireland. And there is now evidence that they can identify many unrecognised health problems.

- People with learning disabilities should where possible be supported to participate in their local community health promotion programmes such as weight management programmes, local sport centres/gyms and so on.

References

Emerson E & Hatton C (2014) *Health Inequalities and People with Learning Disabilities*. Cambridge: Cambridge University Press.

Emerson E, Baines S, Allerton L & Welch V (2012) *Health Inequalities and People with Learning Disabilities in the UK: 2012* [online]. London: IHAL. Available at: www.options-empowers.org/wp-content/uploads/2013/02/Improving-Health-and-Lives-health-inequalities-and-people-with-learning-disabilities-in-the-UK-annual-report.pdf (accessed October 2016).

Hanna L M, Taggart L & Cousins W (2011) Cancer prevention and health promotion for people with intellectual disabilities: an exploratory study of staff knowledge. *Journal of Intellectual Disability Research* **55** (3) 281–291.

Heslop P, Blair P, Fleming P, Hoghton M, Marriott A & Russ L (2013) *Confidential Inquiry into Premature Deaths of People with Learning Disabilities (CIPOLD): Final report* [online]. Available at: www.bris.ac.uk/media-library/sites/cipold/migrated/documents/fullfinalreport.pdf (accessed October 2016).

Korda H & Itani Z (2013) Harnessing social media for health promotion and behavior change. *Health Promotion Practice* **14** (1) 15–23.

Lafferty A, McConkey R & Simpson A (2013) Reducing the barriers to relationships and sexuality education for persons with intellectual disabilities. *Journal of Intellectual Disabilities* **16** (1) 29–43.

Marks B & Sisirak J (2014) Health Promotion and people with intellectual disabilities. In: L Taggart and W Cousins (Eds) *Health Promotion for People with Intellectual and Developmental Disabilities* (pp. 17–30). Maidenhead: McGraw Hill & Open University Press.

McConkey T, Taggart L & Kane M (2015) Optimising the uptake of health checks for people with intellectual disabilities. *Journal of Intellectual Disabilities* **19** (3) 205–214.

Neiger BL, Thackeray R, Van Wagenen SA, Hanson CL, West JH, Barnes MD & Fagen MC (2012) Use of social media in health promotion: purposes, key performance indicators, and evaluation metrics. *Health Promotion Practice* **13** (2) 159–164.

Siperstein GN, Norins J, Corbin S & Shriver T (2003) *Multinational Study of Attitudes toward Individuals with Intellectual Disabilities*. Washington, DC: Special Olympics.

Taggart L & Chaplin E (2014) Substance abuse disorder. In: E Tsakanikos and J McCarthy (Eds) *Handbook of Psychopathology in Intellectual Disability*. New York: Springer Publishing.

Taggart L & Cousins W (2014) *Health Promotion for People with Intellectual and Developmental Disabilities*. Maidenhead: McGraw Hill & Open University Press.

Taggart L & Temple B (2014) Substance abuse. In: L Taggart and W Cousins (Eds) *Health Promotion for People with Intellectual and Developmental Disabilities* (pp. 128–137). Maidenhead: McGraw Hill & Open University Press.

Temple VA & Walkley JW (2003) Physical activity of adults with intellectual disability. *Journal of Intellectual and Developmental Disability* **28** 323–334.

Treviranus J, Stolarick K, Denstedt M, Fichten C & Ascunsion J (2010) *Leveraging Inclusion and Diversity as Canada's Digital Advantage*. Toronto: Inclusive Design Research Centre, Adaptech Research Centre & Martin Prosperity Institute.

Tuffrey-Wijne I, Goulding L, Giatras N, Abraham E, Gillard S, White S, Edwards C & Hollins S (2014) The barriers to and enablers of providing reasonably adjusted health services to people with intellectual disabilities in acute hospitals: evidence from a mixed- methods study. *BMJ Open*. Available at: http://eprints.kingston.ac.uk/28245/1/Tuffrey-Wijne-I-28245.pdf (accessed October 2016).

United Nations General Assembly (2007) Convention on the *Rights of Persons with Disabilities: Resolution adopted by the General Assembly: A / RES / 61 / 106* [online]. Available at: www.un.org/disabilities/convention/signature.shtml (accessed October 2016).

WHO (2016) *Health Promotion*. Available at: www.who.int/topics/health_promotion/en/ (accessed October 2016).

Useful websites and resources

Easyhealth
Provides accessible leaflets and videos on health promotion for people with learning disabilities.
www.easyhealth.org.uk

Health Literacy Toolkit for Low and Middle Income Countries
The toolkit was developed in partnership with the World Health Organization's South-East Asia Regional Office.
www.searo.who.int/entity/healthpromotion/documents/hl_tookit/en/

IASSID (International Association for the Scientific Study of Intellectual and Developmental Disabilities) Health Guidelines for Adults with an Intellectual Disability
https://www.iassidd.org/uploads/legacy/pdf/healthguidelines.pdf

The Improving Health and Lives Learning Disabilities Observatory (IHAL)
IHAL exists to keep watch on the health of people with learning disabilities and the healthcare they receive. www.improvinghealthandlives.org.uk/

New South Wales Council for Intellectual Disability (NSWCID)
NSWCID offers factsheets on common health problems for people with learning disabilities
www.nswcid.org.au

Chapter 5: The Mental Capacity Act (2005)

Steve Hardy, Lesley Brown and Theresa Joyce

Introduction

In a recent court case (Kings College NHS Foundation Trust v C and V [2015] EWCOP 59) a judge agreed that a woman who had led a very 'colourful' life could refuse to have the life-saving treatment of renal dialysis following a suicide attempt. While the judge said the decision to refuse treatment could be called 'unwise', he was very clear that the woman had understood the risks and no one else could make this decision for her.

This fundamental right to make our own choices about many aspects of life is enshrined in the Mental Capacity Act (2005). The act applies to everyone, including people with learning disabilities. The right to make our own decisions is a fundamental principle in our society. We need to ensure that everyone applies this principle to people with learning disabilities, to make sure they understand their rights and receive the information they need to be able to make decisions about their own health.

This chapter explores the principles of the Mental Capacity Act (2005), with a focus on health-related decisions. The chapter's aims are:

- to improve understanding of the Mental Capacity Act (2005)

- to outline how capacity is assessed

- to explain the process for making best interest decisions.

What is the Mental Capacity Act (2005) and why is it important to us?

The Mental Capacity Act (2005) (MCA) provides a legal framework to ensure that people can make decisions themselves. It prevents others from making decisions on someone's behalf when they are able to do so themselves. It also protects those who cannot make a particular decision at a particular time, by setting out responsibilities for professionals, carers and families.

People with learning disabilities have a history of being denied autonomy and choice, and this is still the case today for some people. Making choices is a right that should be able to be taken for granted. However for many vulnerable groups this is not the case. The MCA requires us to give people as much support as possible to help them understand choices and make informed decisions. The MCA also aims to ensure that people who lack capacity are offered the same range of interventions as everyone else. But most importantly (and often forgotten), we are required to follow the MCA because it's the law – not a choice!

Principles of the Mental Capacity Act

The MCA is underpinned by five principles.

1. Every adult has the right to make his or her own decisions and others must assume they can do so unless proved otherwise.
2. People must be supported as much as possible to make their own decisions before anyone concludes that they cannot make their own decisions.
3. People have the right to make what others might regard as unwise or eccentric decisions.
4. Anything done for or on behalf of a person who lacks mental capacity must be done in their best interests.
5. Anything done for or on behalf of people without capacity should be the least restrictive of their basic rights and freedoms.

What is capacity?

Mental capacity is the ability to make a specific decision at a specific time. This includes decisions about day-to-day life – such as when to get up, what to wear or whether to visit the doctor if you're feeling unwell – as well as more serious decisions. It also refers to decisions that may have legal consequences, such as agreeing or refusing to have medical treatment, buying goods or making a will.

Enhancing capacity

When we support someone with a learning disability, we have an important responsibility to help them understand the day-to-day choices they have in their life and what the consequences of these might be. We can use daily routines such as getting dressed, shopping or cooking to give people the experience and understanding of making choices.

Sometimes we will have to support the person to understand a more complicated decision about their health. We can 'enhance' their ability to make informed decisions (without 'telling' them what we think the best option is) by:

- Being willing to talk through the situation and possible choices on a number of occasions and especially in response to the person's questions.

- Using simple words and short sentences that make sense to the person.

- Providing them with information in a format they can understand and remember, such as Easy Read leaflets, photographs and video clips.

- Using tools such as Talking Mats (www.talkingmats.com) to help them weigh up choices and express their views.

- Ensuring any communication aid they use (e.g. photo book, symbol system, signing vocabulary, voice output communication app) includes the right vocabulary for asking and answering questions about the decision.

It may be a good idea to ask your local speech and language therapist to help you with ideas to enhance the person's capacity. If the person already has a speech and language therapy assessment report or a communication passport, make sure you follow its recommendations and, if appropriate, share them with the healthcare professionals involved so they know how best to communicate with the person.

What is a lack of capacity?

A person may be assessed as lacking capacity: this means they may be unable to make a specific decision at a specific time. The person may be unable to make a decision because of a disturbance in the functioning of the mind or brain, which the act defines, and it includes learning disabilities within its definition. However, this does not mean that people with learning disabilities lack capacity. A person

may lack the capacity to make a decision about one issue but not about others; for example, a person may be able to make the decision about which college course to take but lack the capacity to decide whether to have an operation. The loss of capacity may be temporary and/or change over time. However, it is clear that people should be given support to help understand what may be a complex issue, in order to make an informed decision.

Assessing capacity to make decisions about health

We must always start from the principle that the person has capacity. This is an assumption of capacity, and should avoid a status approach to capacity – i.e. 'You have a learning disability and therefore you lack the capacity to make this decision'. When it comes to health decisions, the person responsible for carrying out the capacity assessment will normally be the health professional who will carry out the procedure, for example, a dentist in the case of dental work, surgeon in the case of surgery, or GP in the case of a prescription for medication. However, this can be problematic if the professional assessing an individual's capacity does not know the person well. It is therefore good practice to gain support from others who know the individual well such as a family member, support staff or a community learning disability team (CLDT), who can support the person.

The judgement of capacity is based on the person's ability to understand the nature and effects of the decision to be taken – professionals are required to give the person all the relevant information relating to the decision. They must also give them enough reasonable time to understand and remember the information about the particular decision. The assessment of capacity must be about the particular decision that has to be made at a particular time and not about a range of decisions.

Health professionals are required to make an assessment before carrying out any care or treatment, and the more serious the decision the more formal the assessment should be. There is no set level of formality; common sense should prevail and judgments made should be backed by objective reasoning. There is also no set criteria for the amount of information that should be recorded by the professionals, but again the more serious the decision, the more detailed the information required and recorded.

The MCA lays out a two-stage assessment of capacity. First, a person must have an impairment or disturbance in functioning of the mind or brain. The act provides a list of conditions that fall under these categories and having a 'learning disability' is one of them. But having a learning disability does not automatically mean that a person lacks capacity; it may mean that they just need some extra support to make a decision or they may be able to make it by themselves. Once it is established that the person has a learning disability and that this might make it difficult for them to make a decision, then the second stage of assessment should be carried out: the functional test of capacity. Under this assessment, the person is deemed unable to make a decision for themselves if they are unable to do any of the following:

- To understand the information relevant to the decision.

- To retain information.

- To use or weigh up the information in relation to the risks and benefits of each course of action.

- To communicate what their decision is (and why).

There is no prescribed amount of knowledge that a person has to demonstrate. The judgement is based on the balance of probability (i.e. whether it more likely than not that the person lacks capacity). The MCA process may appear very formal to health professionals and, quite rightly, a health professional should know processes to ensure the rights of the individual are upheld. But the way a person is assessed should be made as informal as possible, giving them every chance to succeed. Remember, it's a conversation with the individual, not an exam.

Case example of a capacity assessment: Sammy

Sammy is a young man with mild to moderate learning disabilities. He has been living in a supported house for the last five years. He is close to his family, and his mum is involved in lots of decisions about his life, for example what activities he does during the day. He has some verbal skills.

Sammy currently has some dental problems, which are causing him a lot of pain, but he refuses to open his mouth for his teeth to be cleaned. Some of the staff team think it would be a good idea to give Sammy an occasional general anaesthetic so that a dentist can clean his teeth and fill any cavities. The other half do not agree with this idea. His mother is in two minds about the procedure, as she does not want him to have an anaesthetic, but she hates to see him in pain.

The dentist responsible for assessing Sammy's capacity to consent has only met him on a handful of occasions and has asked the nurse from the community learning disability team (who has known him for several years) to assist her in the assessment.

Assessing whether Sammy has capacity to make this decision

The nurse asked if he has problems with his teeth, he nodded to indicate he did. The nurse then asked what would happen about his teeth and Sammy replied that they would be taken out. When asked how many he replied 'lots of teeth'. The nurse asked who would do this and Sammy replied 'tooth doctor'. When asked where, he replied 'College Hospital'. He explained that he would have an 'operation'. 'After the operation,' he said, 'I'll feel better'. When asked if he had been to the hospital before, he replied 'twice' and that he had seen 'Christine'. When shown a picture of Christine he recognised her. The nurse asked what Christine had told him and he said that Christine would do 'blood tests' and 'lots of things'. When shown a picture of the weighing scales at the clinic he knew that he had stood on them and they were for measuring weight. The nurse asked Sammy if the hospital staff had asked him if he wanted to have the operation and he replied 'yes'; The nurse asked Sammy what his reply to this was and he said 'yes'. Sammy was asked how his teeth would feel if he had the operation and he replied 'better'. Sammy gave us permission to contact the hospital and find out what would happen and which staff would be involved.

The dentist provided information about the risks, which included that he would be in pain for a few days (but could have painkillers), that there would be blood in his mouth for a few days, that he would have to eat soft foods for a few days and that there was a 1 in 250,000 risk of dying during the course of the procedure. Sammy understood that he would be in pain, that there would be blood and that he would eat foods like scrambled eggs rather than crusty rolls. He was shown a drawing of a big circle, with a tiny part taken out, and it was explained that the circle showed all the people who had the operation and got better. The tiny part showed the people who had the operation and didn't wake up.

The dentist asked Sammy what he understood about the whole procedure before he had the operation. He was able to tell him, using simple language; he did not just answer 'yes/no' questions. The dentist (and the CLDT Nurse) agreed that on the balance of probability Sammy had the capacity to decide whether he wanted to have this dental procedure.

What happens if the person lacks the capacity to make a health decision?

If a person has been assessed as lacking capacity then any action taken, or any decision made for or on behalf of that person, must be made in his or her best interests. The health professional who is to make the decision is known as the 'decision maker' and will normally be the health professional responsible for carrying out the procedure and/or giving the treatment.

The MCA provides a checklist of factors to be considered when making a decision on behalf of someone who lacks capacity. These include a number of considerations and safeguards including:

- anti-discriminatory practice
- considering whether the person might regain capacity
- understanding that even though the person lacks the capacity to make the decision they may be able to contribute their own views and opinions, however small
- considering any wishes or beliefs the person themselves might have
- consulting others (including family and carers)
- considering all relevant circumstances – from previous cases the courts have recommended that the decision maker uses a balance sheet.

All capacity decisions should made in the best interests of the individual and in a way that is least restrictive of the person's rights and freedom of action. Take, for example, a woman with learning disabilities who is experiencing pain every month during menstruation. At this time her behaviour can be described as very challenging and she refuses to engage in activities she normally enjoys. She lacks capacity to manage her menstrual cycles. An answer could be for her to have a hysterectomy. However, this would be an extreme course of action given that there are other less restrictive options to consider. In these situations it is important to consider the irreversibility test: procedures where there is no going back on the decision are often the most restrictive options.

The MCA provides independent mental capacity advocates, also known as IMCAs. An IMCA can be appointed when the person has no family or unpaid carer to participate in decision-making in relation to three specific types of decisions: serious medical treatment, arrangements for provision of NHS accommodation (i.e. hospital or care home) or provision of local authority accommodation. The IMCA has the power to interview the person and examine records and is there to support the individual and their rights, but they are not decision makers.

Previous cases that have gone to court have recommended that decision makers should use a 'balance sheet' approach for any serious decisions, which should include:

- considering the benefits of the procedure

- weighing up the disadvantages (risks) of the procedure

- considering the possible gains and losses and the likelihood of them occurring

- striking a balance between possible gains and losses

- viewing the procedure as in the persons best interests only if the benefits out weigh the disadvantages.

Relevant decisions will vary from case to case. It is not just the outcome that is considered, but what the burdens and benefits of the treatment will be. Other considerations include social welfare – including how any decision will impact (for better or worse) on the way the person lives their life – and the emotional impact; how the person will feel and react. It is important to remember that in life people do make seemingly unwise decisions; it is not for the assessment to judge whether the person should be allowed to do this, only if they have capacity to make the decision and know the risks associated with it.

Summary points

- The Mental Capacity Act (2005) is a law that applies to everyone. The act enshrines the right for individuals to make their own decisions. The principles of the act are:

  - Every adult has the right to make his or her own decisions and others must assume they can do so unless proved otherwise.

  - People must be supported as much as possible to make their own decisions before anyone concludes that they cannot.

  - People have the right to make what others might regard as unwise or unusual decisions.

  - Anything done for or on behalf of a person who lacks mental capacity must be done so in their best interests.

  - Anything done for or on behalf of people without capacity should be the least restrictive of their basic rights and freedoms.

Part II
Common conditions

Chapter 6: Respiratory illness

Daniel Marsden and Sally Wilson

Introduction

This chapter seeks to investigate respiratory conditions: what they are, how they can be treated, and how parents and carers can support people with learning disabilities to manage and live with these conditions.

Respiratory medicine is the speciality concerned with all lung diseases, from diagnosis to treatment and management of the conditions. The respiratory system is vital to sustaining life, and respiration is made up of four main components:

1. The inflow and outflow of air from the atmosphere into the lungs, the inhaled air traveling down the trachea, or windpipe, into the lungs.

2. The delivery of oxygen to the blood and removal of waste from blood.

3. The transporting of oxygen and carbon dioxide within the blood to and from cells in the body.

4. The regulation of this respiration or breathing.

It is important to consider how to minimise the impact of long term conditions and maximise health. There are a number of ways people with learning disabilities can achieve this:

- Eat healthy foods, avoid foods that are high in saturated fat, be aware of food labels, and eat five portions of fresh fruit and vegetables every day.

- Take regular exercise. It is easy to build this up gradually and most GP practices will be able to provide additional guidance on how to achieve this.

- Do not smoke, as this will significantly improve most respiratory conditions. Family or carers should ensure they do not smoke in the same room or car. GP practices are able to advise on local programmes and groups for smoking cessation.

■ Do not drink more than the recommended units of alcohol per week.

As well as assisting with the above changes, those supporting the person can also help reduce the impact of any long term condition by doing the following:

■ If someone with a learning disability has a chest infection, minimise the risk of infection by, for example, keeping them away from day centres or work placements where they may infect other people with learning disabilities.

■ Encourage hand hygiene and oral hygiene, and support hand washing and cleaning of teeth.

■ Encourage slower eating – food cramming can cause choking.

■ The individual should be kept away from smoky or polluted environments; also consider potential irritants, such as air fresheners, in the individual's environment.

■ Consider making sure they have an annual flu jab.

Respiratory health and people with learning disabilities

There are many respiratory conditions that require careful monitoring and treatment; sometimes these conditions are referred to as 'lung disease'. There are a number of common lung diseases, some of which are more prevalent in people with learning disabilities. It has been identified that people with learning disabilities are more likely than those without disabilities to develop respiratory infections or to experience swallowing difficulties. Swallowing difficulties contribute to an increased risk of aspiration, lung infections and pneumonia. Often this is because of an increased risk that food, drink or saliva goes down the 'wrong hole' and can block the airway, making it difficult to breathe, causing choking. Respiratory disease is one of the main causes of death for people with learning disabilities.

People with Down's syndrome are particularly prone to respiratory problems because they are more likely to have lung and respiratory tract abnormalities: as many as 36% of people with Down's syndrome have a respiratory condition. Studies carried out in Ireland (McCarron *et al*, 2013) have shown that they also have a lower immune response and an increase in 'mouth breathing' has been implicated. People with Down's syndrome are more likely to have fistulas – holes between two tubes in the body. This is a particular problem when the hole is between the pipes that take food to the stomach (the oesophagus) and air to the lungs (the trachea) as food or drink can spill across.

People with learning disabilities and physical disability are also more prone to chest infections due to aspiration and reduced mobility. The individual's learning disabilities may have been caused by birth complications such as premature birth or low birth weight and these are associated with respiratory problems throughout the lifespan. People with learning disability may be prescribed medications that reduce how well the lungs work or lower immunity, making breathing more difficult.

People with learning disabilities are more likely to be obese, which can also cause respiratory problems, including reduced lung capacity and greater difficulty in breathing rapidly or deeply for sustained periods of time. Being obese can also cause sleep apnoea and can make asthma worse.

Several other specific conditions affecting people with learning disabilities are associated with breathing problems:

- People who have tuberous sclerosis are more likely to have lung complications.
- Fragile X syndrome is associated with chest wall deformities.
- Cerebral palsy is associated with muscle tightness that can affect breathing.
- People with learning disabilities may not be immunised against infections (for example flu jabs).

Respiratory conditions

As mentioned, there are many different types of respiratory condition, too many to detail in this chapter, but we outline here some of the more common conditions and the main symptoms relating to them.

Asthma: This is a condition where the airways are inflamed and occasionally spasm causing shortness of breath and wheeziness. There are a number of triggers for asthma symptoms – which commonly present as asthma attacks – including allergies to pollen or pet hair, infections, cigarette smoke or pollution. There is also gastric asthma; this is triggered by reflux, which is more common in people with learning disabilities.

Chronic obstructive pulmonary disease (COPD): This relates to a collection of symptoms that cause difficulty in breathing, arising from an inability to inhale and exhale normally. It is usually associated with a persistent cough and wheezing, and the person may also have a feeling of chest tightness.

Emphysema: This is a form of COPD where the resulting lung damage causes air to become trapped in the lungs. There are several symptoms, including shortness of breath, a cough and difficulty breathing, especially during exercise.

Sleep apnoea: This is where the flow of air in and out of the lungs stops during sleep. These pauses in breathing can last for up to 10 seconds and can occur multiple times during the night, often waking the person for a few minutes as the brain triggers the need to breathe. Consequently, people who suffer from sleep apnoea are often very fatigued during the day.

Cystic fibrosis: This is a genetically inherited condition where there is poor clearance of the mucus from the bronchi (the airways leading to the lungs), leading to repeated lung infections.

Aspiration pneumonia: This is an inflammation of the lungs due to bacterial infection, that occurs after food, fluid, vomit or saliva is inhaled into the lungs instead of passing into the stomach. It may also occur due to reflux, where food travels back up the oesophagus, and so can occur sometime after eating. It can cause fever, sweats, wheezing and coughing, which results in reduced oxygen intake, lethargy and altered consciousness.

Assessment and treatment of respiratory diseases

Clinical assessment of any respiratory disease is usually undertaken in GP practices or hospital outpatient clinics, and may include lung function tests, breathing on exertion and arterial blood gas testing in addition to a good history of the condition. History is important as it enables clinicians to understand how the disease may be affecting lifestyle and if there are any psychological issues to consider. Things to note when giving clinicians details about history include how long the condition has been present, what makes it better or worse, what tests have already been completed and what medications have been taken.

People with learning disabilities may not always be able to articulate their symptoms, which can lead to diagnostic overshadowing and respiratory conditions being missed. When people are unable to say what their symptoms are, it becomes important for family members and carers to observe for any changes in behaviour that could indicate physical health problems. In order for families and carers to be able to monitor any symptoms of respiratory distress, they need to know what kind of symptoms to look for, including the number of breaths taken per minute, whether the person's breathing rate changes, if there is any change in skin colour or any observed differences that may indicate an underlying physical cause.

Spirometry is a commonly used breathing test that can be carried out by a practice nurse in a GP surgery. It involves the patient taking a deep breathe in and then breathing out into a tube as fast as they can. The spirometer (the tube they blow into) then measures how much air the patient has exhaled. This test may need to be repeated and the result is then compared with national averages depending on the age and sex of the patient. People with learning disabilities may need extra time to learn what is expected of them and how to do this test accurately. The peak expiratory flow test (PEF or peak flow) is also commonly used in GP practices to measure how fast air can be blown out of the lungs. As with the spirometry, there is a technique to the PEF that may take longer for people with learning disabilities to master. There are several films on YouTube that demonstrate peak flow testing and it may be useful for people with learning disabilities to watch these with a family member or a carer to support their learning.

Asthma medicines are usually given via an inhaler, a device used to breathe the medicine straight into the lungs. Some of the medicines are in aerosol form and some are powder. Some inhalers can be used with a spacer, which is a large plastic tube that can be attached to a face mask, which is especially useful for people who may struggle to seal their lips around the inhaler. Most people with asthma require support to practise the technique of inhaling their medication in order to optimise its effectiveness.

Medications for COPD include inhalers, tablets or liquids. In some cases oxygen may also be prescribed and can be used at home and out in the community. In England there is a home oxygen service that delivers the equipment and offers training in how to use it.

Diagnosis of sleep apnoea usually occurs after the patient has been observed sleeping, or after they have worn a monitoring device at home during the night. People with learning disabilities may need support to become familiar with the testing equipment, as it requires sensors to be placed on the skin in various places to monitor heart rate and breathing rate. Sleep apnoea can be treated using breathing techniques as well as medications. Many people with sleep apnoea need to use breathing machines throughout the night to make sure they get the constant oxygen supply they need while sleeping.

Aspiration pneumonia can occur at any time and is especially prevalent in people with more severe learning disabilities who may have a poor swallow reflex. It can result in the person needing hospital admission for intravenous

(IV) antibiotics, chest physiotherapy and oxygen therapy. Aspiration pneumonia is an acute condition which if left untreated can be life threatening. Speech and language therapists (SLTs) can assess people's swallow and advise on a number of strategies or approaches to improve comfort, safety and general health.

There are a number of ways that a member of staff or a family member can tell if someone is having breathing difficulties:

■ They may be breathing heavily or at a faster rate than normal (normal breathing rate is 12–20 breaths per minute).

■ They may look like they are in distress or having physical difficulty when breathing, such as arching their body to take in breath.

■ Their nostrils may flare out under the effort of breathing in.

■ The gaps between the bones around the neck or chest may be more sucked in than usual under the effort of breathing.

■ A wheezing or whistling sound may be heard when the individual is breathing.

■ They may be coughing. In cases of asthma the individual may have phlegm on their lungs but find that coughing does not bring this up. With an infection they may bring phlegm up that is discoloured or has blood in it.

■ They may complain of having a tight chest.

How family and staff can support the person

Breathing difficulties can require significant support and management for people with learning disability and may be more complicated for those presenting with a number of health problems. It is common for people to experience high levels of anxiety when their breathing is impaired and they may need calm reassurance. This is a natural response, and yet one of the main physical presentations of anxiety is short shallow breathing, which can further exacerbate any underlying respiratory problems. Teaching breathing techniques can really improve anxiety and it is important for family members or carers to attend appointments with a respiratory nurse who will be able to advise on the correct way to breathe.

Learning to relax the breathing can take time and a consistent approach with teaching. If people with respiratory disease are starting to feel anxious it is important to first encourage them to breathe out and empty their lungs before breathing through the nose. Breathing through the nose slows breathing down and avoids hyperventilating – or breathing too quickly. Another useful technique is to ask the person to put one hand on their chest and the other hand on their abdomen, while breathing through their nose. Encourage them to breathe into their abdomen, meaning the hand on their stomach should move and not the hand on their chest. This stretches the diaphragm, which in turn can relax some of the chest muscles that may have tightened, causing the anxiety and breathlessness. Counting while breathing can also help to slow down and regulate the speed of breathing, which reduces the short anxious breathing pattern and re-establishes regular breath rate: for example, count one, two while breathing in, and three, four while breathing out. For additional information about breathing techniques and exercises, local physiotherapy teams will be able to advise and offer support.

When people with learning disabilities are being taught these skills it can take time and consistent reminders to ensure breathing techniques are learnt and breathing is optimised. Pictorial care plans as well as family and carer involvement may support this learning.

Learning how to use inhalers may also involve family and carer support to optimise treatment. Any machines being used to treat sleep apnoea may require a period of desensitisation so the person with a learning disability can get used to the sight and sound of the equipment. There are various machines that can be used to treat sleep apnoea; they involve a well-fitting face mask that can make a noise and which may take a little while for the person to get used to. Similarly, oxygen masks can also take some time to adjust to, and some people prefer to use a nasal cannula to receive their oxygen therapy.

Nationally there have been several 'singing for breathing' groups established to support people with long-term respiratory diseases. These groups encourage the development of breathing techniques that have the added benefit of increasing lung function. Local physiotherapists and asthma nurses will be able to advise further.

As most respiratory diseases are long term conditions, they will require regular outpatient or GP appointments to be kept. Attending appointments can be time-consuming and frightening, and there may be some individual reasonable adjustments needed to make the appointments work for the patient with a learning disability. There are learning disability nurses who work in acute hospitals as acute liaison nurses (ALNs) who will be able to support the implementation of reasonable adjustments for hospital admissions and appointments. In the community, many learning disability community nursing teams have health facilitation nurses who are able to liaise with GP clinics to negotiate reasonable adjustments.

Reasonable adjustments can be small and really simple to implement. They may include, for example, making sure that the person is first on the clinic list, that they are able to wait in the cafe or outside, and that they receive a text or phone call when the consultant is ready.

The learning disability nurse will also be able to help develop a hospital passport, which will include details of conditions, medical history and response to previous treatments. It will also document how the person communicates and copes in healthcare settings. This can be a really useful patient-held record of their specific individual needs, and can support nursing and clinic staff, while being an equally useful prompt for family members and carers.

Conclusion

Respiratory diseases are complex in presentation, diagnosis and management, and this chapter has only skimmed the surface of this topic. However, there are many helpful websites, leaflets and publications for further reading.

In line with the general population, people with learning disabilities are likely to have respiratory disease, but they are more likely to die prematurely as a result of their respiratory condition. This may be in part due to people with learning disabilities not always being able to communicate their symptoms. Therefore it is very important for families and carers to have an understanding of the frequency of respiratory disease among people with learning disabilities and the key symptoms to look out for.

Summary points

- It is important for families and carers to have an understanding about respiratory disease among people with learning disabilities and the key symptoms to look out for in order to support and access help as necessary.

- Seek support from a GP if you have any concerns about a person with learning disability suffering from respiratory disease.

- The local learning disability nursing team can offer further advice and support.

- Physiotherapists can help with teaching breathing techniques.

- Reasonable adjustments can be made to support GP and hospital appointments.

Reference

McCarron M, Swinburne J, Burke E, McGlinchey E, Carroll R & McCallion P (2013) Patterns of multimorbidity in an older population of persons with an intellectual disability: results from the intellectual disability supplement to the Irish longitudinal study on aging (IDS-TILDA). *Research in Developmental Disabilities* **34** (1) 521–527.

Further reading

Douglas G, Nicol F & Robertson C (2009) *Macleod's Clinical Examination* (12th edition). London: Churchill Livingstone.

Farokh EU (2010) *Principles of Respiratory Medicine*. New Delhi: Oxford University Press.

Pikora T, Bourke J, Bathgate K, Foley K, Lennox N & Leonard H (2014) Health conditions and their impact among adolescents and young adults with Down syndrome. *PloS one* **9** (5) 1–8.

Rowland M, Peterson-Besse J, Dobbertin K, Walsh ES & Horner-Johnson W (2014) Health outcomes among subgroups of people with disabilities: a scoping review. *Disability and Health Journal* **7** (2) 136–150.

Smeltzer SC (2009) *Brunner and Suddarth's Handbook of Laboratory and Diagnostic Tests*. Philadelphia, PA: Lippincott Williams & Wilkins.

Uppal H, Chandran S & Potluri R (2015) Risk factors for mortality in Down syndrome. *Journal of Intellectual Disability Research* **59** (9) 873–881.

Chapter 7: Cardiology

Daniel Marsden and Sally Wilson

Introduction

Cardiology is the branch of healthcare that deals with the heart and the impact that it has on health. The heart is a muscle that pumps blood through the arteries and veins to maintain energy and oxygen in all cells in the body. In a healthy body the heart is regulated by the body's needs. As exercise increases, so does the pressure to increase blood and oxygen to the muscles, tissues and organs.

Like any muscle, the heart needs to be exercised, looked after and not overworked. Placing too much stress and strain on the heart over a prolonged period can increase the risk of several heart problems occurring at a younger age such as:

- Heart attacks – this is a medical emergency consisting of a sudden blockage of blood to the heart muscle. This is often caused by a blood clot, will cause damage to the heart and can cause death.

- Heart failure – this occurs when damage to the heart causes blood not to be pumped round the body as it is supposed to.

- Congenital heart disease – where some of the structures of the heart are not properly formed prior to birth.

- Blood pressure – which can cause damage to the valves and arteries. This normally occurs as a result of lifestyle choices such as diet, exercise, alcohol consumption and smoking status.

  - High blood pressure can cause damage to the heart resulting in heart attacks and heart failure, along with strokes, kidney disease and damage to the arteries in the arms and legs.

  - Low blood pressure is not generally so significant, but can cause dizzy spells and fainting.

While these conditions apply to the whole population, this chapter intends to identify the distinct risks that people with learning disabilities can face and those conditions associated with particular syndromes. It will discuss how to identify symptoms at an early stage and also some of the issues that may arise in terms of access to healthcare. There are many ways that these risks can be minimised and mitigated, and some prompts, questions and resources will be presented here to help staff members supporting people with learning disabilities.

Predisposing factors

There are several factors that mean people may be more at risk of developing heart problems:

- **Family history:** if an individual has a family member that has been diagnosed with heart disease before the age of 55, for a male member of the family, or 65 for a female member, this would indicate that further diagnostics and monitoring might be necessary.

- **Ethnic background:** if the individual is from a South Asian background they are 1.5 times more likely to die of heart disease before the age of 75.

- **Age:** research suggests that people in their 40s and 50s are more likely to begin to experience the symptoms of heart disease.

- **Lifestyle choices:** smoking, eating fatty or sugary foods, and consuming more alcohol than is recommended will all increase the chances of damage to the heart and the risks of heart attack or heart failure.

Health checks and detecting heart problems in people with learning disabilities

It is always better to be forewarned of potential heart problems, and there are many ways to monitor or check for issues. If someone falls into two or more of the above 'at-risk' groups, this indicates that GP assessment and monitoring would be beneficial.

There are many different health checks that the GP surgery can offer, including a specific learning disabilities health check which the individual should be invited to have on an annual basis. This is designed to detect any health issues that might occur prior to them becoming a problem. For those between the ages of 40 and 74, the NHS Health Check is also available to help prevent diabetes, heart disease, kidney disease, stroke and dementia. These opportunities are designed for the individual to consider whether there are any changes in lifestyle, medical or social care that might minimise risks to the heart at an earlier age.

When undertaking these checks, it is likely that the GP surgery will already be aware that the person attending has a learning disability. However, when booking the appointment you may wish to explore with them whether there are any elements that might pose a barrier to the collection of the assessment data. Consider, for instance, the following:

- How might the person being supporting to attend the appointment feel about waiting in the waiting room?

- Will the person be asked any questions that can be prepared for prior to the appointment?

- How long is the appointment usually? Will the individual require the same amount of time, or could they need a longer or shorter appointment time, or a more regular/repeat appointment?

- Are there any communication issues that could be planned for?

- While most assessments will be non-invasive, you should check whether a urine, stool or blood sample will be required. What might be the best way of collecting these?

- Questions pertaining to other screening tests may also be discussed. There are some complex legal, ethical and practical considerations for these decisions, relating to further screening procedures. It is the patient's choice whether to have these diagnostics, however issues of capacity and consent will need to be considered. Anyone supporting the individual and the GP surgery might want to consult with local community learning disabilities nurses to support this process.

Within these health checks it is important to include a full review of the medication the individual is taking. Evidence shows that people with learning disabilities are more likely to take one or more medications that are prescribed for other long-term conditions such as epilepsy or a mental health issue (IHaL, 2015). These medications can increase blood pressure.

The health check is also a good opportunity to measure body mass index (BMI), which uses weight and height measurements to work out whether the person's body mass is at a healthy level or not, and gives an indication as to whether they may need to consider a lifestyle change. In general, the greater the BMI number, the greater pressure an individual is putting on their heart. For people with scoliosis (curvature of the spine) and other physical issues, it can be challenging to gain a reliable height to establish BMI. However, the Malnutrition Universal

Screening Tool (MUST) (Bapen, 2011) offers some adjustments that enable a more effective result, using forearm measurements.

It should be noted when measuring BMI that muscle is of a higher density than fat, meaning that for those who do not take exercise or have muscle wastage, a normal BMI could mask a high fat content. It may therefore be beneficial to access the expert advice of a dietician to help interpret this information.

Specific risks to heart health for people with learning disabilities

Along with people with physical disabilities, people who have specific syndromes can also be at a higher risk of heart problems. For instance, research shows that people with Down's syndrome and Williams syndrome are more likely to have congenital heart disease, and people with Down's syndrome and Prader-Willi syndrome are more likely to be overweight (IHaL, 2010). People with Down's syndrome also often have a hole between the different chambers of the heart. In severe cases this can lead to heart failure. It is usually treated and operated on in infancy, but some older adults with Down's syndrome may not have had the corrective surgery needed. If someone has this condition it means their blood has less oxygen in it and they will have trouble doing prolonged, vigorous activity. People with Down's syndrome are also more likely to have heart valve defects. Anyone with these should be under the care of a congenital heart disease specialist.

Keeping the heart healthy

Keeping the heart as healthy as possible is by far the best way of minimising the need to use healthcare services. This involves a series of lifestyle choices:

- **Diet** is a significant factor in keeping the heart healthy. Dietary guidelines recommend eating five portions of fresh fruit and vegetables a day, along with a portion of protein, found in meats and pulses, and a portion of carbohydrates such as bread, potatoes, pasta or rice. Packaged food often contains high levels of fat, sugar and salt which should be consumed in moderation. Food packaging often uses red, amber or green labelling to indicate how much of the recommended daily allowance of fat, salt and carbohydrates it contains. Avoiding 'red signs' or eating in moderation is best. For more information on a healthy diet, see further resources at the end of the chapter.

- **Taking exercise** on a regular basis strengthens the muscles, improves circulation and can have the effect of reducing stress and be beneficial to a healthy heart. There are many excellent online tools that enable novices to set reasonable goals or to track exercise. Couch to 5K is one such example – see resources at the end of the chapter for more details. It is also possible to join clubs or groups that play sports and team games.

- **Being a non-smoker** is key, as smoking causes damage to the arteries, leading to a build-up of fatty material that causes them to narrow. According to NHS Choices (2016) if you smoke, your chances of experiencing heart disease increase by one quarter. This can in turn lead to an increase in blood pressure and can increase the risk of blood-clotting, which can potentially cause heart attacks and strokes.

- **Following current guidance for alcohol consumption** is also recommended, which is no more than 14 units of alcohol for men and women per week. One pint of strong lager can contains three units of alcohol, one pint of standard lager contains two units, a small glass of wine contains 1.5 units, and a single serving of a spirit contains one unit of alcohol. Drinking greater amounts over a prolonged period can cause damage to the heart and its rhythm, increasing blood pressure, and increasing the risk of strokes, liver disease and some cancers. Smartphone apps are available to support monitoring of the number of units consumed, and how much is spent on alcohol, see the resources section for further details.

Enabling individuals to make healthy choices for themselves, for example by taking up and maintaining a sport, giving up smoking or learning how to cook healthier meals, can be a complex issue. First, the individual would need to have some understanding of the possible risks of their lifestyle choices on their heart. Some consideration as to how these messages are conveyed is essential; there are some excellent websites with free downloadable resources to help with this, including the British Heart Foundation and Easyhealth. Like any behavioural change it is important to enable the individual to identify achievable goals, to celebrate when one has been achieved, to maintain this progress and then to move on to the next goal. This is a challenge, but peer support, electronic reminders and monitoring carried out by health professionals can strengthen an individual's resolve.

Symptoms that should prompt urgent action

There are some symptoms that can indicate a more serious heart problem and should prompt urgent action:

- Chest pain (especially while lying flat or sleeping).
- Breathlessness.
- Sweating.
- Pain that spreads to the arm, neck or jaw.
- Light-headedness or dizzy spells.

If someone is experiencing chest pain that spreads, call 999.

Other symptoms that may require attention or support can include:

- dizziness
- fainting
- fast heart rate
- skin appearing a blueish colour
- clubbed fingers – fingers appear like drumsticks with bulging at the tips
- showing less interest in physical activities they used to enjoy like dancing or sports may indicate they are getting worse.

People with learning disabilities are often less able to interpret and verbalise the sensations and experiences they are having. It is therefore important to understand how the person expresses pain, and how much detail might be elicited from them about it. Consider the following:

- Does the person use communication aids?
- Are those supporting the person knowledgeable and experienced at using the communication aids to communicate effectively?
- How can the situation be best explained to healthcare professionals?

While healthcare services continue to become more aware of and adept at making adjustments for people with learning disabilities and their families, this care will remain a collaborative activity, as carers and care workers know what is 'normal' for that individual.

There are several ways to be able to prepare for an urgent admission. Consider the following:

- Is there an agreed Healthcare Passport used in the local area, and is this complete, up-to-date and available?

- Is there information on the healthcare organisation's website about what people with learning disabilities and their carers can expect?

- Does the service have a lead or a link nurse associated? For instance, most hospitals will have a lead for learning disabilities, which in some cases will be called a liaison nurse.

- Does the healthcare organisation understand that the person has learning disabilities? Ringing ahead with this information may help the service to plan and prioritise.

Tests or diagnostics that you might be offered

There are several assessments or diagnostics that might be proposed for someone presenting with heart or circulation problems:

- Taking an individual's pulse can indicate whether the heart is running in a normal rhythm or at the right speed for that individual.

- Normal blood pressure for most adults is between around 120/80. Were it to be above or below this, health professionals will likely be looking at possible causes. High blood pressure over weeks, months or years puts strain on the blood vessels and heart and can cause heart attacks and strokes.

- Blood samples can be taken and tested in a number of ways to establish if the heart has been damaged, to indicate why an individual might have palpitations, to establish whether they have heart failure and whether they have sufficient minerals for a healthy heart.

- A chest x-ray can help determine whether the person's symptoms are due to breathing or heart issues, and can identify any congenital heart problems that started before the individual was born, heart failure or any inflammation of the muscles around the heart.

- An electrocardiogram enables healthcare professionals to understand how the heart muscles and electrical pulses are working, and whether the rhythm indicates that an individual is having or has had a heart attack in the past. This involves having sensors attached to the skin which detect the electrical signals of the heart.

- An echocardiogram uses an ultrasound monitor to look at the heart. This involves placing some lubricating jelly on the chest to help conduct high-frequency sound waves, which bounce off the muscles of the heart to produce an image. The procedure takes about 15 minutes and can help in diagnosing whether an individual has recently had a heart attack, is in heart failure, has damage to the heart valves or has had a heart problem since birth.

- An angiogram allows doctors to look inside the heart to find out if there is any damage. This test can take up to 30 minutes. Using local anaesthetic a small tube is passed via the arm or leg along an artery into the heart. A dye is then pushed through the tube and a series of x-rays are taken to show any damage.

Making adjustments for having these tests

Depending on the circumstances, individuals will have different needs when being supported to have these tests. In emergency situations A&E staff are adept at intervening where people do not understand what is happening and are frightened. In less urgent circumstances, where the person does not understand what might be occurring, healthcare professionals will want to rely on the safeguards of the Mental Capacity Act (2005) to enable a decision to be reached in the individual's best interests and which is the least restrictive course of action possible. Consulting with the local community learning disability team can help with practical problem solving, facilitating diagnostics and care that is adjusted for the needs of the person with learning disabilities, and enabling mainstream healthcare professionals to monitor and maintain health.

Conclusion

Like the general population, as people with learning disabilities get older they will be susceptible to a number of health conditions including heart disease. We know that people with learning disabilities are more likely to experience heart problems at a younger age, that these problems can be associated with particular syndromes and medications taken for other health conditions, and that social and economic issues can lead to unhealthy lifestyle choices. However, there are ways that these risks can be minimised and reduced: through regular health checks at the GP surgery, by understanding how the person being supported might express their symptoms, and by staff or carers being prepared for visits to healthcare services in urgent situations. Specialist learning disability services will often have experience of accessing local healthcare services, diagnostics and treatment, and will be able to signpost and problem solve issues of access.

There are many online resources that help staff and carers and the people they support to take exercise, eat healthily and make other important lifestyle changes to look after their heart.

Summary points

■ Lifestyle choices are important to having and maintaining a healthy heart, encouraging a healthy diet and exercise will help with this.

■ People with learning disabilities are more likely to be vulnerable to heart disease due to associated health issues, and socioeconomic factors.

■ It is important to attend the GP annual health check and to have a health action plan to work to.

■ Having a good understanding of the symptoms of heart disease and how an individual might express these is vital.

■ Community learning disability nurses can support and facilitate access to the relevant tests in difficult or complex situations.

References

Bapen (2011) *The MUST Explanatory Booklet* [online]. Available at: www.bapen.org.uk/pdfs/must/must_explan.pdf (accessed October 2016).

IHaL (2010) *Health Checks for People with Learning Disabilities: A systematic review of evidence* [online]. Available at: https://www.improvinghealthandlives.org.uk/uploads/doc/vid_7646_IHAL2010-04HealthChecksSystemticReview.pdf (accessed October 2016).

IHaL (2015) *Prescribing of Psychotropic Drugs to People with Learning Disabilities and / or Autism by General Practitioners in England* [online]. Available at: https://www.improvinghealthandlives.org.uk/securefiles/160810_1130//Psychotropic%20medication%20and%20people%20with%20learning%20disabilities%20or%20autism.pdf (accessed October 2016).

NHS Choices (2016) *Managing Weight With a Learning Disability* [online]. Available at: www.nhs.uk/Livewell/Disability/Pages/weight-management-learning-disabilities.aspx (accessed October 2016).

Further resources

Easyhealth is a good resource to find 'accessible' health information: www.easyhealth.org.uk

NHS Guidance on a healthy diet: http://www.nhs.uk/livewell/goodfood/Pages/Goodfoodhome.aspx

Couch to 5K: http://www.nhs.uk/Livewell/c25k/Pages/couch-to-5k.aspx

One You Drinks Tracker: http://www.nhs.uk/Tools/Pages/drinks-tracker.aspx

Chapter 8: Diabetes in people with learning disabilities

Maria Truesdale and Laurence Taggart

Introduction

Diabetes is a lifelong condition that causes a person's blood sugar level to become too high. There are two main forms of diabetes: type 1 and type 2. Within the UK there are 3.3 million people diagnosed with diabetes and an estimated 590,000 people who have the condition but are not aware of it. The rapid increase in the number of adults developing type 2 diabetes is due to an ageing population, increasing levels of obesity and a lack of healthy lifestyle. Increasing evidence suggests that people with a learning disability are more likely to develop type 2 diabetes than those without. These individuals require additional support in the everyday management of their condition and to prevent long-term complications in the future.

What causes diabetes?

Diabetes occurs when the body cannot absorb glucose or sugar into the body's cells. The body needs a hormone called insulin to help break the glucose down so that it can be absorbed by the body: type 1 diabetes is where there is no insulin and type 2 diabetes is where there is not enough insulin or it is not working sufficiently. Both conditions are characterised by raised blood sugar.

The causes of type 1 and type 2 diabetes are different. Type 1 diabetes is caused by an autoimmune disorder that develops when the body's immune system attacks and destroys the cells that produce insulin. In contrast, type 2 diabetes develops when the body does not produce enough insulin to maintain a normal blood glucose concentration (called Hb1Ac), or when the body is unable to effectively use the insulin that is produced.

Symptoms of diabetes

If blood sugar or glucose is high (known as hyperglycaemia), individuals are likely to experience a range of physical symptoms such as:

- increased thirst
- headaches
- difficulty concentrating
- blurred vision
- frequent urination
- fatigue
- erectile dysfunction
- weight loss
- mental health symptoms such as mood change, agitation, withdrawal, and verbal and physical aggression
- urine that smells 'sweet' or has a 'fruity odour'.

Less likely symptoms are:

- having thrush – complaining of itchiness around the penis/vagina
- cramps
- skin infections
- constipation.

In the long term, if diabetes is not detected and is left untreated the person may develop blindness, renal failure, infection requiring amputation and heart problems, which can lead to premature death.

For many people with learning disabilities there is a greater dependency upon family and paid carers to recognise the signs and symptoms of diabetes and thereby make a referral to a nurse or GP for a health check. However, many family and paid carers may not know the signs and symptoms of diabetes. In addition, some people with learning disabilities may not display the typical signs and symptoms of diabetes as described above and may exhibit an array of 'challenging behaviours', making it harder for carers to recognise a health problem (Taggart *et al*, 2013).

Prevalence of diabetes

Diabetes affects approximately one in 20 people across the world and rates of diabetes worldwide are predicted to increase from 177 million in 2000 to 366 million by 2030: a global prevalence rate of 6.3%.

Type 1 diabetes is more prevalent in individuals with chromosomal syndromes such as Down's syndrome, Klinefelter syndrome and Prader-Willi syndrome, due to the weight gain associated with these conditions. Type 2 diabetes is also more prevalent in adults with learning disabilities. MacRae *et al* (2015) have reported that they found the prevalence figures of both type 1 and type 2 diabetes to be higher among people with learning disabilities compared to the non-disabled population. Estimates vary between 3%–18% (average 11%) across published studies.

Risk factors

There are a number of known risk factors for developing diabetes in the non-disabled population:

■ family history

■ age

■ ethnicity

■ obesity

■ high cholesterol

■ smoking.

Taggart *et al* (2014) have reported that people with learning disabilities are more likely to be at risk from developing diabetes as a result of:

■ genetic conditions that lead to obesity

■ sedentary (non-active) lifestyles

■ consuming high-fat diets

■ being prescribed antipsychotic medication

■ higher levels of obesity.

Several studies have clearly found that adults with learning disabilities and diabetes are screened less often than is recommended by the national UK clinical guidelines (Taggart *et al*, 2013).

Screening for diabetes

Across England, Wales and Northern Ireland people with learning disabilities should be offered an annual health check. This can help to identify a number of unrecognised health problems, including diabetes, and can also help with diagnosing and managing those who have the condition (Lennox & Robertson, 2014). However, some health checks may not automatically include diabetes screening; this is despite the identified higher prevalence rates of diabetes for this population.

Some people with learning disabilities may not be known to GP practices, thereby making it harder for nurses and GPs to identity them and to offer them an annual health check (McConkey *et al*, 2015). Therefore, a strong argument exists in favour of screening for subjects who are at increased risk for diabetes. Diabetes UK has a brief online questionnaire that assesses a person's risk of developing type 2 diabetes (see http://riskscore.diabetes.org.uk/high-bp), and this could be used with adults with learning disabilities.

Treatment of diabetes

Diet

Diet plays an important part in glucose control. Often, people with learning disabilities do not go food shopping or prepare and cook their own food. Reliance is usually on family or paid carers to plan and cook their meals – and research has shown that many of these carers may not have the appropriate knowledge of nutrition (Hanna *et al*, 2011). Knowledge and education about what a healthy diet is, as well as ongoing encouragement and support from family, paid carers and healthcare staff, is crucial to the success of a person with a learning disability in making healthy food choices and maintaining a healthy diet. Those people with learning disabilities who do go shopping and prepare their own meals may not purchase the most healthy of foods, relying instead on 'convenience foods'. Education about what constitutes a healthy diet is therefore important.

Diet can be improved through a reduction in sugar intake and saturated fats, and eating the recommended five portions of fruit and vegetables a day, in addition to portion control, calorie monitoring and alternative cooking methods (eg. grilling or baking rather than frying foods).

Exercise

Exercise is a good way of helping to reduce weight, which will then reduce high blood glucose. However, many people with a learning disability live sedentary lifestyles and find it difficult to engage in physical activities.

Education on the benefits of physical activity not only to control blood glucose but to help reduce obesity is required for this vulnerable group to stay healthy (Taggart & Cousins, 2014). It is important that people with learning disabilities are aware of the recommended daily amount of exercise and examples of ways in which they could be more physically active. With support from others (family, peers and staff), people with learning disabilities can incorporate various levels of moderate to vigorous healthy exercise into their daily lives, for example, by undertaking some household chores, climbing the stairs or walking. Breaking down the recommended 30 minutes of daily exercise into three ten-minute blocks can make an increase in physical activity achievable.

Medication and concordance

Medication is a core part of diabetes treatment, whether in the form of tablets or insulin injections to reduce blood glucose, high blood pressure or high cholesterol. However, a number of difficulties exist with medication concordance for people with learning disabilities due to their potentially reduced capacity to follow instructions, failure to self-administer prescribed medications and a lack of awareness about the need to reorder medications. Securing concordance with treatment may often involve other agencies, and may rely on family and carers to administer medication.

The type of medication required will depend on the individual's own needs and situation. For some people tablets are not enough to control blood glucose levels and insulin is required. This can be even more problematic for people with learning disabilities and often requires the support of a healthcare team. As insulin is injected into the stomach, buttocks or thigh, individuals with learning disabilities may not have the knowledge and understanding of rotating injection sites to prevent the build-up of lumps under the skin, which may lead to erratic absorption of the insulin that may affect control of blood glucose levels.

Management of diabetes

The key healthcare essentials for effective diabetes management have been identified as follows:

1. Annual blood glucose monitoring.

2. Annual blood pressure monitoring.

3. Annual monitoring of cholesterol.

4. Annual screening for signs of retinopathy (a disease of the retina) – eye tests, in layman's terms.

5. Annual monitoring and review of legs and feet, focusing on skin, circulation and nerve supply.

6. Annual monitoring and review of kidney function, including checking for the presence of protein in the urine as a sign of possible kidney disease.

7. Review and monitoring of weight to identify the need for weight loss.

8. Advice and support to quit smoking.

9. Attendance for regular diabetes review to identify and manage conditions such as heart disease to minimise the risk of stroke.

10. Working with healthcare professionals to develop a clear care plan to support diabetes management to minimise risks and complications.

11. Making use of accessible information about the management of diabetes.

12. Providing for carers to enable the effective management of diabetes.

13. Access to education programmes about diabetes and effective management.

14. Access to information and specialist care when planning a family to ensure effective diabetes control and management.

15. Access to healthcare professionals with knowledge and skills of diabetes to enable effective management.

16. Access to emotional and psychological support from specialist healthcare professionals about issues and concerns about diabetes management and control.

(Adapted from Diabetes UK, 2015)

Although general, the above guidelines should also be adhered to in how diabetes is managed in people with learning disabilities, though reasonable adjustments will have to be made to empower individuals and their carers.

Diabetes can reduce the blood supply to your feet and cause a loss of feeling, therefore another area of importance is foot care. Ideally the person should see a podiatrist once a year and between these times there are ways the individual can take care of their feet:

■ They should be encouraged to observe their feet daily, looking out for sores, cuts, swelling or skin that is hot to the touch or smells. If the person is unable to do this for themselves staff/carers need to do this and report any injuries.

■ Ensure that shoes fit well and that shoes and socks are not too tight.

■ Cut toenails regularly so they do not rub against neighbouring toes causing injury. This should be done by a chiropodist.

■ The individual should be encouraged not to walk barefoot.

■ Only apply moisturising creams to dry skin on the feet; avoid getting it in between toes and ensure that the area between the toes is dry.

■ Feet should be patted dry after bathing rather than rubbed; ensure the gap between the toes is dry.

■ They should be encouraged to avoid alcohol and be made aware of the dangers associated with drinking alcohol.

Easy Read resources

Accessible and easy to read health promotion literature is crucial to enable people with learning disabilities to increase their understanding of what diabetes is, what constitutes a healthy diet, ways they can be physically active, and the importance of medication compliance.

People with learning disabilities often have poor access to information about their diabetes in a format appropriate to their level of understanding. A pictorial information booklet developed by a health facilitator in Northern Ireland has recently been published. It provides diabetes education in a simple, clear manner using pictorial information to aid understanding (see the resources section at the end of this chapter).

Family members, paid staff and healthcare professionals also need to be educated about what diabetes is, healthy diet and promoting physical activity to support and empower the person to be aware of the risk factors of diabetes and to modify their lifestyle behaviours (Taggart *et al*, 2014).

Structured education programmes

There has been a great emphasis on the need for structured education for people with type 2 diabetes in the non-disabled population in the UK and internationally. However, structured education programmes aimed at helping people to self-manage their diabetes have not been targeted at people with a learning disability, despite being identified by NICE guidelines as 'best practice' (NICE, 2004).

Structured education programmes aim to improve people's knowledge, skills and confidence, enabling them to take control of their own condition and integrate effective self-management into their daily lives. DESMOND (Diabetes Self-Management for Ongoing and Newly Diagnosed) is a UK national structured education programme designed for people with type 2 diabetes. It lasts for six hours and supports people to find out more information about diabetes. It is a resource designed to help people manage diabetes-related changes and gives people the opportunity to meet and share experiences with others.

The DESMOND-ID programme is an amended version of the original DESMOND structured education programme (Taggart *et al*, 2015). The ways in which educators deliver the content is adapted to make it accessible for people with a learning disability. There are learning activities to engage participants and an emphasis on using images rather than the written word. Previous work has shown that flexibility is required in delivery and timing of the education sessions in order to meet the learning needs of individuals.

Conclusion

It is well established that people with a learning disability are more susceptible to developing type 2 diabetes as they age due to a number of risk factors. It is paramount that family members and carers of people with learning disabilities are aware of these risk factors and the symptoms of diabetes, for early detection, monitoring and control. Maintaining good control of blood glucose levels, as well as blood pressure and cholesterol levels, is crucial in reducing the risk of diabetic complications. For those who are overweight, weight loss can often help to improve the extent of diabetes symptoms. Although challenges still exist, individuals supporting people with a learning disability and type 1 and type 2 diabetes can help in the management of their condition by facilitating individuals' compliance with taking medication and offering lifestyle advice. In order to achieve this, general health promotion as well as primary prevention of diabetes is needed. The increasing availability of Easy Read resources and the development of structured education programmes specifically for people with a learning disability and their families is one way of addressing the needs of this vulnerable population.

Summary points

■ Empower the person and their carers to understand what diabetes is and its long-term consequences for the individual's health.

■ Focus on weight management/reduction and increasing physical activity.

■ Ensure that user-friendly information is available for both the person with learning disabilities as well as their carers.

■ Encourage the person to participate in an adapted structured education programme to learn how to manage their condition.

References

Diabetes UK (2015) *The Care You Should Receive: 15 healthcare essentials* [online]. Available at: https://www.diabetes.org.uk/Guide-to-diabetes/Monitoring/15-healthcare-essentials/ (accessed October 2016).

Hanna LM, Taggart L & Cousins W (2011) Cancer prevention and health promotion for people with intellectual disabilities: an exploratory study of staff knowledge. *Journal of Intellectual Disability Research* **55** (3) 281–291.

Lennox N & Robertson J (2014) Health checks. In: *Health Promotion for People with Intellectual and Developmental Disabilities* (pp 194–203) Maidenhead: McGraw Hill/Open University Press.

MacRae S, Brown M, Karatzias T, Taggart L, Truesdale-Kennedy M, Walley R, Northway R, Carey M & Davies M (2015) Diabetes in people with intellectual disabilities: a systematic review of the literature. *Research in Developmental Disabilities* **47** 352–374.

McConkey T, Taggart L & Kane M (2015) Optimising the uptake of health checks for people with intellectual disabilities. *Journal of Intellectual Disability* **19** (3) 205–214.

NICE (2004) *Diagnosis and Management of Type 1 Diabetes in Children, Young People and Adults* [online]. London: NICE. Available at: www.nice.org.uk/cg15 (accessed October 2016).

Taggart L, Brown M & Karatzias T (2014) Diabetes. In: Taggart, L. Cousins, W. (Eds) *Health Promotion for People with Intellectual Disabilities* (pp 69-76). Maidenhead: Open University Press/McGraw-Hill.

Taggart L, Coates V, Clarke M, Bunting B, Davies M, Carey M, Northway R, Brown M, Truesdale-Kennedy M, Martin-Stacey L, Scott G & Karatzias T (2015) A study protocol for a pilot randomised trial of a structured education programme for the self-management of type 2 diabetes for adults with intellectual disabilities. *Trials* **16** 148.

Taggart L, Coates V & Truesdale-Kennedy M (2013) Management and quality indicators of diabetes mellitus in people with intellectual disabilities. *Journal of Intellectual Disability Research* **57** 1152–1163.

Taggart L & Cousins W (2014) *Health Promotion for People with Intellectual Disabilities*. Maidenhead: Open University Press/McGraw-Hill.

Websites and useful resources

These are websites that contain user-friendly resources for adults with diabetes.

Diabetes
Diabetes: Pictorial information about type 2 diabetes for people with a learning disability: www.northerntrust.hscni.net/pdf/Diabetes_booklet_for_those_with_a_learning_difficulty.pdf

Pete the Pancreas
www.diabetes.ie/wp-content/uploads/2011/08/15-Jun-2011-Pete-for-children-FINAL-UPLOAD.pdf

Reasonable Adjustments to Diabetes Services for People with Learning Disabilities
Guide to reasonable adjustments published by Improving Health and Lives: www.improvinghealthandlives.org.uk/publications/1176/Making_Reasonable_Adjustments_to_Diabetes_Services_for_People_with_Learning_Disabilities

Type 2 Diabetes: Living a healthier life
A film providing good clear information for people with learning disabilities about diabetes and living with the condition: www.diabetesdvd.org.uk

Chapter 9: Mental health and mental well-being

Eddie Chaplin and Karina Marshall-Tate

Introduction

In the past there was a misconception that people with learning disabilities could not experience mental health problems. Not only is this not true, it is now commonly accepted that people with learning disabilities in fact experience mental health problems at higher rates than the general population (Cooper *et al*, 2007). Mental health problems and how they present in people with learning disabilities may also differ when compared to the general population.

People with learning disabilities who have mental health problems are more likely than the general population to experience increased levels of physical ill-health and they are more likely to experience poorer physical health outcomes. For example, those with a severe mental illness (SMI), which include psychotic disorders such as schizophrenia and bipolar disorder, are more likely to die from physical ill-health within five years, compared with the wider population (British Medical Association, 2014). Conversely, over 4.5 million people in England and Scotland who have a long term physical condition also suffer from a mental health problem. For example, those with long term conditions such as type 1 diabetes or who have had a heart attack are more likely to experience depression than those who have not (British Medical Association, 2014). People with learning disabilities are more likely to receive a poorer service when accessing healthcare and as a result have a greater number of health needs due to poor recognition and management of both mental and physical health conditions (Alborz *et al*, 2005; Baines & Emerson, 2011; Emerson & Glover, 2013). These health inequalities were previously accepted as being a condition of having a learning disability; however there has been shift in these views (Heslop *et al*, 2013; Michael, 2008; PHSO, 2009). It is no longer acceptable for people with learning disabilities to experience these inequalities.

There are a number of reasons why people with learning disabilities might be vulnerable to developing mental health problems. These include:

- being more prone to negative life experiences, for example, bullying
- low socioeconomic status
- lower employment rates
- reliance on others for support
- higher rates of physical health problems
- being socially excluded
- brain injury
- sensory impairments
- neurological conditions such as epilepsy
- poor or maladaptive coping strategies
- poor self-esteem.

Positive mental health

A greater understanding of mental health problems in people with learning disabilities has coincided with an increased interest in positive mental health (mental well-being) and mental health promotion. Mental health promotion seeks to educate and reduce an individual's vulnerability to mental illness and poor mental health by educating them about protective factors and teaching them strategies to build resilience. The list below, adapted from Hardy and Bouras (2002), serves to illustrate potential targets for education and intervention to promote mental well-being for people with learning disabilities:

- adequate nutrition and exercise
- detection and treatment of physical ill-health
- developing and having continuity in relationships
- being involved in and listened to in the care/support planning process
- having ethnic and cultural needs met
- developing social skills
- developing coping skills

- being part of a community or peer group

- having an occupation

- having a stable home life

- being financially stable

- having access to support services when required

- developing assertiveness and self-confidence.

Good mental health can be affected by our socioeconomic and health status, but is not only the absence of stress, poverty and trauma that is important. Good mental health promotion should be inclusive and aim to, wherever possible, bring families and communities together for the person. The NHS has launched a mental health promotion campaign in which they promote five steps to mental well-being. These five steps encourage people to:

1. Connect – with the people around you.

2. Be active – go for a walk or a bike ride.

3. Keep learning – learning new skills can give a sense of achievement and confidence.

4. Give to others – a smile or a kind act or volunteering.

5. Be mindful – be more aware of the present moment, how you feel and what is going on around you

(NHS Choices, 2016)

Often, though, there are barriers to implementing personal mental health strategies that are aimed at improving mental well-being. People with learning disabilities may need additional support in how to look after their mental well-being. Things many of us take for granted – like having a job, being connected and being active, for example – may not be possible for people with learning disabilities, or they may be reliant on support from others to achieve this. Additionally, some individuals with learning disabilities may lack the required knowledge of what to do when feeling unwell and where to go to get help. They may be dependent on others to support them. However many people who support them feel unequipped to recognise the early signs of deterioration in a person's mental health. There are a number of educational leaflets freely available for carers and in an Easy Read format for people with learning disabilities to help them understand more about their condition and treatment.

In the UK, mental health provision is based on the recovery approach. Recovery is a values-led approach that puts the person at the centre of their care and is led by their hopes and dreams. It emphasises supporting the person to be able to live with their illness rather than a health professional relying on the existence or absence of signs and symptoms to determine if an individual is ill or not. Recovery is characterised by hope through personalised networks, similar to circles of support, to help individuals realise their potential and reduce stigma. Recovery focuses on people rather than services, and emphasises the person's strengths rather than their weaknesses. A major focus of the recovery model is education and enabling the individual to participate equally in their treatment, thus supporting self-management, which as a result decreases the need for people to rely on formal services and professional support. Good mental health allows the opportunity for people to play an active part in their community by contributing through work, volunteering and having active social lives – things that are taken for granted by others.

Assessment

People with learning disabilities can find it difficult to describe their feelings and experiences, either through difficulty in communicating their experiences or not realising the significance of changes in them, such as poor sleep or changes in appetite. Therefore, if an individual does access healthcare services because of a health problem, basic information can often be overlooked or not reported during the interview because of a lack of inquiry and corroboration. Because of cognitive impairment, poor memory may also make recalling and recognising symptoms difficult. With this in mind clinicians may be more reliant on reports from family members and carers.

People with learning disabilities may present with atypical signs and symptoms of illnesses. This is when symptoms one may expect appear not to be present and are replaced by another symptom. For example, normally when someone is depressed they will experience changes in appetite and or their sleep pattern; some people with severe learning disabilities may also experience these as well as atypical signs such as self-induced vomiting or aggression (Hurley, 2006; McCarthy & Chaplin, 2015) or self-injurious behaviours. This can include the reporting of physical symptoms or deterioration in their behaviour. Sometimes the problem may have a physical origin so it is therefore important to conduct a full physical examination. This can rule out or identify reasons for the person's presentation. A number of mental and physical illnesses also have an overlap of symptoms. A common example is thyroid problems, which can mimic the extremes of bipolar disorder. When the level of thyroxine is low, then the person may present with depressive symptoms such as apathy, loss of interest in their surroundings or feeling low; whereas those with high levels of the hormone thyroxine may experience manic type symptoms such as excitability, irritability, anxiety, insomnia or psychosis.

For people with mild learning disabilities, assessment is often conducted in the same way as for the wider population, with clinicians working on the assumption that prompt identification and intervention will increase the chances of a positive prognosis. To assist diagnosis there are a number of measures available specifically for people with learning disabilities, including the Glasgow Depression Scale for people with a Learning Disability (GDS-LD0) (Cuthill *et al*, 2003), the Glasgow Anxiety Scale for people with an Intellectual Disability (Mindham & Espie, 2003), and the Psychiatric Assessment Schedule for Adults with Developmental Disability (PAS-ADD) (Moss, 2011). All these tools support clinical decision-making when making a diagnosis. The presentation of mental illness in individuals will change depending on the diagnosis. Below we discuss some of the more common mental illnesses and in Table 9.1 common symptoms are listed according to diagnosis.

Common mental health problems

Table 9.1: Signs and symptoms of mental illness

Mental illness	Common signs and symptoms
Anxiety	■ Restlessness & pacing ■ Avoiding situations/withdrawal ■ Panic attacks/palpitations/headaches ■ Changes to sleep pattern and appetite ■ Chest pain/dry mouth/excessive sweating
Depression	■ Loss of interest in usual activities ■ Low levels of energy ■ Changes to mood ■ Changes to sleep and appetite ■ Feelings of worthlessness or guilt
Psychosis, including schizophrenia	■ Hallucinations – seeing or hearing things that others cannot perceive ■ Changes to sleep, appetite or behaviour ■ Strange or unusual behaviours ■ Strange or unusual beliefs e.g. paranoid delusions

Mental illness	Common signs and symptoms
Bipolar affective disorder	■ Low mood ■ Feelings of worthlessness or despair ■ Changes to sleep, appetite or behaviour ■ Unusual or bizarre beliefs ■ Not sleeping ■ Feeling full of energy and 'constantly on the go' ■ Having lots of thoughts or new ideas

Anxiety

Anxiety disorders are characterised by excessive anxiety, worry and apprehension. The rates of anxiety disorders are thought to be higher in people with learning disabilities, and a recent study reported a rate of 3.8% in this group (Cooper *et al*, 2007). Anxiety disorders affect both men and women at the same rates in people with learning disabilities, compared with the wider population, where women experience higher rates of anxiety.

The assessment of anxiety disorders in people with learning disabilities can be a challenge. And describing their symptoms – particularly mental distress or physical illness, such as palpitations, stomach pains or headaches – can be difficult. When accurate self-report is unavailable, we need to observe for behavioural signs of acute anxiety or sleep disturbance. This may include fidgeting, restlessness, being in a panic, sweating, shaking, etc. Normal anxiety is helpful and helps to protect us. However, having an anxiety disorder means that the person will find it difficult to control their worry and anxiety, which will start to interfere with their everyday life. Other signs and symptoms may include restlessness or feeling on edge, irritability, the mind going blank, muscle tension, and sleep difficulties, such as problems falling asleep or remaining asleep, or having a restless night's sleep.

Anxiety disorders can also be characterised with what are known as somatic or autonomic symptoms. These include dry mouth, difficulty swallowing, sweating, shaking, chest pain, headache, fatigue and changes in urinary frequency. Anxiety will impede the person's quality of life, as they will avoid situations that they think will induce their symptoms for fear of anxiety and the physical symptoms associated with it.

As well as general anxiety disorders, there are other specific anxiety disorders such as phobias. A phobia (an irrational and persistent fear of specific objects or situations) is also an anxiety disorder. Examples of phobias may include having a fear of blood, having injections or of animals. An individual may have a phobia of a specific situation, such as going in a lift or other enclosed place, or travelling by aeroplane. In agoraphobia people have anxiety around an open or public place or situation, usually outside the home, such as an open marketplace or travelling in a train, in which escape may be difficult. Social phobia is fear of failing in social situations or performing in front of other people. Social phobias may arise when people are exposed to unfamiliar people or possible scrutiny by others. Those with severe learning disability may express this fear or anxiety through tantrums, freezing or shrinking from social situations with unfamiliar people.

Also common to anxiety disorders are panic attacks. A panic attack can be described as a discrete period of intense fear or discomfort. In panic disorder people have symptoms of palpitations in which the heart feels like it is racing and pounding. The person may be observed to be sweating, trembling or having difficulty breathing and may hyperventilate. They may complain of chest pain or feeling dizzy, or may look as if they are going to collapse. They can sometimes have feelings of unreality or being detached from oneself, or fear that they are going to lose control. They may complain of a fear of dying or numbness sensations with observed chills or hot flushes. Extreme panic may result in aggression and destructive behaviour such as lashing out of the arms and legs and head-banging. People with learning disabilities are more likely to express anxiety somatically rather than emotionally, so will often describe the physical symptoms rather than thoughts of impending dread or doom.

Depression

When assessing for depression it is important to enquire about the person's mood in recent weeks or whether they have lost interest in usual activities or become more irritable in their mood. Often, for people who are depressed, a change in their activity levels will occur. The person may be agitated, pacing and fidgety or their movements may slow down completely. They may report a loss of energy or fatigue, and may be observed spending an excessive amount of time just sitting with no engagement in activities. As a result depression is likely to impact on that persons day-to-day functioning in terms of attending the day service or any work placement they may have. It is also important to consider biological symptoms. For example, does the person have any significant weight loss or weight gain? Is there any change in their sleep pattern, such as early-morning awakening or sleeping excessively?

The person may describe feeling worthless or express inappropriate guilt by saying they are bad or should be punished for some past event. They may seek constant reassurance from carers and make lots of negative self-statements about themselves. People with severe learning disability might not be able to express these feelings of guilt or worthlessness but may show a slowing-down in their activities or reduction in their self-care skills; they may be more distracted and find it increasingly difficult to concentrate or complete day-to-day tasks. Some atypical signs may be self-injurious behaviours such as pulling out hair or head banging.

People who have depression may also experience thoughts of death or suicidal ideas or make plans to commit suicide, and may make threats to harm or kill themselves that may be impulsive in nature. If there are ever any concerns that a person with learning disabilities is experiencing these thoughts and feelings then they should be supported to seek medical help through their GP or in an emergency via accident and emergency services.

Psychosis

The prevalence rates of psychotic disorders in people with learning disabilities are greater than in the wider population. In schizophrenia, probably one of the most widely known psychotic disorders, the rates are estimated at 3% in people with learning disabilities compared to 1% in the general population. Cooper *et al* (2007) reported a figure of 4.4% for people with learning disabilities suffering from psychotic disorders. In terms of assessment, people with learning disabilities may find it difficult to report or understand symptoms seen in psychosis such as hallucinations or to describe delusional beliefs. Delusions are false beliefs that are not explained by culture or experience and for which the person rejects any alternative explanation. These can be paranoid in nature, for example, believing that a person is out to harm them or that they are being controlled. Delusions may be less elaborate than in those without learning disabilities, which can be explained in some part due to poorer expectations and opportunities. For example, someone who does not know about AIDS or other viruses, could not hold the delusion that these are being transmitted by aliens. This may be an issue, as fantasy can be mistaken for delusions and vice versa, in people with learning disability. For example, if someone with a learning disability says they are a policeman this will often be taken as fantasy or play. However it is worth bearing in mind that delusions are a reflection of what is happening or within the scope of the person's understanding of the world. Therefore those with limited opportunities may present with less complex delusions. Reporting symptoms can also be an issue particularly where the person is unaware of the significance or that any changes are taking place in the first place, whether it is the content of their thoughts, or other signs and symptoms mentioned earlier. This makes it more difficult to know what is relevant to report to clinicians.

Some people may also show behaviours that lead people to believe (wrongly) that they are responding to hallucinations. For example, the echoed speech seen in people with autism may give the impression they are holding a conversation, when in fact they are repeating fragments of speech they have heard earlier. A diagnosis of schizophrenia is difficult in people with severe/ profound and multiple learning disabilities, due to reduced communication skills and difficulty in sharing their experiences. In this type of scenario observation is key, including monitoring of biological indicators of poor mental health, such as changes in sleep or diet. Behaviours seen in people with autism may be similar to those we see in people with schizophrenia and there have been a number of cases where people with autism have been incorrectly diagnosed as having schizophrenia.

Bipolar disorder is another psychotic disorder in which the person experiences periods of depression and hypomania, which is characterised by periods of elation, excess energy and bizarre beliefs that can often be grandiose. Physical health is also an issue, as exhaustion may occur in severe cases where hypomania or mania occurs. At this point the person may be constantly on the go, not eating or sleeping, and may be a physical risk to themselves.

Supporting mental health management

An essential part of the health management of people with mental illness is the inclusion of physical health as part of the process. Often, routine examination as part of a mental or physical health assessment has uncovered undiagnosed conditions. It is likely that having learning disabilities and a mental health problem means the person will have poorer health outcomes in general. The importance of annual health checks for people with learning disabilities (described in previous chapters) serves to highlight how crucial they are in improving health outcomes. Another important issue in terms of physical healthcare is the monitoring of medication and side effects. Some medication used to treat mental health problems can have adverse side effects or increase the individual's likelihood of being diagnosed with long term physical conditions. For those supporting someone with a learning disability, it is important to find out more about this from a GP or local health team. The questions to ask may include:

- What is the medication being prescribed for?

- What are the potential side effects?

- Is there anything the person can do to stop side effects happening or to reduce them if they occur?

- Will the medication affect the person day-to-day – for example, can they still go for lunch at the pub?

- How long will the person be on the medication and when will it be reviewed?

- How will the person know that it is working?

- Will the person need to have blood tests?

Sometimes people with learning disabilities are prescribed drugs for challenging behaviour that are normally used to treat mental illness. Public Health England and many learning disabilities health and social care staff have been concerned for some time about this practice, particularly in the light of the Winterbourne View scandal. In July 2015, NHS England published findings from reports from three public bodies, which highlighted that there is a much higher incidence of prescribing of these medicines among people with learning disabilities than the wider population, often without justification, and that these medicines are used for a long time without review. Table 9.2 provides a breakdown of common medications used for mental health problems.

Table 9.2: Examples of medication commonly used to treat mental illness

Drug group	Generic name	Manufacturer name	Side effects
Antidepressants	Citalopram Fluvoxamine Paroxetine Fluoxetine Sertraline Clomipramine Amitriptyline Venlafaxine	Celexa Luvox Paxil Prozac Zoloft Anafranil Elavil Effexor	■ Nausea and vomiting ■ Weight gain ■ Diarrhoea ■ Sleepiness ■ Sexual problems

Drug group	Generic name	Manufacturer name	Side effects
Antipsychotics	Clozapine Haloperidol Risperidone Quetiapine Trifluoperazine Olanzapine	Clozaril Haldol Risperdal Seroquel Stelazine Zyprexa	■ Drowsiness ■ Dizziness ■ Restlessness ■ Weight gain ■ Dry mouth ■ Constipation ■ Nausea ■ Vomiting ■ Blurred vision ■ Low blood pressure ■ Seizures People on antipsychotics will need regular physical checks, including blood tests for white blood cell count. These fight infection and low white cell count is a common side effect of antipsychotic medications. The person should also have their weight, glucose levels and lipid levels monitored regularly by a doctor. For some of the older types of antipsychotics such as chlorpromazine and haloperidol, side effects may include Parkinson's type symptoms, such as: ■ Tics ■ Tremors ■ Rigidity ■ Muscle spasms ■ Restlessness

Drug group	Generic name	Manufacturer name	Side effects
Mood stabilisers	Lamatrogine Lithium carbonate Carbamazepine	Lamictal Lithium Tegretol Carbotrol	■ Itching and rash ■ Excessive thirst, which can lead to excessive drinking ■ Frequent urination ■ Tremor (shakiness) of the hands ■ Nausea and vomiting ■ Slurred speech ■ Fast, slow, irregular or pounding heartbeat ■ Blackouts ■ Seizures ■ Hallucinations ■ Confusion ■ Swelling of the eyes, face, lips, tongue, throat, hands, feet, ankles or lower legs Lithium can cause several side effects, which can be serious. Because of this those prescribed lithium will require regular blood testing of lithium levels. Over recent years there has been an increase in prescribing drugs traditionally used for epilepsy, which are also mood stabilisers.
Anxiolytics	Lorazepam Buspirone Clonazepam Diazepam Alprazolam	Ativan BuSpar Klonopin Valium Xanax	■ Nausea ■ Blurred vision ■ Headache ■ Confusion ■ Tiredness ■ Nightmares

Adapted from *An Introduction to Supporting the Mental Health of People with Intellectual Disabilities* (Chaplin, Marshall-Tate & Hardy, 2016)

While medication for mental illness can help an individual with challenging behaviour when in crisis, it should be a last resort and its continuing and/or long term use should be avoided (unless a mental illness has been diagnosed). There is little evidence for to support its use and the potential side effects can be severe (Public Health England, 2015; Sheehan *et al*, 2015). Asking the questions listed on p.92 can help to ensure that medications are correctly prescribed and accurately documented to enable their effective use and review.

If an individual with learning disabilities displays challenging behaviours and does not have a mental illness then alternative measures should be used, such as psychological and environmental interventions, interventions to treat coexisting health problems or sleep problems, and positive behaviour support (NICE, 2015).

If there are problems due to medication, it is best to seek medical help as soon as possible. Something simple, such as adjusting the dose or switching to a new medicine, may help. Side effects can include dry mouth, restlessness and irritability but also more serious effects such as weight gain, which can increase risks of conditions like diabetes and some blood disorders.

Conclusion

People with learning disabilities are at greater risk of developing mental health problems, resulting in an increased need for effective mental health and well-being strategies. There has been an abundance of policy and directives on mental health promotion over the last decade, however we need to ensure that these are applied to the specific needs of people with learning disabilities, who should be included in consultations so that they are empowered to take control of their lives and thus promote their own mental health.

There have been a number of good practice examples of mental health care but often these are not shared. There are a number of local forums for people with learning disabilities that focus on promoting positive mental health, such as the Tuesday Group. The group is made up of adults with learning disabilities who have used mental health services coming together to teach others about staying safe and well and to talk about their own experiences. The Tuesday Group has not only been well received by participants but has provided a voice for people with learning disabilities, through conferences, publications and consultations, giving them a say in the development and evaluation of local and national policy and initiatives for mental health.

Summary points

- Everyone has mental health needs and when these needs are not met it increases the risk of developing mental health problems.

- Good mental health is the foundation for individual well-being and helps the person to realise their own potential, cope with the normal stresses of life, work productively and make a contribution to their community.

- People with learning disabilities are at increased risk of mental ill-health.

- Mental health promotion is designed to enhance the mental well-being of individuals, families, organisations or communities.

- Mental health promotion aims to prevent mental health problems from occurring by supporting the individual to build resilience or reduce the impact of mental illness on their day-to-day life.

- Mental health promotion materials should be available in an accessible format and courses or programmes should be adapted to meet the needs of people with learning disability.

References

Alborz A, McNally R & Glendinning C (2005) Access to health care for people with learning disabilities in the UK: mapping the issues and reviewing the evidence. *Journal of Health Services Research & Policy* **10** 173–182.

Baines S & Emerson E (2011) Health inequalities and people with learning disabilities in the UK. *Tizard Learning Disabilities Review* **16** (1) 42–48.

British Medical Association (2014) *Recognising the Importance of Physical Health in Mental Health and Intellectual Disabilities: Achieving parity of outcomes*. London: BMA Board of Science.

Chaplin E, Marshall-Tate K & Hardy S (2016) *An Introduction to Supporting the Mental Health of People with Intellectual Disabilities: A guide for professionals, support staff and families*. Brighton: Pavilion Publishing and Media Ltd.

Cooper SA, Smiley E, Morrison J, Williamson A & Allan L (2007) Mental ill-health in adults with intellectual disabilities: prevalence and associated factors. *British Journal of Psychiatry* **190** 27–35.

Cuthill FM, Espie CA & Cooper SA, (2003) Development and psychometric properties of the Glasgow Depression Scale for People with a Learning Disability: individual and carer supplement versions. *British Journal of Psychiatry* **182** 347–353.

Emerson E & Glover G (2013) *Reducing Premature Mortality in People with Learning Disabilities: effective interventions and reasonable adjustments* [online]. London: NHS England. Available at: https://www.england.nhs.uk/wp-content/uploads/2014/09/info-ld-interventions.pdf (accessed October 2016).

Hardy S & Bouras N (2002) The presentation and assessment of mental health problems in people with learning disabilities. *Learning Disability Practice* **5** (3) 33–38.

Heslop P, Blair P, Fleming P, Hoghton M, Marriott A & Russ L (2013) *Confidential Inquiry into Premature Deaths of People with Learning Disabilities (CIPOLD): Final report* [online]. Bristol: Norah Fry. Available at: www.bris.ac.uk/media-library/sites/cipold/migrated/documents/fullfinalreport.pdf (accessed October 2016).

Hurley AD (2006) Mood disorders in intellectual disability. *Current Opinion in Psychiatry* **19** (5) 465–469.

McCarthy J & Chaplin E (2015) Anxiety disorders. In; C Hemmings and N Bouras (eds) *Psychiatric and Behavioural Disorders in Intellectual and Developmental Disabilities* (pp89–98). Cambridge: Cambridge University Press.

Michael J (2008) *Healthcare for All: Report of the Independent Inquiry into Access to Healthcare for People with Learning Disabilities*. London: Department of Health.

Mindham J & Espie CA (2003) Glasgow Anxiety Scale for People with an Intellectual Disability (GAS-ID): development and psychometric properties of a new measure for use with people with mild intellectual disability. *Journal of Intellectual Disability Research* **47** (1) 22–30.

Moss S (2011) *PAS-ADD Clinical Interview*. Brighton: Pavilion Publishing and Media Ltd.

NICE (2015) *Challenging Behaviour and Learning Disabilities: Prevention and interventions for people with learning disabilities whose behaviour challenges*. NICE guideline [NG11]. London: NICE.

NHS Choices (2016) *Five Steps to Mental Wellbeing* [online]. Available at: www.nhs.uk/conditions/stress-anxiety-depression/pages/improve-mental-wellbeing.aspx (accessed October 2016).

NHS England (2015) *Urgent Action Pledged on Over-medication of People with Learning Disabilities* Available at: https://www.england.nhs.uk/2015/07/14/urgent-pledge/ (accessed October 2016).

Parliamentary and Health Service Ombudsman (PHSO) (2009) *Six Lives: The provision of public services to people with learning disabilities*. London: TSO.

Public Health England (2015) *Prescribing of Psychotropic Drugs to People with Learning Disabilities and / or Autism by General Practitioners in England* [online]. PHE publications gateway number: 2015105.

Sheehan R, Hassiotis A, Walters K, Osborn D, Strydom A & Horsfall L (2015) Mental illness, challenging behaviour, and psychotropic drug prescribing in people with intellectual disability: UK population based cohort study. *BMJ* **351**: h4326.

Chapter 10: Caring for the person with epilepsy and learning disability

Tony Hollands

Introduction

People with learning disabilities have an increased risk of developing epilepsy. Around one per cent of the general population have a diagnosis of epilepsy, but for people with learning disabilities their risk of developing seizures due to epilepsy is 26 times greater (McGrother *et al*, 2006). The risk of having epilepsy increases with the severity of the learning disability, and up to half of people with profound learning disability also have epilepsy (de Boer *et al*, 2008). People with learning disabilities are more likely to have epilepsy associated with structural abnormalities of the brain, leading to more frequent, and more difficult to control, seizures. Sixty eight per cent experience ongoing seizures despite treatment (McGrother *et al*, 2006), resulting in the need for poly-therapy: treatment with more than one anti-epileptic drug (AED) in an effort to control seizures. This may lead to an increased risk of side effects or interactions between AEDs and other medications, which could have an effect on the person's health. Due to more frequent seizures in this group, more intensive management and an increased focus on reducing risk is required.

This chapter will focus on the assessment, management and support of people with epilepsy and learning disabilities, concentrating on first aid, seizure rescue medication, seizure triggers, support with taking AEDs, attending medical appointments, advocacy and home risk assessment.

Support with epilepsy clinic appointments

The doctor treating epilepsy, often a neurologist or a psychiatrist in learning disabilities, will rarely see their patient's seizures, therefore the individual's carer, whether family member or support worker, are the eyes and ears of the epilepsy team. There are a number of tools available to assist with recording seizures, from seizure observation forms that can provide a detailed eye witness account (with questions to answer about onset, seizure description and recovery), to monthly recording forms or seizure diaries. Video footage of seizures can be extremely helpful when viewed in clinic. With smartphones now widely available and capable of capturing very clear images, filming seizures is becoming easier, but issues of privacy, mental capacity and consent must be considered. The most common mistake made when recording a person's seizures is to assume that their seizures are of a certain type, just because it has always been said that they have experience that particular seizure type. For instance, because the person experiences blank staring episodes their seizures may have been recorded as absence seizures, but blank staring can also occur in complex focal seizures. What distinguishes the two seizure types is the length of the seizure and other involuntary behaviours that occur with the staring – such as semi-purposeful movements like lip-smacking or clothes plucking. The seizure type is fundamental to the selection of the correct medical treatment for different seizures; without the correct information seizures may not respond to treatment or may even worsen.

Preparation for the clinic appointment is essential. At the very least seizure recording charts or diaries and a list of medication with doses are required. It is equally important for the carer escorting the person with epilepsy to know the person in their care. The carer must have spent a reasonable time supporting the individual in order to be aware of any changes that may have occurred. Treating epilepsy is not just about counting seizures – although being seizure-free is most likely to improve quality of life (Birbeck *et al*, 2002) – we must also consider the effects of individual seizures on quality of life, for example changes in behaviour prior to seizures, and how long it takes for a person to recover completely. Many people with epilepsy and seizures that are difficult to control may take several days to return to their normal level of functioning, for example, to be free of headaches, to respond normally and to have normal energy levels.

Knowing the person and their abilities is also extremely important in order for the carer to be able to act as an advocate. The person with epilepsy and learning disability needs to be involved, as far as possible, in decisions about their treatment and management of their condition. All involved in their care have a responsibility to assess capacity with making decisions. The carer is a key individual in the assessment process and must have knowledge of the person's abilities in order to assist the epilepsy team in reaching decisions around capacity. Of course, the carer will also have a key role in supporting the individual with the decisions they make, or in any best interest process.

First aid for seizures

Carers who support people with epilepsy and learning disabilities are required to complete first aid training that must include basic life support. However, basic life support alone would be insufficient without general epilepsy awareness training that includes understanding and recognising different seizure types.

Seizure types are broadly classified into focal (formerly known as partial) and generalised seizures (see Tables 10.1 & 10.2). Each seizure requires a different first aid response depending on the effects on the person's levels of consciousness during the seizure and the risk of injury to the individual.

Table 10.1: Focal (partial) seizures and symptoms.

Type of focal seizure	Symptoms
Simple focal seizure	Consciousness not impaired, with alteration in emotion, sensation (sensory), vision, movement and behaviour depending on area of brain involved.
Complex focal seizure	Features as seen in simple focal seizures (above) but with impaired consciousness. Confusion, and automatisms – semi-purposeful repetitive behaviours may be present depending on area of brain involved.
Focal seizure with secondary generalisation	A focal seizure which develops (due to the spread of epileptiform activity in the brain) into a generalised seizure, usually a tonic clonic seizure.

Table 10.2: Generalised seizures and symptoms.

Type of generalised seizure	Symptoms
Tonic clonic	Complete loss of consciousness, rigidity and rhythmical jerking of the whole body. Often tongue bite and/or urinary incontinence. Followed by confusion and drowsiness.
Tonic	Sudden brief rigidity of the whole body, with complete loss of consciousness. Will fall if standing followed by rapid recovery. Injuries to back of head common.
Atonic	Sudden brief loss of muscle tone (body goes floppy), complete loss of consciousness, if standing will fall followed by a rapid recovery, injuries to forehead and face common.
Myoclonic	Sudden, single jerks (often violent) of mainly upper body, if standing could fall, may feel dazed for few seconds before rapid recovery.
Clonic	Repetitive jerking (often rhythmical) and usually affecting the whole body. Complete loss of consciousness followed by confusion and drowsiness.
Absence	Sudden vacant stare, abrupt interruption of consciousness, usually lasting less than 5 seconds with rapid recovery.

Both tables based on the Commission on Classification and Terminology of the International League Against Epilepsy (1981) and ILAE commission report (Berg *et al*, 2010).

Broadly speaking, in a simple focal seizure the person experiences no alteration in their levels of consciousness. They will often experience changes in sensation such as numbness, tingling, a strange taste or smell, or a rising sensation from deep in the abdomen, but will be aware of what is happening to them. In a complex focal seizure, the seizure may commence as a simple focal seizure, but as epileptiform or electrical activity spreads in the brain, consciousness is impaired, leading to confusion, unresponsiveness and automatisms (performing of repetitive behaviours) such as lip-smacking, clothes-plucking or rubbing of the nose or hair.

In generalised seizures the epileptiform discharges in the brain are widespread and the person loses consciousness, but this varies with different types of generalised seizures. For instance, in a generalised absence seizure loss of consciousness may last less than five seconds, and will be so brief the person having the seizure will not know what has happened. Observers may recognise just a brief staring episode. Whereas in a generalised tonic-clonic seizure the person's muscles may suddenly stiffen for a few seconds – if standing they will fall – and then the whole body jerks rhythmically. They will lose consciousness completely, often taking a prolonged period of time to recover fully. The person will not have any recollection of what has happened to them.

First aid response is dictated by the person's levels of consciousness and the seizure type. In most cases, for focal seizures and non-convulsive generalised seizures, such as absences and myoclonic seizures, the priority is making sure the person is safe and away from danger. In generalised tonic-clonic and tonic seizures, however, the first aid priorities are to maintain the person's airway, breathing and circulation. Within any seizure type there can be a risk of experiencing prolonged or repeated seizures, and generalised tonic-clonic seizures in particular require an urgent response by contacting an ambulance and/or administering seizure rescue medication, if prescribed.

Please note: when describing levels of consciousness in people with severe learning disability, always attempt to engage with the person and assess against their normal levels of awareness. For a person with a mild learning disability obtain their recollections after the seizure. Remember that if the person has their eyes opened in a fixed stare during a seizure, such as in a tonic clonic seizure, that despite eyes opened, they are still almost certainly unconscious.

Rescue medication for seizures

As people with epilepsy and learning disability are at increased risk of more frequent and more difficult-to-control seizures, they may be prescribed seizure rescue medication. For many years the first-line treatment for prolonged or repeated seizures was rectal diazepam. However, medication given rectally, although often effective, can be difficult to administer, and the whole process is undignified for the patient and uncomfortable for the person administering the medication. More recently another benzodiazepine, midazolam, has become the first-line drug for prolonged repeated seizures, administered into the buccal cavity (in the side of the mouth between the inside of the cheek and lower gum). Not only easier to administer and more dignified, buccal midazolam can also be used for people who are users of wheelchairs, without having to try and struggle to remove them first, which is obviously not without risk of injury to the person being treated, but also to the carer.

Carers must undergo training in the administration of buccal midazolam. Training guidance is standardised and set out in *A Guideline on Training Standards for the Administration of Buccal Midazolam* (JEC, 2012). Training will include epilepsy awareness and recognising seizures, first aid and the administration procedure for the medication, as well as, importantly, understanding side effects of the medication, recovery of the person with epilepsy and when to contact the emergency services for assistance. The safe use of the drug to control seizures is a priority of training, not just the administration procedure. A prerequisite for attending training in the administration of buccal midazolam is that carers must have attended first aid training that includes basic life support.

There must always be an individual buccal midazolam administration plan, signed by the prescribing doctor, in place. This should be understood by carers administering the rescue medication. The individual plan must include seizure descriptions and classifications (types), and in what situations to administer any medication – for example, after five minutes, or if one seizure follows another without recovery in between. An ambulance would usually be called if it is the first time buccal midazolam is being administered (in case of any adverse reaction or it fails to control the seizures) or, if administered previously, if the seizures continue for a further five minutes after administration. All medications have potential side effects that patients must be warned of, but not all patients experience side effects. Often, central nervous system side effects can be quite subtle, such as increased tiredness, difficulties with co-ordination or balance, and visual disturbances. If the carer is not familiar with the person's normal levels of cognitive function, mobility, moods and behaviour, they will not be able to detect and report any changes to the epilepsy team. Please see the first aid guidelines for tonic clonic seizures at the end of this chapter.

Epileptic seizure triggers

Most seizures are of sudden onset, and many people with epilepsy are not aware of their seizure triggers. We have to be clear about what we mean by seizure triggers. There are a group of epilepsies, known as reflex epilepsies, that occur consistently in response to certain stimuli. Probably the most well known are seizures brought on by photosensitivity, with specific stimuli or triggers being flashing images or patterns of light. This affects around three percent of all people with epilepsy, with females affected more so than males (Shorvon, 2005). However, there are also much rarer reflex epilepsies, such as eating and reading epilepsy.

In general epilepsy care we need to consider situations in which seizures may increase in frequency. These situations are referred to as seizure precipitants. (Although they are often referred to as seizure triggers, this is technically incorrect.) So what situations are more likely to increase the frequency of seizures for people with learning disabilities?

Those with epilepsy who do not have learning disabilities will usually be able to work out for themselves, perhaps with some help from family, friends or from professionals supporting them, what makes their seizures worse or better. But in many cases, people with a learning disability will not be able to recognise their own seizure precipitants. Therefore, an important role of carers in epilepsy care for people with learning disability, is for them to know what can precipitate seizures. This will mean getting to know what type of seizures the person has and their usual frequencies, and monitoring the person closely to try and understand what increases and reduces the likelihood of seizures.

Situations associated with increased likelihood of seizures in people with learning disability and epilepsy include:

■ illness

■ tiredness

■ during the night

■ during sleep

■ while falling asleep or on waking

■ menstruation

■ constipation

■ stress

■ excitement

■ pain

■ anxiety

- alcohol

- some recreational drugs.

Illingworth *et al* (2014) identified illness as the most common situation likely to increase seizures in a study of 100 people with epilepsy and learning disability.

Support with taking anti-epileptic drugs

If doses of medication taken to control epileptic seizures are missed, then clearly control may be lost. Often though, the high level of risk to the individual with epilepsy is not fully appreciated. The person may not only experience more seizures, but the seizures may be more severe, and could even lead to status epilepticus or sudden unexpected death in epilepsy (SUDEP) – see the section on epilepsy and risk.

If doses of medication are missed, there is usually one of two possible causes: the first is forgetting to take medication (or carers forgetting to administer medication) and the second is medication refusals. Carers must recognise the severe risks to the person with epilepsy and learning disability of not taking AEDs regularly. A person with a mild learning disability may acquire the skills to self-medicate and become independent in this area of their life, whereas a person with a severe learning disability is likely to need their medication administered to them by their carer.

Monitored Dosage Systems, or Dosette packs, are an extremely helpful tool to reduce the risks of an individual forgetting to take medication or a carer forgetting to administer it. The packs are divided into sections to hold tablets, which are arranged in a grid, with seven columns for the days of the week, and four rows for morning, lunch, dinner and night. The packs are prefilled with medication by the chemist and the prescriptions can be sent directly to the pharmacy from the GP. The packs, if used correctly, will help the person take medication at the prescribed time; however, they can be problematic if the person is undergoing frequent medication changes, as they can delay these changes.

Of course the packs will not alert someone to take their medication, but there are a number of devices or apps for mobile phones that can be set up to remind the patient or carer of the dose time. Other devices include dose boxes that automatically open at the times doses are due, but these may need to be filled by the person with epilepsy themselves or their carer.

Medication refusals by the person with epilepsy and learning disability may require a comprehensive assessment of the reason for the refusals. Efforts can be made to encourage the person to take their medication every 15-30 minutes up until six hours after the original dose time, and as long as the medication is taken twice daily – every 12 hours – there should be six hours before the next dose. Do not double up on doses, and always check with the prescribing doctor or nurse (Epilepsy Society, 2015). A later dose is preferable to a missed dose: missed doses eventually lead to a lowering of drug levels and possible loss of seizure control.

Risk assessment

The National Institute of Clinical Excellence (NICE), make specific recommendations on the management of risk for people with epilepsy and learning disabilities (2012). The key areas of risk to be assessed can be found in the summary at the end of this chapter. The carer, with support from the epilepsy team, needs to develop individual risk management plans.

At the beginning of this chapter we addressed the risks associated with different seizure types, including prolonged repeated seizures, or status epilepticus, and SUDEP. SUDEP is defined as:

> *'Sudden, unexpected, witnessed or unwitnessed, non-traumatic, non-drowning death in a patient with epilepsy, with or without evidence of a seizure and, excluding status epilepticus (prolonged seizures) in which post-mortem examination does not reveal a toxicological or anatomic cause for death.'*
> (Nashef, 1997, p.56)

SUDEP affects one in 1,000 people with epilepsy, but for people with learning disabilities the risks can be higher, due to seizures that are often difficult to control. For those with severe epilepsy the risk of SUDEP increases to one in 200 (NICE, 2012). For the person with epilepsy and learning disability, any risk assessment needs to include the following aspects of daily living that may place the person at increased risk, due to seizures and possibly due to their learning disability as well. Risk factors for SUDEP must also be addressed in the epilepsy risk assessment.

Recommendations on assessing risk for people with epilepsy and learning disability should include:

- bathing and showering (to reduce the risk of drowning during a seizure a shower is safer)

- preparing food
- using electrical equipment
- managing prolonged or serial seizures
- the impact of epilepsy in social settings
- SUDEP
- the suitability of independent living, where the rights of the child, young person or adult are balanced with the role of the carer.

(NICE, 2012)

Risk factors for SUDEP include:

- young age
- generalised tonic-clonic seizures
- uncontrolled epilepsy
- learning disability
- seizures occurring during sleep
- unwitnessed seizures
- poor adherence to anti-epileptic medication.

(Shorvon, 1997)

Telecare devices such as under-mattress seizure detection alarms, which can detect tonic-clonic seizures may allow carers to be alerted to the person with epilepsy having a seizure in their sleep, or when resting on their bed. Similar devices are available to be placed in easy chairs. Other useful devices include listening monitors (such as infant monitors) or different forms of CCTV, although a capacity assessment may be required before deciding on their use, or a best interest decision reached. Seizures which do not involve rhythmical jerking movements or involve the person making a loud noise, may ultimately require regular checks throughout the night by carers.

Conclusion

Carers of people with learning disabilities and epilepsy have a vital role in ensuring the people in their care receive the best treatment and management for their epilepsy. They need to be aware of the different types of epilepsy and how it may present differently in individuals, and be aware of a care plan.

Summary points

- Obtain epilepsy awareness training and, if required, training in the administration of seizure rescue medication, such as buccal midazolam or rectal diazepam.

- Ensure you are able understand different seizure types and recognise the seizures experienced by the person in your care.

- Enable the person with learning disability and epilepsy in your care to live as full and independent a life as possible, and at the same time understand the risks posed by seizures, so risks can be properly assessed and effectively managed.

- Ensure you know the person in your care well, and have the required information about the person's seizures, medication, general health and well-being before attending appointments with the team treating their epilepsy. This will enable you to help the person explain their progress to the doctor or nurse, and enable you to truly act in the person's best interests.

References

Berg AT, Berkovic SF, Brodie MJ, Buchhalter J, Cross JH, van Emde Boas W, Engel J, French J, Glauser TA, Mathern GW, Moshé SL, Nordli D, Plouin P & Scheffer IE (2010) Revised terminology and concepts for organization of seizures and epilepsies: report of the ILAE Commission on Classification and Terminology. *Epilepsia* **51** (4) 676–685.

Birbeck GL, Hays RD, Cui X & Vickery BG (2002) Seizure reduction and quality of life improvements in people with epilepsy. *Epilepsia* **43** (5) 535–538.

de Boer HM, Mula M & Sander JW (2008) The global burden and stigma of epilepsy. *Epilepsy and Behaviour* **12** (2006) 540–546.

Commission on Classification and Terminology of the International League Against Epilepsy (1981) Proposal for revised clinical and electrographic classification of epileptic seizures. *Epilepsia* **22** (4) 489–501.

Epilepsy Society (2015) *Strategies and Tools for Taking Epilepsy Medication / AEDs* [online]. Available at: https://www.epilepsysociety.org.uk/strategies-and-tools-taking-medication#.V17Bl5ErK00 (accessed October 2016).

Illingworth JL, Watson P & Ring H (2014) Why do seizures occur when they do? Situations perceived to be associated with increased or decreased likelihood in people with epilepsy and intellectual disability. *Epilepsy and Behaviour* **39** 78–84.

Joint Epilepsy Council of the UK and Ireland (2012) *Working Together for Epilepsy: A guideline on training standards for the administration of buccal midazolam.* Leeds: JEC.

McGrother CW, Bhaumik S, Thorp CF, Hauck A, Branford D & Watson JM (2006) Epilepsy in adults with intellectual disabilities: prevalence, associations and service implications. *Seizure* **15** (6) 376–386.

Nashef L (1997) Sudden unexpected death in epilepsy: terminology and definitions. *Epilepsia* **38** (11 Suppl) 56–58.

NICE (2012) *The Epilepsies: The diagnosis and management of the epilepsies in adults and children in primary and secondary care*. CG137. London: NICE.

Shorvon SD (1997) Risk factors for sudden unexpected death in epilepsy. *Epilepsia* **38** (Suppl.11) 520–522.

Shorvon SD (2005) *Handbook of Epilepsy Treatment* (second edition). Oxford: Blackwell Publishing.

Appendix

First aid for generalised tonic-clonic seizures (convulsive seizures)

1. Stay calm.

2. Look around – is the person in a dangerous place? If not, don't move them.

3. Move objects like furniture away from them.

4. Note the time the seizure starts.

5. Stay with them. If they don't collapse but seem blank or confused gently guide them away from any danger. Speak quietly and calmly.

6. Cushion their head with something soft if they have collapsed to the ground.

7. Don't hold them down.

8. Don't put anything in their mouth.

9. Check the time again. If a convulsive (shaking) seizure doesn't stop after five minutes call for an ambulance – dial 999.

10. After the seizure has stopped, put the person in the recovery position and check that their breathing is returning to normal. Gently check their mouth to see that nothing is blocking their airway such as food or false teeth. If their breathing sounds difficult after the seizure has stopped, call for an ambulance. Stay with them until they are fully recovered.

(Epilepsy Society, 2015)

For information on first aid for all seizure types see www.epilepsysociety.org.uk or www.epilepsy.org.uk

Chapter 11: Cancer

Peter Woodward

Introduction

There are hundreds of different types of cancer, ranging from those that are well known and high on the public health agenda, such as lung, cervical, breast, testicular, bowel and skin cancers, to much rarer cancers with a lower prevalence rate. People with learning disabilities are prone to developing cancers just as anyone else can, but the types of cancers that are seen in people with learning disabilities may vary. For instance, lung cancer, which is associated with smoking tobacco, is seen in lower rates in people with learning disabilities who are less likely to smoke. Instead, cancers of the oesophagus and stomach are seen in higher numbers in people with learning disabilities due to differences in anatomy and physiology or infections that are seen in people with learning disabilities (see Chapter 12 on gastrointestinal disorders). This chapter discusses how cancers may develop and why different cancers develop in people with learning disabilities. Finally, it examines the difficulties in assessing for cancers in people with learning disabilities and the problems involved in treating cancer.

How cancer develops

The body is made up of trillions of cells, which divide to produce fresh cells as they are needed. For instance, the skin is constantly renewing itself as old cells die and new ones take their place. Cancer occurs when one of the body's cells becomes damaged over time. The cell can be damaged by accident when dividing normally or it can be damaged by external factors such as radiation, tobacco smoke, alcohol or chemicals. If the cell becomes damaged it may die or pass the damage on to its 'daughter' cells. These damaged cells may not affect how the cell functions but are one step further away from being healthy. These cells can become damaged still further as the person ages, and in some cases the damage causes the cells to reproduce excessively.

Normally, healthy cells will only reproduce as needed but cancer cells will keep reproducing. If the cells carry on reproducing they form lumps in the body. If the lump has a blood vessel nearby it can be fed by the blood supply causing it to enlarge still further. These lumps can be dangerous because as they continue to expand they can put pressure on organs or cause blockages in the body. It is possible that some of the cancerous growth can break off and travel around the body in the blood stream. When these fragments get to blood vessels that are very small, such as those in the lungs or the brain, they can lodge there and will continue to expand where they have lodged, making fresh growths.

It can take a long time for a cell to become cancerous; because of this most cancers are associated with older age and the risk of getting cancer increases with each year. There are some cancers that are associated with childhood, like leukaemia, and others like testicular cancer which is normally seen prior to middle-age in men.

Some people may be born with a mutation in their cells already, which may be genetic. This does not mean the individual will definitely develop cancer but it may increase the chance of developing cancer over a lifetime.

Possible risk factors for cancer

There are many factors that increase the likelihood of getting cancer, some of which are listed below:

■ Tobacco contact, but usually breathing in tobacco smoke.

■ Viruses such as the human papilloma virus associated with cervical cancer.

■ A diet that is high in processed meats; over-cooking food, for example, by barbecuing; or a diet with too little fibre.

■ A poor diet and lack of exercise – obesity is also a risk factor and is associated with cancer of the bowel, oesophagus, kidney, gall bladder and pancreas.

■ Excessive alcohol consumption, which can affect the mouth, liver, breast, bowel and throat.

■ Working in dangerous environments where an individual may be exposed to asbestos, dust, chemicals or dyes.

■ Exposure to hormones such as oestrogen as part of postmenopausal therapy, which can affect the breasts or prostate.

■ Infections such as *helicobacter pylori* (see Chapter 12) or hepatitis b and c, which can lead to health complications that can later cause cancer.

■ Radiation, which could be due to sunlight, x-rays, radon gas or even through radiotherapy used to treat cancer.

■ Age can interact with all of the above as someone can be exposed to a carcinogen at 20 years old and not develop cancer until much later in life, or they may be exposed everyday of their life and still not get cancer until they are much older. For example, some workers who were exposed to asbestos in the 1960s developed asbestosis in later life.

Cancer in people with learning disabilities

It is very difficult to get an exact picture of how many people with learning disabilities develop cancer. In the wider population about a quarter of people develop cancer and of these 50% will die as a result, making it one of the major causes of death. Many studies have found that people with learning disabilities are less likely to develop cancer – about half as many – and it is the third highest cause of death. Other studies have found that the rates of cancer are similar in people with learning disabilities. It also needs to be considered that in the past, people with learning disabilities would die at a significantly younger age, which means many of the older studies looked at people who had not reached old age, in which case one would expect to see lower rates of cancer. There is also an argument that because less people with learning disabilities smoke they will not develop lung cancer. This means that if rates of cancer are the same in people with learning disabilities as they are in the wider public, they may have higher rates of other cancers to account for the lower rates of lung cancer.

People with learning disabilities are more likely to develop some types of cancers in higher rates than are seen in the wider population and less likely to develop other cancers than would be expected.

Cancers seen in lower levels in people with learning disabilities

Skin cancer is seen in lower levels. This is because skin cancer is often caused by exposure to ultraviolet rays. People with learning disabilities are less likely to holiday abroad in sunny destinations or to use sunbeds. They are often kept out of the sun or avoid it if they are on medication that makes them sensitive to the sun. It is not that people with learning disabilities cannot develop skin cancer, they are just less likely to make lifestyle choices associated with skin cancer.

People with learning disabilities are less likely to smoke and this means there are also lower levels of mouth, throat and lung cancer. People with mild learning disabilities are more likely to smoke than people with more severe learning disabilities and this is reflected by slightly higher rates of lung cancer in people with mild learning disabilities.

Women with learning disabilities have been found to have lower rates of cervical cancer. This may be accountable to being less likely to being in a sexual relationship where they could be exposed to the human papilloma virus. Women with Down's syndrome may be at lower risk of breast cancer.

Cancers seen in higher levels in people with learning disabilities

People with learning disabilities can develop cancer for exactly the same reasons as the wider public. However, there are some additional reasons why they may or may not develop cancers. For example, some genetic syndromes can make the development of cancer more likely. This may be due to a genetic reason or to environmental factors in conjunction with the syndrome. For example, people with Down's syndrome are more likely to develop cancer of the gall bladder for genetic reasons. They are also more likely to be obese and obesity is associated with cancer. This is where genetic and environmental factors can combine to cause cancer. Some syndromes are associated with lower rates of hormones like oestrogen and testosterone. These are often treated with hormone replacement therapy, which can lead to certain cancers such as breast cancer in women or prostate cancer in men.

Down's syndrome is more studied in relation to cancers, and there are some that should be looked out for, particularly in the very young, such as leukaemia which is 20 times more likely in people with Down's syndrome. Other cancers seen in higher numbers in people with Down's syndrome are cancer of the retina, cancers of the lymphatic system, pancreatic cancer, cancer of the gall bladder and bone tumours. Men with Down's syndrome are more likely to develop cancer of the penis and testicles.

Gastrointestinal cancers may be twice as high in people with learning disabilities. This is due to other health complications causing cancer. For example, gastro-oesophageal reflux disease, where stomach acid leaves the stomach and burns the lining of the oesophagus, can damage the oesophagus and is thought to cause cancer. The *Helicobacter pylori* infection can cause stomach ulcers which are in turn thought to cause cancer of the stomach. Please see Chapter 12 on gastro-intestinal disorders for more on these conditions.

Chronic constipation, like a number of other risk factors, is often associated with more severe and profound learning disabilities. It is known that constipation can lead to the development of cancer of the colon and rectum. However, it is not clear whether this causes higher levels of these cancers in people with learning disabilities, as people with more severe learning disabilities tend to die at a younger age.

Because people with learning disabilities have a different profile of cancers, it of course does not mean that carers should be complacent. People with learning disabilities can and do develop all sorts of cancer. It is important to know which ones may be more prevalent so that carers can observe for the signs and symptoms of these.

Identifying and assessing for cancer

Identifying cancer in people with learning disabilities, like many health problems, can be more difficult if the individual does not report feelings of pain or discomfort. Carers need to be alert to the types of cancers that are seen in higher numbers in people with learning disabilities. If they care for someone who has a syndrome they should research to see if there are any cancers associated with this syndrome and be on the lookout for signs and symptoms of these. Most syndromes have advice pages available on the internet.

An individual may not realise they have cancer and symptoms will depend on where the cancer is located, how far advanced it is and if it is affecting any organs, nerves or tissue. For example, a very small brain tumour may cause symptoms but a tumour in the pancreas can go unnoticed until it is at an advanced stage. Other cancers are easier to detect, for example, skin cancers that can be seen or cancers that affect the liver. If the cancer has spread around the body there may be symptoms in other parts of the body to the initial cancer site.

Regular screening can help detection. Examples are screening of the cervix, mammograms, blood tests to detect for prostate cancer and tests to look for small amounts of blood in the faeces, which can indicate gastrointestinal cancers. Some of these are more invasive or painful, such as mammograms or cervical smears. Women with learning disabilities may be put off because of the discomfort caused or not seeing the point of having a screening test if they do not feel ill. Others with more severe learning disabilities may not be considered at risk so may not be offered cervical screening because they are not sexually active. Levels of cervical and breast screening have been found to be lower in people with learning disabilities.

Some lumps are detected through self-examination and people with learning disabilities can be taught to self-examine their breasts or testicles for lumps. There is advice available via the internet on carrying out self-examinations, including versions adapted for people with learning disabilities (see www. easyhealth.org.uk for examples). Learning disability nurses or sexual health groups run by the local community learning disabilities team may be able to provide advice on this too.

Some cancers such as breast, testicular or skin cancers are often discovered by an individual's partner during sexual foreplay. However, people with learning disabilities are less likely to be in a sexual relationship, making this route of detection less likely. Support staff may be put off examining the people under their care, worrying about issues of consent or what may be considered abuse. However, skin cancers can be seen, as can large testicular lumps, and support staff should be vigilant when supporting individuals with their personal hygiene.

Carers should be concerned if they observe dark faeces, which may indicate that blood from further up the digestive tract is in the stool. If blood is seen in vomit or faeces medical advice should be sought.

When a doctor carries out examinations they may feel for lumps or carry out blood tests that may look for changes in hormonal levels or for changes in the immune system. If a cancer is suspected, a biopsy may be carried out where a sample of the growth is taken away for testing.

Table 11.1 shows some of the signs and symptoms associated with some gastrointestinal cancers. It can be seen that it is often not obvious that someone has cancer or that the symptoms can be mistaken for something else.

Table 11.1: Signs and symptoms of gastrointestinal cancers

Signs and symptoms of stomach cancer	Signs and symptoms of oesophageal cancer	Cancer of the pancreas
■ Indigestion ■ Excessive stomach acid ■ Chest pains ■ Belching ■ Feeling full and having a loss of appetite ■ Weight loss ■ Feeling sick or vomiting ■ Blood in stools ■ Blood in vomit	■ Often does not cause problems until it is at quite an advanced stage ■ Trouble swallowing or feeling that food is stuck ■ Pain/pressure in the chest ■ Weight loss ■ Loss of appetite ■ Vomiting ■ Blood in vomit or stools ■ Hiccups ■ Coughing/choking ■ Indigestion/heartburn	■ Weight loss ■ Jaundice or yellowing of the skin or whites of the eyes ■ Urine that is dark or faeces that are a lighter colour ■ Feeling sick or vomiting ■ Itching ■ Abdominal pain ■ Back pain ■ Enlarged lymph nodes in the neck

Treatment of cancer

If a cancer is discovered and it is at an early enough stage, the aim of treatment is to try to remove, kill or reduce the cancerous growth. There are various methods for doing this, which are discussed below. Some of the treatments may be used in combination.

Surgery is used to remove the cancer completely by cutting it out of the body. This can be an operation carried out under general anaesthetic or it may be done under local anaesthetic, for example, when removing a growth from the skin. Some types of cancer cannot be operated on, such as leukaemia and lymphoma.

Chemotherapy is the use of chemical drugs to target the cancerous growth. This type of drug targets rapidly dividing cells; unfortunately, it can be toxic to all cells, healthy or cancerous, so may kills other rapidly growing cells in the body. This can make side effects particularly unpleasant and other drugs may have to be given to counter the side effects. Chemotherapy may be used where the cancer has spread or is at risk of spreading.

Radiotherapy is the use of radiation to try to kill or reduce the size of a growth. This can be done by using a beam of radiation and pointing it at the part of the body where the cancerous growth is. This method is quite painless but involves the individual remaining still while the therapy takes place. Another option is inserting a radioactive piece of material into the body next to the growth; alternatively a radioactive substance can be injected into the body or the person can drink it. Although the radiation does not cause pain, the procedure to insert it may cause discomfort. The radiation damages the DNA of the cancer cells causing them to die. Radiotherapy may be used with surgery to either shrink the growth before surgery or to make sure all of the growth is dead following surgery.

Immunotherapy is a newer treatment for cancer, which is used to boost the body's natural defence systems to detect and kill cancers. This may be through helping the body to recognise cancer as a problem, or using the immune system to carry radiation or chemical drugs directly to the cancerous growth. Types of immunotherapy can be used to create a vaccine for cancer or to create viruses that kill the cancer, although this can have some side effects.

As well as direct treatments to tackle the cancer, other medications can be given to help deal with pain, sickness or any other health conditions the person may develop, such as constipation. Hormones may also be used, for example, in the treatment of prostate cancer. Vaccines can be given for conditions that may cause cancer such as hepatitis or the human papilloma virus.

There are a number of complementary or alternative therapies that can be offered when someone has cancer. These may be used to help the person to come to terms with their illness or to give the individual relief from pain or the side effects of medication. This could be through counselling or support groups, or offering massage, acupuncture or aromatherapy. Unfortunately, people with learning disabilities often do not get offered the full range of alternative therapies that are available. These should be explored when supporting someone who has cancer.

Because of the many problems involved in detecting cancer in people with learning disabilities, diagnosis may not happen until it is too late. This may mean that the cancer cannot be treated or that the treatment will have side effects that outweigh the benefits. In this case the individual may be offered palliative care (see Chapter 13).

Cancer prevention

The ideal scenario is to prevent cancer occurring in the first place. People with learning disabilities should be encouraged to have a healthy lifestyle in terms of weight, smoking, sun exposure, diet and exercise. Advice from the government about healthy living should apply to people with learning disabilities too. There should be greater vigilance with regards to gastro-oesophageal reflux and *Helicobacter pylori* infection. When an individual has a syndrome that is associated with a particular cancer, carers and professionals should be aware of the symptoms.

Conclusion

People with learning disabilities may be slightly less likely to have cancer than the wider population. However, with increases in life expectancy, the occurrence of cancer in people with learning disabilities will rise. The types of cancers that people with learning disabilities are most likely to develop can differ from those seen more prevalently in the wider population. Because of this, there needs to be a greater awareness and vigilance for these types of cancers. Diagnosing can be problematic, with cancers often spotted too late, and when it is, people with learning disabilities may not be offered the full range of treatments and palliative care.

Summary points

- Carers should encourage a healthy lifestyle in people with learning disabilities.

- Carers should be aware of the types of cancers seen in higher levels in people with learning disabilities, such as gastro-intestinal cancers.

- Carers should be aware of the symptoms of gastro-oesophageal reflux disease and *Helicobacter pylori* infection and seek to have these treated at an early stage.

- If someone has a syndrome that is associated with a particular cancer, carers should look out for the signs and symptoms of this and encourage regular health check-ups.

- Carers should empower people with learning disabilities to carry out self-examination and encourage attendance for screening.

Chapter 12: Gastrointestinal disorders

Peter Woodward

Introduction

For the purpose of this chapter, 'gastrointestinal' refers to the transit of food once it has successfully left the mouth, passed through to the stomach, travelled through the small and large intestines, and on to where it is finally evacuated. People with learning disabilities can have the full range of gastrointestinal problems that the whole population can develop. In addition to this, people with learning disabilities have some gastrointestinal conditions that are seen in higher levels than would usually be expected. This chapter will address the additional problems of gastro-oesophageal reflux disease, *Helicobacter pylori* infection and constipation. Problems due to swallowing are discussed in Chapter 14 on dysphagia, and at this point it is assumed that an individual has successfully swallowed.

Gastro-oesophageal reflux disease (GORD)

The oesophagus is the pipe that food and drink travels down when it leaves the mouth to get to the stomach. When it reaches the stomach a ring of muscle (sphincter) opens, allowing the food to enter, and closes afterwards like a valve (see Figure 12.1). Sometimes the contents of the stomach travel back up through this opening, which can then cause damage to the oesophagus. This is called gastro-oesophageal reflux disease, abbreviated to GORD. (Within the US the term GERD may be used due to the alternative spelling of 'esophageal'.)

Often people will experience a mild form of GORD and may refer to this as heartburn. The discomfort has nothing to do with the heart, however, and is caused by stomach acid coming into contact with the lining of the oesophagus.

The stomach has a coating of mucous that helps to protect it from this acid but the oesophagus is not protected and the acid can cause burning. This can lead to pain in the upper throat or across the chest. In severe cases where this occurs again and again over a period of time, the oesophagus can develop ulcers, causing further pain and making the passage of food more difficult. It is thought that continued damage to the oesophagus due to GORD can cause cancer.

GORD can be triggered by a number of lifestyle choices, such as smoking and drinking alcohol or coffee, which can relax the valve at the top of the stomach. Eating particular foods, such as spicy or acidic foods, can be a trigger, as can eating very large amounts. Other triggers could be pregnancy or bending over, where additional pressure is put on the stomach, particularly if it is full. An individual eating a large meal late at night accompanied by wine and coffee many find that they suffer with GORD, especially when they then lay flat in bed.

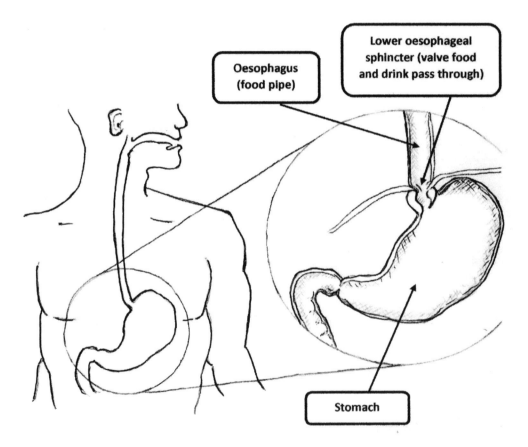

Oesophagus (food pipe)

Lower oesophageal sphincter (valve food and drink pass through)

Stomach

Figure 12.1: Diagram of oesophagus and stomach

GORD is seen in much higher levels in people with learning disabilities. This is usually due to differences in the person's body that cause pressure to be put on the stomach or affect the valve of muscle, as well as other factors leading to the valve relaxing too much. For example, GORD is seen in much higher levels in people with some syndromes like Fragile X, Cornelia de Lange and cerebral palsy, where the control of the valve may not be as strong. Often medications like epilepsy drugs or benzodiazepines can have a relaxing effect, making GORD more likely. If the individual has curvature of the spine, which is seen in people with more profound learning disabilities, this can put additional pressure on the stomach. There is an association between the stomach infection *Helicobacter pylori* (discussed later in the chapter) and GORD. Some people with learning disabilities may have a number of these factors working against them, leading to a much higher likelihood of having GORD.

It may be assumed that someone who is fed via a percutaneous endoscopic gastronomy (PEG) (a tube that allows liquid food to be fed directly into the stomach) would not develop GORD. However, an individual who is PEG-fed could still develop GORD if liquid is allowed to fill the stomach quicker than it can drain away. This may be more apparent during night-time feeding when the person is lying flat, allowing liquid to pool against the ring of muscle at the top of the stomach.

Identifying and assessing GORD

If the individual can describe their feelings they may complain of having heartburn or a burning taste in their throat or mouth from the stomach acid. They may say that it burns when they have hot drinks, that they find it difficult to swallow or that the passage of food to their stomach is painful. Others close to the individual may notice that they have bad breath that smells of vomit. They may notice that the person is sick after eating meals. Their dentist may notice that their teeth are eroded by the acid.

In more serious cases the walls of the oesophagus can become inflamed and irritated, but this can only be seen with a camera. Breathing problems can worsen as a result of GORD and asthma may increase. Complications can occur when the contents of the stomach comes back up and then enters the lungs; this is particularly dangerous as it can cause serious infection. In some cases hand-mouthing (putting the hand into the mouth/sucking the hand) has been associated with GORD (Swender *et al*, 2006). The less the individual can communicate about the pain, the more those caring for the individual will have to try to observe for these signs of discomfort.

If carers note any of the above, particularly recurrent vomiting, they should consult with the individual's doctor to get a more comprehensive assessment.

Assessing for GORD can be difficult. A doctor may try to pass a camera down the throat to look at damage to the oesophagus or use a monitor to detect stomach acid in the oesophagus. Some of the cells in the oesophagus may be taken to test for changes that could lead to cancer. These assessments are uncomfortable and can be more difficult the more severe the person's learning disabilities. A best interest meeting may be required to decide if these tests should be done if the individual lacks the capacity to make this decision themselves.

Case study: David

David is a middle-aged man with a severe learning disability. He has cerebral palsy and epilepsy, is overweight, and lives in a residential home for people with learning disabilities. He has limited verbal communication and can say some keywords; sometimes he has behaviour that the staff in the service find challenging.

David is at a higher risk of having GORD because he has cerebral palsy – this means he has trouble controlling the muscles in his body. This includes the ring of muscle that is meant to keep the stomach closed, which will not close properly. David also receives medication for his epilepsy that relaxes his muscles further still. If he has a seizure he is given midazolam which causes further muscle relaxation. David being overweight puts additional pressure on his stomach, and tasks like bending to put on his shoes will increase this pressure further still.

The staff where David lives feel that he has limited enjoyment in life but know that he enjoys eating. They are happy for Simon to have second and third helpings of meals, meaning that he will often eat very large portion sizes. Added to this, David often has a dry mouth due to his epilepsy medication and will drink large amounts of water. Often he is very full which contributes to the pressure that builds up in his stomach.

David will often suffer with GORD, causing him pain and tightness across the chest. He has trouble expressing this and will often shout or moan for long periods of time. The staff team deal with this by giving him snacks and drinks, assuming that he is hungry.

The GORD has been caused by a number of factors due not only to David's syndrome but to his medication, weight gain and the way the staff team work with David.

If this continues over a long period of time the acid will begin to erode David's oesophagus, he could develop ulcers and may also develop swallowing problems or even cancer.

Treatment of GORD

If a diagnosis of GORD is confirmed there are several treatment options, ranging from dietary changes through to surgery. GORD may be reduced by making changes to diet, such as trying to avoid large meals or trigger foods and drinks like alcohol, coffee or spicy foods. Elevating the head of the bed at night can assist in keeping stomach contents lower in the stomach. Avoiding bending or exercise after eating can prevent pressure being put on a full stomach. Over-the-counter antacids, heartburn and indigestion relief may help too, but these may need to be taken in consultation with the individual's doctor, pharmacist or in line with medication protocols in a residential or day service. The thickening of foods or liquids, making it more difficult for these to travel back up the oesophagus once in the stomach, may also be recommended.

If changes in lifestyle are not successful at reducing GORD an individual may require prescribed medication. These medications are designed to reduce the amount of stomach acid that the body produces. Omeprazole and lansoprazole are common drugs that reduce the amount of stomach acid produced. Others are available and there are drugs that may be used in combination with these to promote healing of the oesophagus. Other drugs may speed up the emptying of the stomach.

In severe and prolonged cases of GORD surgery may be necessary. This could be in order to strengthen the valve (the sphincter) at the top of the stomach – an operation called nissen fundoplication. This involves wrapping the upper part of the stomach around the lower part of the oesophagus to reinforce the sphincter muscle. Another option is injecting a gel or plastic in order to make the oesophagus narrower. Corrective surgery to improve posture may also help if this is exerting pressure on the stomach.

Any further medication or surgery should be used in conjunction with lifestyle changes, and the individual should always be encouraged to watch their diet, lose weight if necessary and cut back or stop smoking.

The individual may require ongoing regular monitoring to check the oesophagus is still okay.

> ### Case study: Interventions for David
>
> David's case was discussed earlier. After reviewing David's lifestyle, there are some interventions that could be suggested. These would then need to be agreed with David or done in his best interests. The interventions should be person-centred and should look at being least restrictive to his lifestyle. They could include the following:
>
> - David could have smaller meals spread throughout the day.
> - He should avoid spicy foods or any other trigger foods like coffee.
> - David should not eat after dinner so that he does not go to bed on a full stomach.
> - David should be encouraged to take only small sips of drinks at meal times.
> - David should be encouraged to lose weight – if this is by exercising he should not exercise on a full stomach.
> - If David's GORD is worse at night the head end of his bed could be elevated by 10–15 cm.
>
> If lifestyle changes do not work, medical or surgical interventions may need to be considered:
>
> - David could be prescribed a medicine like omeprazole or lansoprazole that reduces the amount of stomach acid he produces. These are considered safe to use in the long term.
> - Any other health conditions that could be making the GORD worse should be treated, such as *Helicobacter pylori* or a hiatus hernia, which may need surgery.
> - If none of the other interventions work and David is considered to be at risk of further complications, nissen fundoplication may be suggested. This is usually done by keyhole surgery.

Helicobacter pylori

Helicobacter pylori (often shortened to *H. pylori*) is a bacterium found in the stomach. As many as half the world's population (usually in developing countries) carry this stomach bacterium and the majority will not suffer any discomfort from it. Many will not know they have *Helicobacter pylori* and the symptoms of *Helicobacter pylori* infection are similar to those of indigestion. People who are ill due to *Helicobacter pylori* will often suffer from bloating accompanied by belching, and may suffer from nausea or stomach cramps. Heartburn is also a symptom and *Helicobacter pylori* is associated with GORD. Weight loss may be another indicator of *Helicobacter pylori* infection.

If *Helicobacter pylori* goes untreated it can lead to complications. The infection can increase the likelihood of stomach ulcers and it is believed that untreated ulcers can lead to stomach cancer. If someone has a stomach ulcer the symptoms listed above will be more extreme; an individual may refuse to eat because it is too painful or they may vomit. There may be blood in the vomit or their stools may be sticky and dark in colour.

People with learning disabilities are more likely to be infected with *Helicobacter pylori*. It is not known exactly how it is passed on but it is assumed that it is transmitted mouth to mouth via saliva or from faeces to mouth. This could be by someone with poor personal hygiene infecting objects that they touch and another individual passing the infection to their own mouth when they touch food or put their hands in their mouth. People with more severe learning disabilities are more likely to contract *Helicobacter pylori*, as are those who use crowded services like day centres or live-in residential services with other people with learning disabilities. Infection with *Helicobacter pylori* can be an occupational risk when working with people with learning disabilities. In one study, 82% of people living in an institution and 27% of staff were found to be infected (Bohmer *et al*, 1997), which is higher than should be expected. Risk of staff becoming infected with *Helicobacter pylori* is increased with the length of time in employment and increased level of direct contact with people with learning disabilities who are infected.

Case study: Rosemary Lodge

Rosemary Lodge is a residential home for people with learning disabilities. When the local long-stay hospital for people with learning disabilities closed down in the 1990s, five of the men and women who lived there moved to Rosemary Lodge. Sarah moved in recently from her family home.

All the people that live at Rosemary Lodge have severe learning disabilities. They share two communal bathrooms, toilets and sinks. They eat together in the same dining room and use the same kitchen.

One of the men living at Rosemary Lodge started losing weight and one day vomited blood. When medical investigations were conducted doctors found that he was infected with *Helicobacter pylori* and had developed a stomach ulcer. The GP suggested that the other people living at Rosemary Lodge be tested as well. Staff held a best interests meeting and agreed that at their next health check-up the other residents would be tested for *Helicobacter pylori* too.

It was found that everyone that lived at Rosemary Lodge had the *Helicobacter pylori* infection except for Sarah – this was probably because Sarah had not lived there for long.

Assessment for *Helicobacter pylori*

There are tests to confirm the presence of *Helicobacter pylori*. One involves giving the individual a tablet and analysing their breath. This test requires the co-operation of the individual so may be more difficult to do with people with more severe learning disabilities. The individual's stools may be tested; however, this test is not always accurate. Blood tests are another option but will also require the person's co-operation. Given the high prevalence of *Helicobacter pylori* in people with learning disabilities, it may be appropriate to test for this whenever an individual is required to give a blood test for other medical reasons.

Some doctors may treat the condition without assessment if they have a firm belief that the individual has *Helicobacter pylori*, taking into consideration that the treatment could be less invasive than the assessment.

After an individual has been found to test positive and treated for the infection, it is recommended that retests are performed every three to five years, as it is likely that an individual with learning disabilities will become reinfected. If an individual has GORD they may be treated for *Helicobacter pylori* at the same time, as some of the medicines used to treat GORD and *Helicobacter pylori* are the same, and there is a greater likelihood of having both conditions together.

Treatment for *Helicobacter pylori*

Helicobacter pylori is treated with a medication to reduce stomach acid (as with GORD) and antibiotics at the same time. The course of treatment can last from five to 10 days and sometimes other medications or several antibiotics are used (Gasparetto *et al*, 2012). Carers should always try to encourage good personal hygiene and be aware that cross-infection might be caused by saliva or faecal matter. Tests may be necessary after treatment because some people can remain infected after treatment. Reinfection from *Helicobacter pylori* can be seven times more likely in people with learning disabilities, particularly if they share day centres or their home with other people with learning disabilities (Wallace *et al*, 2004).

> ### Case study: Interventions for Rosemary Lodge
>
> The staff working at Rosemary Lodge looked at changing some of their working practices:
>
> ■ They encouraged everyone to wash their hands prior to meals.
>
> ■ They changed the soap dispensers, taps and hand-dryers in the toilets to make them easier to use.
>
> ■ They swapped the hand soaps to include antibacterial agents and washed down door handles and toilet flushes regularly.
>
> ■ They applied to have every room fitted with an en suite toilet and bathroom.
>
> ■ All the toilets were fitted with self-closing lids to prevent the contents spraying out when flushed. All cosmetics and toothbrushes were kept in a separate room where there were no flushing toilets.
>
> ■ One of the men living at Rosemary Lodge had trouble wiping after using the toilet and the occupational therapist suggested a devise that could assist with this.
>
> ■ Everyone living there who was infected was given medication to get rid of the *Helicobacter pylori* and were retested afterwards.
>
> ■ A test for *Helicobacter pylori* was to be carried out every three years to coincide with an individual's annual health check.

Constipation

At some point most people will experience constipation and it is often thought of as more of a discomfort than a serious health problem. However, if undiagnosed or untreated it can cause serious health problems. Someone can be considered to have constipation if they pass fewer than three stools in a week, if they need to strain in order to pass a stool more than once in every four occasions of using the toilet, or if they pass hard or pebble-like stools more than once in every four occasions.

Constipation can be caused by a variety of reasons, for example:

■ A poor diet that does not include enough fibre.

■ Dehydration – this may be due to not drinking enough fluids or consuming fluids that can cause dehydration such as alcohol; in people with learning disabilities excessive salivation or drooling could cause dehydration.

■ Not exercising or moving about enough or spending all day sitting or lying down.

■ Some medications, such as antiepileptics, antidepressants, antipsychotics, pain killers, iron tablets, calcium supplements or aluminium antacids – a number of these medications are used in higher quantities by people with learning disabilities.

■ Putting off going to the toilet or ignoring the urge to go.

■ Changes in routine, such as changes in work pattern, that disrupt the regular use of the toilet or stop someone going to the toilet when they want to – for example, someone with a learning disability who usually uses the toilet at 8am but starts travelling to the day centre three days a week at this time may no longer be able to go as they normally do.

There are a number of situations in which someone may not use the toilet when needed, for example:

■ They may have fear of using the toilet due to pain in passing a stool.

■ They may have fear of using the toilet because of something bad that has happened in a toilet in the past. For example, they could have been traumatised by abuse that took place in a toilet.

■ They may not have enough privacy, such as in a residential home where locks are disabled and staff can walk in.

■ Some people do not like using public toilets or going in unfamiliar places.

■ The toilet may not be adapted to an individual's needs. For example, often disabled toilets are higher from the floor to aid getting on and off; however, others may find these are too high and may fear falling.

■ An individual who is deeply engrossed in an activity like watching their favourite television programme may put off going.

Constipation is likely to increase as an individual gets older and people who are overweight or underweight have an increased likelihood of having constipation. A number of physical health problems are associated with constipation, including muscular dystrophy, multiple sclerosis, Parkinson's disease, bowel disease, irritable bowel syndrome (IBS), spina bifida, cerebral palsy, cystic fibrosis, diabetes, hypothyroidism and low muscle tone.

Individuals with swallowing difficulties or who are fed via PEG may have a diet lower in fibre and fluids or have a puréed diet that does not stimulate the bowel in the necessary way. Constipation is seen in higher levels in people with profound learning disabilities who may have skeletal deformities, problems with muscle control, problems squatting or sitting on the toilet, as well as many of the other problems listed above.

Identifying whether someone has constipation

Someone with learning disabilities who has good communication should be able to describe any discomfort they have in using the toilet. This does not mean that they will openly discuss any problems they are having and they may not feel that it is something that they can talk about. There are some things to consider when assessing whether someone has constipation:

■ Observe the toilet after use (this may mean observing someone's pad when they are being changed):

■ Do they pass hard pellet-like stools?

■ Is there fresh, bright red blood in the bowl, where they have hurt themselves straining?

■ Does the individual strain or sound like they are straining when using the toilet?

■ Do they spend a long time using the toilet?

■ Do they avoid or put off going to the toilet?

■ Do they have bad breath despite having good dental/oral hygiene?

■ Does their underwear have soiling or staining on it even though they have not used the toilet? This could be a sign of faecal matter leaking out around compacted faeces.

■ Do they ever insert a finger into their anus? This may be an attempt to remove faeces.

■ Does the individual have a swollen or bloated abdomen? You may notice this through their waistband being too tight.

■ Does the person pass wind excessively? This can also be a sign of constipation.

If someone is suspected to have constipation it can be a good idea to encourage them to keep a diary of their toilet use or do this for them. It is easy for someone to forget when they used the toilet last and this information may not get passed on from one shift to another. The diary should state when the person used the toilet, if they were in any pain or discomfort, and information about the type of stool that they passed. The different types of stool are described in the Bristol Stool Chart/Scale. This is readily available on the internet and describes seven different stool types. Types one and two are associated with constipation and types three and four are ideal stools.

If it is suspected that someone has recurrent constipation they will need to be seen by their GP. Evidence from a diary, including information on the type of stools that the individual passes, may help the GP in making a diagnosis. If the individual consents, taking photographs may assist when trying to describe things like colour, consistency, evidence of mucous or other issues with the individual's stool. It may also help the GP to know what the individual's average diet or fluid intake looks like, and if there have been changes in diet or mobility recently. These can be recorded in the diary too.

The GP may want to carry out a physical examination. This may just involve feeling the individual's abdomen or could involve more invasive examinations such as inserting a finger into the individual's rectum. Although this should not be painful it could cause discomfort of distress. Other investigations might include blood tests or other procedures to rule out other health problems. If the individual does not have capacity to consent to this the GP would need to hold a best interests meeting.

A test can be carried out where a coloured 'marker' is drunk and then observed for how long it takes to travel through the digestive system. If it takes an excessively long time this can be an indicator of constipation.

Complications

Faecal impaction can occur when a collection of hard, dry stools cause an obstruction in the rectum meaning that other stools cannot pass. If an individual has faecal impaction there may be swelling around the rectum or bleeding. The individual may be incontinent where they leak softer or liquid stools (overflow diarrhoea). This may be seen as soiling of underwear, giving the false impression that the individual is passing stools as normal. Carers should also observe for blood on underclothes. If anyone presents these symptoms, medical advice should be sought immediately.

Haemorrhoids or 'piles' may occur due to attempting to pass hard stools. These are caused by swollen blood vessels and cause pain and even bleeding. Signs that someone may have piles are swelling around the anus, bleeding, complaining of pain or itching and excessively scratching the area. If an individual has haemorrhoids medical advice should be sought from their GP.

Interventions for constipation

Constipation may be countered with changes in dietary habits and measures to make the use of the toilet as stress free as possible. These may be used in conjunction with medication prescribed by a GP.

Carers should encourage an increase in the amount of fibre in the diet to 18–30 grams a day. Fibre intake can be increased by eating more fruit, vegetables, some cereals and switching to more wholemeal and whole grain products. One study carried out with children with learning disabilities who had a low-fibre diet, showed that laxative use was reduced by a third by adding a 50-gram bowl of All-Bran to breakfast time (Tse *et al*, 2000). Information on high-fibre diets, including meal plans, are available on the internet. Advice can also be sought from a GP or dietician. The individual should be encouraged to drink more fluids, preferably water. Individuals should aim to consume at least two litres a day while cutting back or avoiding drinks that dehydrate, such as alcoholic beverages and caffeinated drinks. Very salty foods should be avoided. Individuals should be encouraged to exercise or at least increase any movement that they currently do.

The toilet should ensure privacy and reduce any levels of stress the individual may feel. The best times to pass a stool are first thing in the morning, or within 30 minutes of eating a meal or taking laxatives (discussed later). When using the toilet, squatting is the ideal position for passing stools; this can be assisted by providing a footstall to raise the feet and allowing the individual to lean forward and rest their elbows on their thighs. The individual should be praised for appropriate use of the toilet as well as for maintaining an appropriate diet and exercising.

Medications for constipation

There are a number of different types of laxatives, which work in different ways. These are usually given in an order of preference and if working in the individual's best interests the least invasive method should be used first. In the case of someone with a learning disability, their GP should be consulted rather than opting for over-the-counter remedies. The GP may recommend the use of 'stronger' laxatives, or a combination, depending on how seriously they view the problem. Laxatives may need two to three days to start working.

The first laxative to be recommended is usually a bulk-forming laxative; these help retain fluid in the stools so they are softer and easier to pass. The individual will need to drink enough fluids to make them effective. They are usually fibre supplements such as ispaghula (psyllium) husk, inulin fibre, methylcellulose, linseeds, wheat dextrin or sterculia. The next type of laxative that may be used is an osmotic laxative, which increases the amount of fluid in the bowels, softening the stool and increasing stimulation to want to go to the toilet. Examples include lactulose and macrogols. Once again, the individual needs to drink enough fluids for this type of laxative to work effectively.

If bulk-forming and osmotic laxatives are helping to soften the stool but the individual still has difficulty passing, their GP may prescribe stimulant laxatives such as senna, bisacodyl or sodium picosulphate. These stimulate the bowel muscles to push harder than normal. They should work within 6–12 hours and are often given at night ready for the morning. These may also be prescribed as suppositories: small capsule medicines that are inserted into the anus and dissolve at body temperature to be absorbed into the blood vessels. They work much faster – typically in 20–60 minutes.

Enemas are larger amounts of fluid that are injected via a small tube through the anus into the bowel. They usually work like osmotic laxatives/faecal softeners or can sometimes be oil-based to help lubricate the stool's passage. The individual should lie on their left side with their knees bent up towards their chest if possible, so the fluid can flow into the descending colon more effectively. The use of suppositories and enemas may need to be administered by a community nurse or specific training would be required.

Laxatives are usually only prescribed on a short-term basis. In some cases people with learning disabilities have been taking these for longer periods of time and if this is the case their continued use should be checked with the GP, who should have a reason for why they are being used in the long term. This may be due to counteracting the side effects of a long-term medication or a medical complaint. Where long-term use of laxatives has been in place it may be possible to reduce them very gradually over time if changes to diet and lifestyle are implemented. If the individual is taking more than one type of laxative they may have to be reduced in turn. The GP must be consulted before deciding to do this.

The GP may also recommend that the person uses painkillers prior to going to the toilet, and this requires planning ahead, ready for when they may need to go. Some painkillers cause constipation as a side effect so cannot be used. A local anaesthetic ointment or a muscle relaxant can be prescribed to ease the pain and help relax the muscles around the anus. The GP must be consulted regarding this. Faecal impaction is usually treated with high doses of osmotic laxatives followed by a stimulant laxative. Suppositories and enemas are also often used.

Case study: Simon

Simon is a twenty-five-year-old man with severe learning disabilities, Down's syndrome and autism. Simon also has epilepsy and is on medication for this. He lives at home with his parents and attends a day centre during the week. Simon has a very limited diet and will only eat foods that have a dry texture. Simon's parents have difficulty finding foods that he will eat. This has led to him having a very monotonous diet mostly consisting of toasted white bread. Since he left school Simon has been rather inactive and over the last 10 years he has become overweight.

Simon is known to his local community learning disabilities team and his parents have spoken to his learning disability nurse as they are concerned that Simon has constipation. The nurse has asked his parents to keep a diary of Simon's food and drink intake, his activity levels, and how often he uses the toilet and the type of stools that he produces.

From the diary it is apparent that he is only passing stools once or twice a week and that these are hard and small. There is often bright red blood in the bowl when he does use it. Simon's nurse accompanies him to the GP and explains the situation. The following interventions are put into place:

■ Simon receives bulk-forming and osmotic laxatives and is given stimulant laxatives that his parents are to give him if he has not been to the toilet for more than three days. These have been initially prescribed in the short term and it is hoped that with changes to Simon's diet they will be withdrawn in the long term.

■ A test has also been carried out to see if Simon has hypothyroidism which is seen in higher levels in people with Down's syndrome and is often associated with constipation. This has been confirmed and Simon has been started on medication to treat this.

■ Simon has also developed haemorrhoids and he is given an ointment to help with this.

■ Simon's parents have begun to introduce more fibre into his diet. Initially this has been through swapping to white bread with added fibre and slowly moving to wholemeal bread. Other foods have been introduced, such as breakfast cereals, which Simon will eat dry. He has also tolerated dried fruit like raisins and dates and these have been slowly introduced. As a reward Simon receives a foot rub, which he enjoys, every time he eats a food high in fibre, whenever he drinks a glass of water and every time he uses the toilet.

■ Simon's parents have started taking him to the local swimming baths and have encouraged him to walk more.

■ A step has been put in the toilet for Simon to rest his feet on in order to improve his position while using the toilet, and a radio has been put in the toilet so he can listen to music while using the toilet. Simon's parents have also fitted a lock on the door, which they had been reluctant to do as they thought Simon would get locked in. The lock can still be opened by a screwdriver in the event of an emergency.

Simon's bowel movements have become more regular and the laxatives have been withdrawn with just some additional fibre being added to a drink in the morning.

Conclusion

People with learning disabilities can suffer from a wide range of gastrointestinal problems, just as anyone can. In particular, they are more likely to have GORD, *Helicobacter pylori* infection and constipation. These may be even more apparent if the individual has a more severe learning disability. If untreated these can cause serious health problems and even death. Carers should be vigilant for the symptoms of these conditions and seek medical advice should they believe there is a problem.

Summary points

■ For a variety of reasons people with learning disabilities are more likely to contract *Helicobacter pylori*, develop GORD and have constipation. Carers should be alert to the signs and symptoms associated with these.

■ Good hygiene, a healthy diet and sensible eating practices can help prevent these conditions developing.

■ Screening for these conditions should make up part of an individual's annual health check.

■ Given that *Helicobacter pylori* is so prevalent, it could be recommended that it should be screened for whenever someone has a blood test for any other reason.

References

Bohmer C, Klinkenberg-Knol E, Kuipers E, Niezen de Boer M, Schuckink-Kool F & Meuwissen S (1997) The prevalence of Helicobacter infection among inhabitants and healthy employees of institutes for the intellectually disabled. *American Journal of Gastroenterology* **92** (6) 1000–1004.

Gasparetto M, Pescarin M & Guariso G (2012) *Helicobacter pylori* eradication therapy: current availabilities. *Gastroenterology* **2012** 1–8.

Swender S, Matson J, Mayville S, Gonzalez M & McDowell D (2006) A functional assessment of handmouthing among persons with severe and profound intellectual disability. *Journal of Intellectual & Developmental Disability* **31** (2) 95–100.

Tse P, Leung S, Chan T, Sien A & Chan A (2000) Dietary fibre intake and constipation in children with severe developmental disabilities. *Journal of Paediatric Child Health* **36** (3) 236–239.

Wallace R, Schluter P & Webb P (2004) Recurrence of Helicobacter infection in adults with intellectual disability. *Internal Medicine Journal* **34** (3) 132–133.

Chapter 13: End of life care

Renee Francis, Eddie Chaplin and
Karina Marshall-Tate

Introduction

Although there are increased mortality and morbidity rates for people with
learning disabilities, life expectancy has increased. This means that people
with learning disabilities will also be prone to diseases associated with ageing,
which changes how we approach end of life care. It also means that learning
disability staff, who may not have had experience in end of life care, and palliative
care staff, who may not have had experience in providing care to people with
learning disabilities, are now finding that they are meeting new challenges in
their practice. From the other chapters we have seen that people with learning
disabilities suffer higher rates of physical comorbidity with a rise in illness
associated with poor lifestyles. We also know that there are many incidents of
premature deaths that could reasonably have been expected to be prevented, for
example, deaths through epilepsy or aspiration of fluids and/or foods on the lungs.
For many people with learning disabilities, good end of life care has not been
available, denying them their right to a dignified and peaceful death. This chapter
considers some of the issues and best practice for supporting people at the end of
life. The term 'end of life' is used to mean different things, from the last year of life
to the last hours or days. The latter is the meaning used in this chapter.

Although the number of people with learning disabilities is increasing, it is still
the case that the rates of illness for people with learning disabilities often differ
to the general public. Cancer provides a useful illustration of this. Overall cancer
rates in people with learning disabilities are roughly the same as the general
population. However, some cancers, such as those affecting the gastrointestinal
system, are more common in people with learning disabilities. Breast cancer
can be more common in women with learning disabilities, as they are still
less likely to have had children or to breastfeed and therefore do not have the
protective factors these provide. This picture can change again when we look at
specific conditions. People with Down's syndrome, for example, are more likely

to contract leukaemia than the rest of the population. They are at decreased risk of developing solid tumours, however, which means that women with Down's syndrome are less likely to get breast cancer, regardless of having children or breastfeeding (Emmerich, 2010). The picture changes again when we consider other conditions such as dementia. People with learning disabilities are up to five times more likely to develop dementia than the general population. People with Down's syndrome are at even greater risk, not only of being diagnosed with dementia, but of developing it at a much earlier age than others in both the general and wider learning disabilities population.

Many of the issues and barriers identified in previous chapters remain a factor for a number of care providers at the end of life. These link to a lack of awareness of the needs of people with learning disabilities, which can extend to how we communicate, the assumptions we make about behaviour or presentation being due to the learning disability (diagnostic overshadowing), as well as unawareness of the diseases people with learning disabilities may be more prone to; as a result care providers can make poor decisions based on inadequate or inaccurate assessment. Often, family carers and agencies who support people with learning disabilities within both health and social care settings lack the training to recognise the early warning signs of both serious physical and mental health conditions.

In terms of palliative or end of life care, everyone within society should have equal access to a service that meets their needs at this time of life. For people with learning disabilities there are issues that health and social care professionals need to be aware of in order to give appropriate support at this time. This should be done on a person-by-person basis, but the following are common issues that should be taken into account.

Level of communication

- Can the person express their wishes?

- Is the information that is offered accessible and in plain English?

- Does the person have verbal language or are there any special considerations, for example, the need to sign?

Level of ability

Does the person have difficulty with cognition? This includes memory, recall of information and understanding. It is also helpful to consider whether this is a permanent difficulty, or whether the person's level of cognition fluctuates depending on their illness progression or any treatment they are undergoing.

Level of capacity and ability to give informed consent to treatment

The information given about the Mental Capacity Act (2005) in Chapter 5 also applies here. In addition, it is worth remembering that people may not have capacity for all decisions they may be faced with. For example, someone may understand the need to take paracetamol to treat a headache; however, the same person might struggle to understand when faced with a treatment decision where there are a number of choices as to how to proceed, all of which may have different potential consequences. Also, as individuals near the end of life their level of capacity may change, for example, if they have dementia. Often a person's level of capacity will have already declined when decisions about end of life, such as stopping or changing treatment, need to be made. For those for whom capacity is an issue, the best interests of the person are taken into account. When a lack of capacity has become an issue as the condition has progressed, there may be an advanced directive in place that must be taken into account. For those making decisions in the person's best interest, there is a need to consult anyone the person wishes to be consulted, as well as those engaged closely in the person's care and anyone appointed by the court, such as the registered lasting power of attorney. Whether the person has capacity or not, there is a need for regular review.

Recognising the end of life

Previously there has been a point at which care becomes palliative to signal the person is dying; often this has been a sign for the person and those close to them that the end of life is near. However, the guidance from the Leadership Alliance for the Care of Dying People (LACDP, 2014) felt this distinction to be at times unhelpful and that care should be continuous. However, in the Confidential Inquiry into Premature Deaths of People with Learning Disabilities (Heslop *et al*, 2013), it was noted that for a number of people with learning disabilities, difficulties in identifying that the individual was dying meant that an end of life care pathway was not used. It is also important that the person and family be informed when it is felt the person is dying, as many complaints and much unresolved grief comes from the fact that those around the person did not realise they were dying. When explaining about the likelihood of death, it is good to include best and worst case scenarios should there be any uncertainty or when it is difficult to judge. When death is imminent many people will continue to make or be involved in plans for those close to them and will include their loved ones in the planning process as much as possible. It is therefore important that life continues to follow as normal a pattern as the person is used to, as much as possible. This includes ensuring food and fluid intake, unless in doing so there is a risk of harm to the person that outweighs the benefits. Sometimes this can become confused with treatment that may prolong life, where decisions need to be made on whether to withdraw or start new treatments. These are complex and difficult decisions, and should wherever possible be made in accordance with the person's wishes. These can include decisions about whether to restart chemotherapy where this poses a greater risk to the person, or the decision to resuscitate or not. It is important to recognise that a person's disability should not be a consideration in the decision-making process, that would be a clear violation of the person's human rights.

Best practice for end of life care

Until 2014, end of life care was delivered using the Liverpool Care Pathway for the Dying Patient (LCP). However, there was criticism in a number of care settings that it had become a tick box exercise and not conducive to providing individualised care (LACDP, 2014). The National Institute for Health and Care Excellence also noted that there were concerns about:

- cases where the decision as to whether the person was dying was not being made or reviewed by experienced clinicians, even where the person had the potential to improve

- undue sedation of the dying person due to overuse of symptom-controlling medications

- perceptions that withdrawal of fluids and essential medications were causing the dying person additional distress.

(NICE, 2015)

Following the independent review and subsequent withdrawal of the LCP, work has been done by a number of organisations to develop best practice frameworks to care for the dying person. *One Chance to Get it Right: Improving people's experience of care in the last few days and hours of life* (LACDP, 2014) was developed by a coalition of 21 national organisations committed to improving end of life care and support for families. The approach is based upon the following five priorities for care, and relates to the final few days and hours of life.

Priorities for the care of the dying person

1. This possibility is recognised and communicated clearly, decisions made and actions taken in accordance with the person's needs and wishes, and these are regularly reviewed and decisions revised accordingly.

2. Sensitive communication takes place between staff and the dying person, and those identified as important to them.

3. The dying person, and those identified as important to them, are involved in decisions about treatment and care to the extent that the dying person wants.

4. The needs of families and others identified as important to the dying person are actively explored, respected and met as far as possible.

5. An individual plan of care, which includes food and drink, symptom control, and psychological, social and spiritual support, is agreed, co-ordinated and delivered with compassion.

(LACDP, 2014)

These priorities aim to bring back decision-making to the person who is dying, according to their needs and wishes. Although care delivery is based on the premise that the person will die in the next few days or hours, continued communication remains essential so that the individual and those close to them can continue to make informed choices about their care. Communication at this time will need to be sensitive and, given the issues faced by some people with learning disabilities around memory and understanding, adjustment to individual clinicians' approaches may be necessary to ensure the person or the people looking after their best interests (if there is an issue of capacity) understand. Even if there are no such issues, the family should be central to this process (assuming the person dying wishes this).

The focus on care to meet the persons' dying wishes is wide and can include:

■ being sensitive to families' and carers' needs

■ good physical healthcare, which may include other conditions the person has that are not necessarily related to their life-limiting condition

■ assistance with personal care

■ diet

■ pain and symptom control based on individual need rather than as routine

■ preventative care, for example prevention of pressure areas when the individual begins to spend more time in bed

■ psychological support and time to talk

■ spiritual needs.

NICE (2015) have also produced an evidence-based guideline, *Care for the Dying Adult in the Last Days of Life*, which is aimed at all healthcare professionals and care workers involved in the end of life care of a dying person in an NHS setting. The guideline is particularly aimed at workers who have not received specialist training in end of life care, for example, those working in primary care or care homes, recognising the multidisciplinary and multi-agency nature of good end of life care. The guideline includes recommendations about:

- How medical staff can holistically assess that someone is approaching the end of their life (or, indeed, that their health is improving, even temporarily).

- Communicating with the individual, their family and significant others, and the rest of the multidisciplinary team in a way that facilitates shared decision-making and meets the individual's needs.

- Maintaining hydration for as long as the person wishes and can safely manage this.

- Medication optimisation: this might include stopping previously prescribed medications that are no longer effective or may be causing harm. Medication can be an important part of symptom control for pain, breathlessness, anxiety or nausea and vomiting. The guidelines also state that non-pharmacological interventions can also be effective and should be considered in collaboration with dying individuals and those close to them. In relation to pain management, the guidelines also specifically mention that for people who cannot verbally express that they are in pain, such as some people with learning disabilities or dementia, a validated behavioural pain assessment (such as DIS-DAT) should be used.

(NICE, 2015)

Although both the LACDP and NICE are writing about the care of anyone at end of life, we can see that both emphasise the importance of good communication, shared decision-making and individual care, much as we have discussed in other chapters in relation to supporting people with learning disabilities.

In addition to these overarching guidelines from the LACDP and NICE, the European Association for Palliative Care (EAPC) Taskforce on People with Intellectual Disabilities has produced Europe-wide consensus norms identifying best practice in end of life care specifically for people with learning disabilities (Tuffrey-Wijne & McLaughlin, 2015). Bearing in mind the emphasis that the LACDP and NICE place on good communication and individualised care, it is not surprising that the EAPC assert that if services can get end of life care right for people with learning disabilities, then they will be able to get it right for anyone.

The EAPC consensus norms focus on:

■ Ensuring that people with learning disabilities have equity of access to palliative care services, with services making reasonable adjustments to enable this to happen.

■ Giving special attention to meeting the communication needs of people with learning disabilities, whether verbally or non-verbally.

■ Ensuring that health and social care professionals can recognise when palliative care is necessary and when the individual is entering end of life and the dying phase, with the individual having a person-centred care plan in place to support them at every stage.

■ Assessing the physical, emotional, social and spiritual needs of people with learning disabilities, along with any additional needs that might arise as part of their impairment, and ensuring that reasonable adjustments are made so that these needs can be met.

■ Accurately assessing and managing pain and other symptoms, and supporting carers to recognise symptoms, while being aware of the risk of diagnostic overshadowing.

■ Recognising that symptom management might be more complex in people with learning disabilities due to comorbidities, making collaboration between professionals and the people who know the person well even more important.

■ Ensuring that people with learning disabilities are assumed to have capacity unless proven otherwise, and that they are provided with all the necessary support, including advocacy, to be involved in decision-making.

■ Identifying with the person their important relationships early on so that significant others can be fully involved in end of life care – this may include people with whom the person has not had contact, and if this is the case, the person's wishes should be respected.

■ Collaboration between services, including medical and nursing staff, paid care staff, family carers and faith leaders.

■ Ensuring that there is support for families and carers that recognises their loss.

■ Creating opportunities to involve the person and their significant others in advance care planning that includes holistic planning for future care needs and wishes for what will happen after the person dies.

■ Recognition that the person's death will affect other people with learning disabilities that the person knows, and that these friends will also need bereavement support.

(Tuffrey-Wijne & McLaughlin, 2015)

The consensus norms also note that for all of this to happen, there needs to be appropriate training for staff and for people with learning disabilities themselves, so that they are better able to talk about illness, death and dying. Additionally, services need to be managed so that the palliative care needs of people with learning disabilities can be met, which could also involve palliative care services doing active outreach to find people with learning disabilities and palliative care needs in their areas.

In all of the guidance there is a common theme of the need to take a dynamic approach that allows clinicians and others involved in the person's last days to respond and adapt to the individual's changing needs and wishes. It should also be an end of a longer care process for people who know their condition is life-threatening and who have put in place measures to help come to terms with this and complete their affairs.

Practical steps

In terms of care delivery, there are a number of practical steps that can be taken to ensure the person's wishes are followed. One area often neglected outside of specialist services is advance care planning, which not only lets individuals communicate their end of life care preferences but also their wishes following their death. This can also be an issue in general, with people often reporting excellent cancer care but finding that the other agencies supporting cancer services such as GPs, district nurses, and health and social care providers are often not to the same standard or that care between these agencies can be fragmented. It is essential to the concept of advance care planning that specialist and generic services work collaboratively to be able to respond to the changing needs and wishes of the person. In terms of practical considerations, there are a number of areas that the person is likely to require support with, including:

- Appointments, for example:
  - Double appointments to allow more time for effective communication.
  - Multiple appointments with different professionals (eg. oncologist, surgeon, specialist nurse). Having photographs of the different health professionals or clinic areas can help individuals to understand which appointment they will be attending.
- Physical health, pain relief and symptom control:
  - Being responsive to the person's changing energy levels. They may experience increased fatigue and need to rest more, but will have other times when they are more awake and wanting to be more active.

- Being vigilant about good infection control practice, such as hand washing, as some individuals may have reduced immunity, especially if they have been undergoing chemotherapy.

- Being aware that the person might have increased pain sensitivity, possibly as a side effect of treatment. This should be taken into account when supporting the individual's mobility. It may also mean activities the person used to enjoy might need to be adapted to enable participation.

- Medication prescribing may be more complex due to overlap of drugs used in end of life and mental health care.

- Psychological and social needs and preparing for death:

  - Supporting the person to review their life or to write a letter to people important to them. For all of us, it is important to feel that we are leaving something behind for those that we love. Supporting individuals to record their life story or to write letters to the people important to them can help them to feel that significant people in their lives will have something to remember them by.

  - Making and acting upon a list of things the person wants to do with other people before he or she dies. This might include a holiday or it might include making contact with family or friends with whom the person has lost touch.

  - Maintaining the person's independence to whatever degree possible.

- Spiritual care: this may include formal rites within the person's religion or more informal one-to-one support from a faith leader.

- Ensuring that carers, whether family members or paid carers, have access to support to express and manage their feelings.

For many people there is a choice whether to die at home. It is important that healthcare staff are mindful that they should seek to maintain the person's independence and function for as long as possible. Often there may be pressure to discharge people to care homes as decisions can be made on function at the present time rather than based on what may be achieved following rehabilitation or physiotherapy. Decisions made on the basis of prognosis rather than current state may increase the person's independence, as well as their general well-being, for longer, helped by being in familiar surroundings.

Interventions following death

After death, it is still important to carry out the person's wishes. If the person has died at home, it may be necessary to move the body to somewhere more private. Religious and cultural customs should also be followed in regard to how the body is prepared and by whom. The death will need to be confirmed by a doctor who will sign the medical certificate, which is needed to register the death. If the person has not been seen by a doctor in the previous 14 days, the doctor will refer the case to the coroner for a post mortem.

Conclusion

By working in partnership with individuals with learning disabilities and their families, carers and significant others, we can ensure that we provide care at the end of life that meets their needs in a holistic way. It is a privilege to be allowed into someone's life at a time when they and their loved ones are potentially vulnerable, and to show them the respect that the dignity of their life should be accorded.

Summary points

■ Communication needs to be adapted to enable the person with learning disabilities to participate as much as possible in decisions about their end of life care.

■ The principles of the Mental Capacity Act (2005) need to be followed. It should be assumed that the person with learning disabilities has capacity to consent and be involved in treatment decisions unless proven otherwise. When individuals lack capacity, decisions must be made in their best interests.

■ People should be supported to follow their normal pattern of life and to maintain their independence as much as possible.

■ Advance care planning should be used to support people through their end of life. The care plan should be holistic and responsive to changes in the person's condition.

■ Involving families and other people who know the person well can help to ensure that care continues to meet the person's needs, including ensuring that symptoms are managed appropriately.

References

Emmerich M (2010) Medical conditions in adults near the end of life. In: S Friedman and D Helm (Eds) *End-of-life Care for Children and Adults with Intellectual and Developmental Disabilities* (pp 75–91). Washington, DC: American Association on Intellectual and Developmental Disabilities.

Heslop P, Blair P, Fleming P, Hoghton M, Marriott A & Russ L (2013) *Confidential Inquiry into Premature Deaths of People with Learning Disabilities (CIPOLD)*. Bristol: Norah Fry Research Centre.

Leadership Alliance for the Care of Dying People (2014) *One Chance to Get it Right: Improving people's experience of care in the last few days and hours of life* [online]. Available at: https://www.gov.uk/government/uploads/system/uploads/attachment_data/file/323188/One_chance_to_get_it_right.pdf (accessed October 2016).

National Institute for Health and Care Excellence (2015) *Care of Dying Adults in the Last Days of Life* [online]. Available at: https://www.nice.org.uk/guidance/ng31?unlid=63448395420161011192124 (accessed October 2016).

Tuffrey-Wijne I & McLaughlin D (2015) *Consensus Norms for Palliative Care of People with Intellectual Disabilities in Europe: EAPC white paper*. Milan: EAPC ONLUS.

Chapter 14: Dysphagia

Lesley Brown

Introduction

Being able to eat, drink and swallow without discomfort or anxiety is something that we usually take for granted. However, for some people with learning disabilities and their carers, mealtimes can be tiring and stressful. The individual may have recently developed difficulties with chewing and/or swallowing as a result of a change in their health or medication. More commonly, however, they will have long-standing (chronic) and possibly worsening problems (Chadwick & Jolliffe, 2009; Sheppard, 2002; 2006) that may make it a challenge for them to eat and drink enough to keep healthy. During and after meals they may gag, cough, or become out of breath, fatigued or reluctant to eat and drink. These difficulties may mean they are more prone to chest infections or choking, which can be serious enough to lead to hospital admissions and can be potentially life-threatening.

Difficulties with eating, drinking and swallowing are commonly referred to as dysphagia. It is important that individuals with dysphagia are recognised, assessed and provided with advice to maximise the chances of them eating and drinking comfortably and safely.

The normal eating, drinking and swallowing process

Imagine that you can smell your favourite meal being cooked and then can see the delicious looking plate of food being put on the table in front of you. Your mouth is probably watering even before you begin to eat. You sit up, lift up your head, move the fork to your mouth and as you take the first mouthful, notice the temperature, taste and texture. You use your tongue to move the food around your mouth while the movement of your jaw enables you to chew. Your closed lips stop the food falling out of your mouth and your cheeks help to keep the food on the teeth. The nerves in your mouth tell your brain where the food is, which stops you biting your tongue, lips or cheeks. As the saliva gets mixed with the food, your tongue begins to shape it into a ball and then pushes it up against the roof of your mouth (called the hard palate). Gradually the ball of food is pushed by the tongue and pulled by suction (like a vacuum) to the back of the mouth. At this stage your soft palate (the floppy part of the roof of your mouth right at the back) lifts up so that briefly you are not able to breathe through your nose. Quickly, your swallowing reflex makes your voice box (larynx), which is at the top of the tube to your lungs (the airway or trachea), lift up and close so that the food does not go down the wrong way. At the same time, the valve at the top of the tube that goes to your stomach (the oesophagus) is pulled open to receive the ball of food. Once this happens, everything returns to 'rest' position and normal breathing resumes. Rings of muscles in the food pipe push the food down into your stomach. You then take a mouthful of drink and a similar process occurs even more quickly, as the fluid flows at a much faster rate.

This 'normal' process involves a complicated sequence of nerve impulses and muscle movements that have to be closely co-ordinated with breathing. The process will vary depending on what you are eating and drinking, how quickly you eat and drink, and your general health. Very occasionally these movements may be mistimed as you eat or drink and you may find yourself biting your cheek or tongue, swallowing a hard lump or coughing on something going down the wrong way. Think about what this feels like both physically and emotionally. What would it be like if it happened at every mealtime? What might the long-term consequences be?

Dysphagia among people with learning disabilities

Who experiences dysphagia?

Dysphagia is more common among people with learning disabilities than in the general population (Sheppard, 2006). Some groups are especially vulnerable and need closer monitoring (Chadwick & Jolliffe, 2009). These include:

- people with profound and multiple learning disabilities (PMLD)

- people with physical disability, principally cerebral palsy, and especially as they enter their 30s (Sheppard, 2002)

- people with dementia

- people taking certain medications that may reduce their alertness, cause them to have a dry mouth or even directly affect the swallowing mechanism

(especially some antipsychotics/neuroleptics, benzodiazepines and muscle relaxants)

■ people with epilepsy, immediately before or after a seizure (some anti-epilepsy drugs may also increase swallowing difficulties)

■ people who have had a stroke or been diagnosed with a deteriorating condition such as Parkinson's disease

■ people with respiratory health conditions such as chronic obstructive pulmonary disease (COPD)

■ people with syndromes that affect the anatomy of their face, mouth or throat.

Individuals with existing dysphagia who usually manage well with guidelines in place, may have more difficulties when they are unwell, especially if the ill-health affects their breathing. As with all health issues among people with learning disabilities, difficulties with receptive and expressive communication can make it difficult for individuals to understand questions about suspected dysphagia and/or to report symptoms. Carers of people who are at a very early stage of communication development or who do not volunteer information – for example, people on the autism spectrum – need to be especially vigilant for signs of dysphagia. Equally, any individual reporting discomfort, anxiety or choking at mealtimes or when taking medication should be always taken seriously.

What are the risks and consequences of dysphagia for people with learning disabilities?

In 2004 the National Patient Safety Agency listed dysphagia as one of the top five factors that might risk the health of someone with learning disabilities. They also described how some health symptoms, such as coughing at mealtimes, may be overlooked, presumed to be part of the person's learning disability or just seen as something they have always done. All six of the individuals highlighted in Mencap's report *Death by Indifference* had difficulty with eating and poor oral intake, which may have made a contribution to their death (Mencap, 2007).

Difficulties with eating, drinking and swallowing can impact negatively on a person's general health by increasing the likelihood of:

■ weight loss

■ malnutrition

■ dehydration

- constipation
- urinary tract infections
- increased vulnerability for and delayed healing of pressure areas
- incorrect drug levels
- anxiety and/or depression.

In some circumstance, food, drink, medication or saliva may go down the wrong way into the airway or lungs. This is known as 'aspiration'. The body's natural reaction to this is to produce a cough to push the aspirated material out. Some people may have 'silent aspiration', which means they do not cough. Aspiration may lead to:

- aspiration pneumonitis (inflammation of the lungs)
- chest infections
- aspiration pneumonia (infection of the lungs; infection from aspiration is most usually in the bottom of the right lung)
- chronic lung disease.

Researchers have shown that chest infections are among the leading causes of death for people with learning disabilities. Often these individuals die younger than those in the general population (Heslop *et al*, 2013; Hollins *et al*, 1998).

Although there is a strong association between aspiration and chest infections/ pneumonia, the link is not straightforward, as we all aspirate at some time without negative consequences. Aspiration in itself should be viewed as one of a number of risk factors (Chadwick & Jolliffe, 2009). Other factors may help predict those individuals with dysphagia who are most likely to develop aspiration pneumonia (Brockett, 2006; Langmore *et al*, 1998). Those who are most at risk could include:

- people who are dependent on others to eat and drink (i.e. those who have to be supported to eat and drink)
- people who are dependent on others for oral care
- people who have poor oral care/decayed teeth (as they will have more bacteria in their mouth, which could be aspirated)
- people with multiple medical conditions (e.g. chronic heart or lung disease)
- people with weakened or supressed immune reactions

- people with impaired defence mechanisms to protect the airway and lungs
- people who take multiple medications
- people who are immobile
- people who smoke.

People with swallowing difficulties often also have problems with reflux and/or regurgitation (stomach contents coming back up into the throat or mouth). This can lead to an inflammation in the throat (oesophagitis) which can be very painful and may mean the person is reluctant to eat or drink. They may also be at risk of aspirating refluxed stomach contents.

People with dysphagia may be more at risk of choking, especially if their chewing skills are very limited and/or they eat inappropriate food. Some individuals may eat very quickly, overfill their mouth and/or eat non-food items (pica), which can also lead to choking. There are examples of people with learning disabilities dying following choking incidents.

Dysphagia warning signs

When supporting somebody with learning disabilities to eat or drink, it is important to look out for the following warning signs.

Warning signs during or after eating, drinking or taking medication could include:

- avoidance or refusal of certain foods/fluids
- difficulty keeping fluid/food/medication in the mouth and/or excessive drooling
- difficulty chewing adequately or prolonged chewing
- unco-ordinated or pumping tongue movements
- food or medication becoming 'stuck' in the cheeks, roof of the mouth or around teeth
- food/fluid/medication coming out of the nose
- taking a long time to start the swallow
- noisy or effortful swallow
- gagging, retching, regurgitation or vomiting
- coughing or choking during or after eating, drinking or taking medication

- inability to cough or very weak, ineffective cough

- difficulty breathing, increased breath rate, decreased oxygen saturation, cyanosis, breathing that sounds wheezy or raspy stridor

- watery eyes

- slight changes in facial colour

- wet or gurgling voice

- multiple swallows needed per mouthful

- reported discomfort or pain during or after swallowing or grimacing facial expression

- sensation of food getting 'stuck' in the throat or chest

- oral hypo/hyper sensitivity (i.e. either not feeling what's in the mouth or being over sensitive)

- anxiety/panic.

Warning signs that may develop over time could include:

- lack of interest in or attention to food and drink

- restricted diet

- increased time taken to eat/drink

- food refusal

- weight loss

- recurrent chest infections

- aspiration pneumonia

- choking incidents.

Assessment

Medical assessment

As with any health issue, you should always seek advice from the person's GP in the first instance. Depending on the symptoms that the person is reporting or you are observing, you may also need to support the person to see their dentist.

The GP may carry out blood tests or send the person for a chest x-ray. They may prescribe antibiotics or anti-reflux medication.

The GP may refer the person on to a hospital consultant, such as an ear, nose and throat (ENT), gastroenterology or chest specialist. These doctors may discuss performing investigations with the person such as an endoscopy or a barium swallow. These are designed to detect changes in the health and structure of the throat.

Specialist speech and language therapy dysphagia assessment

Dysphagia trained speech and language therapists (SLTs) have specialist skills in the assessment and management of dysphagia. Depending on how services are organised locally the person's GP may need to make a referral. In many cases, however, the SLT in the local learning disability team will accept a referral from the person themselves or anyone who knows them. They may ask a carer to fill in a form or may gather basic information from a carer over the phone.

The SLT will arrange to meet with the person and their carers to find out about their general health and the type of mealtime problems they are having. They will want to observe the person eating and drinking, but will be mindful of any anxiety or difficulties this might cause. They may discuss videoing the person as part of their assessment. Often, people eat in a variety of different locations and are supported by a number of different carers. It is likely the SLT will want to see the person in each location and gather information from as many carers as possible. If the person is able to copy face and mouth movements, the therapist might ask the individual to do so to see how their muscles and nerves are working.

The SLT might ask the person or their carers to keep a record of what the person is eating and drinking and any symptoms they may have.

Sometimes SLTs will arrange for the person to have a videofluoroscopy, which is a video x-ray of the person's swallow. This would be carried out at a local hospital. The procedure involves the person eating and drinking as normal, while sat beside the x-ray machine. Depending on the individual's needs, the SLT may arrange for a visit to the hospital before the appointment to reduce anxiety.

Multidisciplinary team (MDT) assessment

Depending on the person's disabilities and difficulties, the SLT will usually involve other members of the MDT. This could include:

- physiotherapist – to assess the person's posture, positioning, movement and possibly chest health

- occupational therapist – to assess the person's sensory and motor processing skills/difficulties, seating and mealtime equipment

- dietitian – to assess the person's nutritional and hydration needs

- community nurse – to assess the person's general health and medication management, and to support any further medical investigations

- dentist or dental therapist – to assess the person's oral health.

Management

Dysphagia care plan

The SLT and MDT will work with the person and their carers to trial and agree a dysphagia care plan (sometimes called eating and drinking guidelines). It may be necessary to consider the person's capacity to decide about how their dysphagia should be managed. If they are found to lack capacity, decisions will need to be made in their best interest. The person's preferences will nevertheless be taken into account and the least restrictive option will always be sought.

A dysphagia care plan may include information and guidance about:

- the types of difficulties the person has and the possible associated risks

- the level of carer knowledge and experience needed to support the individual

- appropriate equipment (eg. utensils, crockery, cups etc.)

- environmental considerations (eg. positioning in the room, background noise, others present etc.)

- seating and positioning both during and after the meal

- texture modification of food and drink

- nutritional and hydration requirements

- type of assistance required, pacing, bolus size and any special feeding techniques
- giving of medication – timing and format
- oral hygiene
- management of reflux when necessary
- maintenance of respiratory health.

The format of the dysphagia care plan will depend on the person and their circumstances. An Easy Read version may be provided for the person. Some SLTs provide a 'mealtime placemat care plan', which can be especially helpful if the person is supported in a variety of locations by a wide range of carers.

It is essential to take the person's dysphagia care plan with them if they are admitted to hospital.

Risk feeding

Some individuals struggle to eat and drink without aspirating or choking. Nevertheless the decision may be made (either by the person themselves, through a best interest process or following medical investigation) that they should continue to eat and drink. In this case, 'risk feeding' care plans may be developed, which recognise the person's significant difficulties but aim to manage them as best as possible. It is especially important that carers supporting these individuals are aware of the appropriate first aid response to choking.

Alternative feeding

In some cases the person's swallow may be deemed to be 'unsafe' and/or they may be unable to eat and drink enough to be well nourished and hydrated. Alternatives to eating and drinking may be explored, either alongside limited oral intake or oral tasters. Most commonly this will be a PEG (percutaneous endoscopic gastrostomy) which is a feeding tube that is placed through the abdominal wall into the stomach.

Conclusion

Dysphagia is common among people with learning disabilities. If not recognised and managed appropriately it can contribute to poor general health and may place the person at risk of hospital admissions or choking incidents. Carers should be aware of the signs of dysphagia and know how to refer the person for specialist assessment and advice.

Summary points

■ Eating, drinking and swallowing involves a complex sequence of nerve impulses and muscle movements that must be carefully co-ordinated with breathing.

■ Any difficulty with the eating, drinking and swallowing process is known as dysphagia.

■ Dysphagia is common among people with learning disabilities and can make them more vulnerable to a range of health issues, including chest infections.

■ Many people have long-term dysphagia, which can worsen with age or deteriorating health.

■ People with learning disabilities who have suspected dysphagia should be referred for assessment by a specialist speech and language therapist and multidisciplinary team colleagues.

■ A dysphagia care plan (or eating and drinking guidelines) should be in place for individuals who have dysphagia.

References

Brockett R (2006) Patients at risk of aspiration. In: J Cichero and B Murdoch (Eds) *Dysphagia: Foundation, theory and practice* (pp.112–125). Chichester: John Wiley & Sons, Ltd.

Chadwick DD & Joliffe J (2009) A descriptive investigation of dysphagia in adults with intellectual disabilities. *Journal of Intellectual Disability Research* **53** (1) 29–43.

Heslop P, Blair P, Fleming P, Hoghton M, Marriott A & Russ L (2013) *Confidential Inquiry into Premature Deaths of People with Learning Disabilities (CIPOLD): Final report*. Bristol: Norah Fry. Available at: www.bris.ac.uk/media-library/sites/cipold/migrated/documents/fullfinalreport.pdf (accessed June 2016).

Hollins S, Attard MT, von Fraunhofer N, McGuigan S & Sedgwick P (1998) Mortality in people with learning disability: Risks, causes and death certification findings in London. *Developmental Medicine and Child Neurology* **40** 50–56.

Langmore SE, Terpenning MS, Schork A, Chen Y, Murray JT, Lopatin D & Loesche WJ (1998) Predictors of aspiration pneumonia: how important is dysphagia? *Dysphagia* **13** (2) 69–81.

Mencap (2007) *Death by Indifference*. London: Mencap.

NPSA (2007) *Swallowing Problems? Resources for clients and carers. Ensuring safer practice for adults with learning disabilities who have dysphagia*. London: National Patient Safety Agency. Available at: www.nrls.npsa.nhs.uk/resources/?EntryId45=59823 (accessed June 2016).

Sheppard JJ (2002) Swallowing and feeding in older people with lifelong disability. *Advances in Speech and Language Pathology* **4** 119–121.

Sheppard JJ (2006) Developmental disability and swallowing disorders in adults. In: J Cichero and B Murdoch (Eds) *Dysphagia: Foundation, theory and practice* (pp. 299–318). Chichester: John Wiley & Sons, Ltd.

Chapter 15: Hearing and sight problems in people with learning disabilities

Mark Gray

In this chapter we will explore the common, but not often recognised, problems of hearing and sight loss and its impact on a person with a learning disability. Often an individual's ability to communicate is affected or even appears to magnify the degree of learning disability the individual has. This is particularly the case if it is not taken into account that a person struggles to see or hear in any assessment being undertaken of their ability.

Hearing loss

Action on Hearing Loss (formerly known as the Royal National Institute for Deaf People (RNID)) estimates that 7.5 million people have some degree of hearing loss in the wider population of the UK (Emerson & Robertson, 2011). The key factors are the ageing process and now increasingly the lifestyle choices of the young, exposing them to greater levels of noise. The Foundation for People with Learning Disabilities estimate that around 40% of people with learning disabilities are affected by hearing loss. Again, much is age related but increasingly hearing loss forms part of the problems associated with prematurity and complex needs from birth.

While many staff who work with adults with learning disabilities are aware of people with poor hearing, it is possible that their own service user's sensory impairments have not been noticed. The purpose of this chapter is to encourage families and staff to 'take a second look' at people with severe learning disabilities, or who function as if profoundly disabled. It is possible that many have unidentified hearing problems and may benefit from help to improve their hearing which has not previously been offered.

People with learning disabilities are very dependent upon their hearing and it may be the key sense used by some people to understand their world. It is therefore vital that potential hearing problems are identified and appropriate help is offered as soon as possible.

Prevalence of sensory impairment in people with learning disabilities

People with learning disabilities are prone to both hearing and sight problems, particularly if they have Down's syndrome, rubella syndrome or cerebral palsy (RNIB Multiple Disability Service, 2003). Studies consistently reveal that around 40% of people with severe learning disabilities have hearing problems (RNIB Multiple Disability Service, 2001). It has long been known that the more the more severe a person's learning disabilities the more likely they are to have sight or hearing problems.

Unfortunately, many people with learning disabilities frequently go through their lives unnecessarily impaired because people have not recognised hearing loss or visual problems or have not sought help, perhaps because they do not know whom to approach.

Hearing loss in people with learning disabilities

The more people can hear, the easier it is for them to have control over their own lives and to learn and acquire skills. Since more health providers are setting up special services to meet the hearing needs of people with learning disabilities, it is a good idea to enquire from GPs, social services, speech therapists or audiology departments whether such a service is working near you.

People who have always had poor hearing may not be aware that other people hear better than they do. It is not unusual to meet adults who have always found conversation and listening difficult because they have not received appropriate medical care nor been taught to use their hearing more effectively by focusing on sounds, rather than using vision or other senses which have become more prominent.

People with learning disabilities are now also living long enough to acquire hearing problems as part of the ordinary ageing process; in particular they are likely to develop a condition called presbyacusis, which is a sensorineural deafness affecting the nerves in the inner ear consistent with ageing. People with Down's syndrome tend to get some of the symptoms of ageing earlier in life than the 'general population', so they need careful monitoring from their 30s onwards.

Many people with learning disabilities who experience symptoms consistent with being deaf or hard of hearing may have relatively simple problems such as too much wax in their ears. Others may have long-standing ear infections that should be treated as soon as possible. Some people may need hearing aids or even surgery. Wearing hearing aids will not always restore lost hearing but they can greatly assist people's ability to communicate and function successfully in certain situations, although they may still need skilled help. People with learning disabilities will take time to adjust to wearing carefully prescribed and fitted hearing aids, but they are not the only ones who need to be helped and encouraged to get used to them – parents and carers need to be aware of the properties of the types of hearing aids prescribed and what situations or settings they need to be used in.

Symptoms indicating undiagnosed hearing problems

Many people find it difficult to understand what it means to be deaf or hard of hearing. Often hearing problems can be masked by communication difficulties or people appearing isolated and withdrawn, or having behaviour that is very challenging; for instance, someone may lash out suddenly, primarily because they did not hear another's approach, or if visually impaired as well because they could not see them approaching either. Some people have been incorrectly diagnosed as being on the autistic spectrum on the basis that they do not respond to voices or visual images in front of them.

Some people's balance and co-ordination may also be affected or the person may hit or bang the side of their head near their ears frequently.

Some people respond to tones and timbres of voices because of a preference for certain frequency ranges, so may prefer to be around male voices or female voices. However, a common problem that is especially prevalent for people in residential support is wax build up. Carers are often not allowed to support people with personal care of the ears, leading to a form of conductive hearing loss caused by the wax build-up, which can easily be avoided or treated.

How to tell if a person with a learning disability is deaf or hard of hearing

The following checklist was first designed by the RNIB Multiple Disability Service in 2003 and was designed to make family and carers of people with a learning difficulty aware of possible signs of hearing problems. However, it is important to note that some people with a learning disability may have no outward signs of their hearing impairment, while other people display various clues.

One major problem in looking for hearing problems is that the person may have considerable variations in their hearing depending on their environment, health, medication and so on. This means that staff may find that the checklists give different results on different days, or even at different times on the same day.

Checklists emphasise possible differences between people with 'ordinary hearing' and people with hearing problems. There is no intention to stigmatise people in any way. However, these lists are a response to the limited medical screening of people with learning disabilities, and the need for vigilance to prevent their quality of life being undermined by unidentified or unaddressed sensory impairments.

When using the checklist, if the person you support shows several signs indicated in the lists it may be that you need to help them to make an appointment with the GP for an audiology referral. Whilst the checklist is not exact or in fact all-encompassing, many of these signs and symptoms are indeed the most common.

RNIB Checklist

Appearance of ears

- No ears at all.

- Very small ears.

- Closed or partially closed ears.

- Unusually shaped ears.

- Scarred ears or ears that appear damaged.

- Discharging ears (fluid or pus coming from the pinna).

- Ears with an unpleasant smell.

Speech

- Does not speak at all.

- Speaks very loudly or shouts.

- Speaks very quietly or whispers.

- Speaks in a monotonous voice – a dull, single, expressionless tone.

- Speech that others find unintelligible or hard to understand.

- Unusual pronunciation of certain words.

- Poor communication skills.

- Limited vocabulary.

Behaviour

- Breathes through mouth rather than nose.

- Frequent catarrh – having a 'blocked-up' nose.

- Frequent touching of ears – e.g. poking, banging or rubbing etc.

- Bangs or slaps side of face.

- Puts objects (such as knitting needles or pencils) into ears.

- Unusual head movements – cranes neck to hear.

- Hears better on one side than the other.

- Puts fingers (pointing upwards) under ear lobes.

- 'Ear-bending' – putting the ear lobes flat.

- Cups hand behind ear to amplify sound.

- Short attention span.

- Poor self-care skills.

- Poor balance.

- Appears to be listening for sounds that no one else can hear.

- Puts hand over one ear, or a hand over each ear for no apparent reason.

Changes in behaviour

- Dramatic changes in behaviour – may have become 'a different person'.

- Seems confused.

- Increasing lack of co-operation in a person who was previously co-operative.

■ Seems depressed for no apparent reason.

Responses to other people

■ Hears people who speak close to them, or into one ear.

■ Watches people's faces very closely.

■ Has difficulty hearing people if their face and mouth cannot be seen.

■ Has difficulty recognising voices – even people they know well.

■ Needs to see people speaking to hear them or recognise their voice.

■ Ignores people who are not within sight.

■ Is startled by people coming up close or touching them from behind or the side.

■ Does not respond when called by name.

■ Does not respond to verbal instructions.

■ Hears high-pitched voices best – hears women and children better than men.

■ Hears deep voices best – hears men better than women and children.

■ Hears people sometimes, but not always.

Understanding

■ Seems to hear or understand certain people's voices, not others.

■ Misses parts of conversation.

■ Takes time to 'tune in' and understand what is being said.

■ Understands people best who have expressive faces/body language.

■ Needs visual prompts – e.g. being shown a cup when offered a drink.

■ May have difficulty understanding when people change the subject in conversation.

Responses to sounds in the environment

■ Obvious problems in hearing – e.g. cannot hear distant sounds, or near sounds.

■ Needs to sit very close to the television or music, or needs to have it turned up loud.

■ Hears better in quiet areas or without background noise.

■ Hears better in well-lit settings than in dark or poorly lit areas.

■ Hears high pitch sounds better.

- Hears deep sounds better.

- Does not recognise certain sounds or responds inappropriately.

- Cannot identify where sounds come from.

- Seems to hear sounds sometimes but not always.

- Avoids loud noise, or finds it painful, putting fingers into ears or hands over ears.

- Flinches or seems distressed by loud noise.

Support for people with learning disabilities and hearing problems

Much can be done to help people with learning disabilities use their hearing more effectively – reducing the impact of their disabilities and allowing them to have greater control over their lives.

People requiring hearing assessment, hearing aids and hearing aid management advice should in the first place be seen by their GP. The GP will examine them for problems such as wax build up or ear infection and refer them to a hospital ear, nose and throat (ENT) department if necessary. If it is clear that there are no physical complications or underlying disease, a GP may be able to refer the person directly to an audiology department.

It is perhaps not surprising that many GPs are not aware of the prevalence of hearing problems in the population of people with a learning disability.

GPs may also be unaware of the necessity of diagnosis and how this can be achieved. The same is also true of some ENT departments. However, this picture is changing and many GPs will have a number of learning disabled people on their lists, as people increasingly live in the community (and have been living in the community for quite a while now) and have annual health checks. It is hoped that education about the special needs of people with learning disabilities will be made much more generally available. In the meantime, staff should not accept comments such as, 'there is nothing we can do', or 'it really doesn't matter – it won't make any difference'. They should seek help from speech therapists, hearing therapists and particularly enquire about special audiological services.

When visiting an ENT department it is often useful for a speech therapist who knows the individual to accompany the carer or staff member. Anyone attending clinics or appointments with a person with learning disabilities should be able to communicate with that person and be able to provide information on his/her background. There is nothing more difficult and annoying for doctors and workers involved with hearing tests to be told: 'I don't know anything about her. I only met her yesterday'.

A hearing test will provide information about what a person can hear in a 'clinical test'. However, most of us do not live in perfect clinical settings, so it is worth asking hearing therapists about 'functional hearing'. They can advise on what a person hears throughout their day and suggest ways to help people use their hearing more effectively by suggesting training methods and sessions whereby you can focus on listening skills rather than vision and other sensory information. As hearing problems often affect an individual's communication and social skills, advice from speech and language therapists should be sought.

If a hearing aid is prescribed and no hearing therapist is available, speech therapists are usually willing to give help and advice on individual people who will often have initial difficulty. In fact, it may take several months for someone to learn to use an aid and it needs to be established what type of aid it is, where it's best used and when it should not be worn. For some who have hearing aids the type of aid worn very much affects a person's ability to respond to social situations. Very few people with learning disabilities are prescribed digital aids and often have analogue aids which amplify all sounds in the vicinity which can be distressing if around road traffic or in a busy place. Sudden sounds can be alarming and make people jump or sometimes cause physical pain. It is important to ask for digital aids to ensure that people have equality of access. The tests might be more difficult to achieve, however the additional time and effort will pay off and support from the local health facilitation nursing service for people with learning difficulties will often help to get around a lot of the issues.

People will need help in getting orientated to using an aid and it is best done gradually rather than being made to be worn all the time which can result in it being immediately rejected and never used. Families and carers need to work with the audiologist and/or speech and language therapist to work on a step-by-step programme of support to suit the individual's needs.

People with a learning disability whose hearing loss turns out to be more profound will need support in other areas, such as using pictures or signs. This will require training of anyone supporting the individual to use the many sign systems and symbol vocabularies that are available.

Visual impairment and learning disability

People with learning disabilities are ten times more likely to have a visual impairment than the wider population group (Seeability, 2013). Depending on the degree of learning disabilities, and in some cases the person's syndrome or ethnic origin, then the probability can increase sharply. Visual impairment across the spectrum of the population of those with a learning disability falls into three clear categories where support and understanding of the type of condition is required:

1. Refractive errors

These require glasses or contact lenses and regular eye health check-ups to prevent common eye diseases associated with ageing.

2. Congenital and cortical visual impairment

These are eye conditions requiring possible medical intervention and/or certification of visual impairment and environmental, communication and mobility support. Congenital impairment is present from birth or as part of a syndrome presentation, and cortical is brain damage related, sometimes called cerebral or cognitive visual impairment.

3. Age-related visual impairments

These are conditions which affect vision as part of the ageing process and can be corrected by glasses, medical intervention or will be sight threatening and require certification, rehabilitation support for mobility communication and environmental adaptations.

Age-related eye diseases

During an eye test the optometrist will check the retina of the eye to look for early signs of disease such as macular degeneration (loss of central vision as part of ageing) or retinopathies (disorders of the retina causing blind spots, high blood pressure and diabetes, which cause blood spots to appear on your retina, making your vision dark and patchy). They can also see if the lens is becoming opaque and detect the onset of conditions such as cataracts. These are the age related conditions that can occur for all of us, however some people with learning disabilities are particularly susceptible to both refractive and age related conditions much earlier than the rest of the population and should have regular, preferably annual, eye checks. This is particularly the case for people with cerebral palsy, Down's syndrome, rubella syndrome, Cornelia De Lange syndrome and Laurence Moon Bardet Biedl syndrome, to name just a few.

Congenital and cortical visual problems

Where people with learning disabilities have the greatest variation from the rest of society with regards their eye health is in the incidence and type of visual disabilities described in this section. Primarily these conditions are present from birth and are usually a co-morbidity factor related to the type of syndrome that the young child presents with. Some conditions such as congenital cataracts can be treated if confirmed early enough and vision may develop normally or with refractive correction.

For many children who have cortical errors there is a problem with the brain interpreting what the eye is seeing. Around 79% of all children with profound and multiple learning disabilities are believed to experience cortical visual problems and around 50% in those with a severe learning disability.

Cortical visual impairment varies in its presentation from an individual being totally blind, to seeing just light and dark. Symptoms includes:

- Seeing moving images but not stationary images, and vice versa. This will affect communication development and determine whether a person will use signs or symbols.

- Reverse visual perception (seeing upside down).

- Stereo visual problems (blurred vision/double vision) caused by the brain being unable to edit the images from a dominant eye.

- Colour blindness or perception problems.

- Visual field distortions (such as a lack of field in one eye or both eyes).

- Poor depth perception.

- Night vision problems.

- Daylight visual problems (glare).

- Contrast problems.

- Intermittent sight.

A person can have some or all of these symptoms and often cannot express what they are seeing. We can usually only find out through observation of behaviour and specialist functional assessments by orthoptists based in general hospitals or specialist vision workers.

After vision testing

There are two key routes of vision testing; an acuity test and a functional test. Following the eye tests, particularly acuity tests, there may be several options you will be asked to consider.

Most tests finish with a follow up assessment a year to 18 months later, which means there is no change to an existing condition or the eyes are fine.

Sometimes a hospital appointment is required. This could be for further assessment, referral to an ophthalmologist (eye consultant) for examination and treatment which could be medication eye drops or an operation. The latter will require further planning and preparation.

The referral could be for further certification as visually impaired or blind, in which case the individual will receive important paperwork that will trigger a series of events. This is called the Certificate of Visual Impairment or CVI. It contains the diagnosis and prognosis in some cases. A copy always stays with the person, and one goes to the GP, one copy goes to the Office for National Statistics, and informs the ONS census, one copy goes to social services and one stays on the hospital file. The local authority copy should trigger a visit by a rehabilitation officer for the visually impaired (ROVI). They may be employed by the local voluntary blind agency under contract, by the local authority direct or if the person is a school age child, a 'teacher for visual impairment' might visit home or school.

Their visit will be to determine what equipment, coaching and skills development a person will need and what adaptations may be required to help a person be as independent as possible within their home or school.

They will work with families and support workers to make a support plan and scheme of activities to learn and develop new skills, which may include walking with a cane, making drinks with a liquid level indicator, teaching methods to find a way around the home without help. If at school then suggestions will be made to assist with accessing the curriculum and providing home school support. They may also teach staff and family guiding skills for when you are travelling out in public and will inform you of helpful benefits and organisations.

Conclusion

In this chapter we have explored the common problems of hearing and sight loss and its impact on a person with a learning disability. These cover a wide range of sensory impairments that offer different challenges for those who are afflicted by these conditions and their supporters. To that end we have also focused as well on how to support people, and informed readers of a number of organisations where help and assistance may be obtained.

Summary points

- People with learning disabilities are at a high risk of developing hearing and sight problems.

- Many people with learning disabilities are not having their eyes or ears checked and are developing conditions which are preventable, causing people to appear more disabled than they actually are.

- Having poor sight and hearing limits an individual's ability to communicate, make choices, carry out simple self-help tasks and interact with others.

- People with a learning disability require more support to keep, attend and have successful appointments. The person accompanying the individual should be aware of the range of tests and equipment or aids available and be prepared to ask questions on the individual's behalf.

- Seeking support from health facilitation nurses, particularly for hearing tests at the hospital, will usually ensure that health outcomes are much improved.

References

Emerson E & Robertson J (2011) *The Estimated Prevalence of Visual Impairment among People with Learning Disabilities in the UK* [online]. IHAL/Department of Health. Available at: https://www.rnib.org.uk/sites/default/files/Emerson%20report.pdf (accessed October 2016).

RNIB Multiple Disability Service (2001) *Looking for Hearing Problems in People with Learning Disabilities*. Factsheet.

RNIB Multiple Disability Service (2003) *Looking for Eye Problems*. Factsheet.

Seeability (2013) *Vision and People with Learning Disabilities: Guidance for GPs* [online]. Available at: https://www.seeability.org/uploads/files/PDFs_Books_non_Easy_Read/RCGP_Guidance_for_GPs.pdf (accessed October 2016).

Chapter 16: Postural care

Sarah Clayton

Introduction

Postural care is a gentle, effective and respectful intervention used to protect an individual's body shape. The position in which children lie was first identified as a contributory factor in the development of body shape distortion in 1976:

'It is suggested that the 'squint' baby syndrome and the 'windswept' child syndrome in children with cerebral palsy are stages of the same syndrome and that in both the deformities are caused by the effect of gravity on an immobile growing child, rather than spasticity or muscle imbalance. Asymmetrical deformity should therefore be amenable to physiotherapeutic intervention…'
(Fulford & Brown, 1976)

Recommendation nine of the *Confidential Inquiry into Premature Death of People with Learning Disabilities* (Heslop *et al*, 2013) identified the high risk of premature mortality is associated with respiratory infection for people with learning disabilities. As part of the recommendation, it's stated that clinical commissioning groups (CCGs) 'must ensure they are commissioning sufficient, and sufficiently expert, preventative services for people with learning disabilities regarding their high risk of respiratory illness. This would include expert, proactive postural care support' (Heslop *et al*, 2013).

Any person who finds it difficult to move effectively is at risk of developing changes in body shape due to the impact of gravity on their body. The way a person's body shape responds to gravity is highly predictable and as such amenable to intervention. The most influential contributory factor is the position in which a person sleeps. If the amount of time spent in the lying position is calculated, it is estimated that children spend on average three times longer in bed than they do in school (Clayton & Goldsmith, 2008). It is evident that individuals with complex disability spend far longer in the lying position than the general population and that their inability to change position independently is much reduced. Supporting a person to access appropriate, person-centred postural care can be challenging. It is helpful to think of the individual elements of the process in order to identify gaps or to provide direction.

There are five distinct stages to postural care provision:

- Identification of need.

- Measurement of body symmetry using the Goldsmith Indices.

- Training and support for those providing day-to-day care.

- Equipment provision.

- Review process.

Any person providing day-to-day care for individuals should be able to identify warning signs or factors that put people more at risk. The Mansfield Checklist provides a simple-to-use tool that can support people to raise concerns with healthcare practitioners (Clayton, 2000). The checklist also appears on page 28 of the *Royal College of General Practitioners Step by Step Guide for GP Practices, Annual Health Checks for People with a Learning Disability* (Hoghton & RCGP Learning Disabilities Group, 2010) so should be considered when individuals have their annual health check.

The Mansfield Checklist

If you answer yes to any of these questions, the person you are thinking of may benefit from postural care.

Does their body stay in a limited number of positions? Yes ☐ No ☐

Additional information – describe the equipment they use, the opportunities they have to move or change position during the day or any reasons why the person is restricted to a limited number of positions.

Do their knees seem to be drawn to one side? Yes ☐ No ☐

Or inwards? Yes ☐ No ☐

Or outwards? Yes ☐ No ☐

Additional information – describe the position of the person's legs, any difficulties this causes and any opportunity the person might have to change this position during the day.

Are their arms and hands in a position in which they could function normally? Yes ☐ No ☐

Additional information – is there any impact on the person's positioning when they function? Does the person's position impact on their ability to function?

Does their head seem to turn mainly to one side? Yes ☐ No ☐

To their right? Yes ☐ No ☐

To their left? Yes ☐ No ☐

Additional information – does this cause any difficulties with regards to communication or swallowing? Yes ☐ No ☐

Does the body tend to extend backwards? Yes ☐ No ☐

Flex forwards? Yes ☐ No ☐

To the right? Yes ☐ No ☐

To the left? Yes ☐ No ☐

Additional information – does the person experience primitive reflexes? Yes ☐ No ☐

If so, in which circumstances?

Do these movements cause additional difficulties for the person? Yes ☐ No ☐

Are they difficult to control? Yes ☐ No ☐

Is the body shape already asymmetric? Yes ☐ No ☐

Additional information – please describe existing distortion of body shape that the person may already experience, any surgical intervention that has been undertaken and any ongoing difficulties caused by existing distortion of body shape.

Traditionally in the UK, service providers have used an individual's function as the primary indicator as to their risk of developing changes in body shape. Individuals who have a Gross Motor Function Classification Scale (GMFCS) (Palisano *et al*, 1997) of four or five are usually considered to be eligible for support. The scale categorises children into one of five groups ranging from GMFCS 1; those who can walk, run, jump, and climb stairs but who have some impairment of speed, balance or co-ordination, through to GMFCS 5; those who use wheelchairs for all mobility and who need postural support in order to be able to sit comfortably.

The use of a person's functional ability risks excluding huge swathes of the population whose function is better developed but whose body shape is distorted. One solution is to routinely measure the body symmetry of those who access physiotherapy and occupational therapy services and use this as the indicator as to whether the person is at risk. There is no doubt that a person's function is maximised if their body shape is symmetrical but these two aspects of an individual's needs must be considered separately.

Goldsmith Indices of Body Symmetry

If body shape is to be protected it is essential to have a method by which we can measure the effect of positioning strategies. The Goldsmith Indices of Body Symmetry is a validated and objective measure that can be used as children and young people grow and develop (Goldsmith *et al*, 1992). Maintaining symmetry will safeguard the internal capacity of the abdomen and thorax, and in turn protect the function of the internal organs. Monitoring body symmetry plays an essential part in the prevention of premature death.

The chest is a relatively soft, highly mobile structure which changes shape immediately and predictably in different lying positions. For example if a person lies on their stomach (prone) their chest will be wider and flatter than if the same person lies on their back (supine). When people with typical movement then sit or stand their chest springs back to its normal shape, this is a feature called recoil. The less movement a person has, the greater the risk that they will begin to lose this recoil – their chest will start to gradually adapt to their lying posture in all positions. All other aspects of life then become more difficult as the person's ability to sit and stand and carry out daily living tasks. To protect and restore chest shape, positioning strategies are used to apply forces in the lying posture (Clayton & Goldsmith, 2010).

The Goldsmith Indices of Body Symmetry:

1. Provide the individual with a simple and reliable method of measuring and recording their body symmetry.

2. Provide feedback to those providing postural care for the individual.

3. Increase sensitivity to the early signs of asymmetry, and raise awareness of the processes of its development.

4. Enable the individual and their first circle of support to plan postural care on the basis of objective measurements.

5. Provide data essential for the scientific evaluation of the effects of postural care

Measurement of body symmetry is usually carried out by physiotherapists or occupational therapists. It is helpful to therapists if those providing day-to-day support are able to identify any changes in symmetry; regular photographs are a good way to monitor small, often unnoticed changes. Any changes in body shape could indicate that there is a problem with the equipment being used to support the person or that the person's needs have changed. If a person is spending considerably more time in bed, for example if they have been unwell, it is important to consider whether they are being adequately supported.

Measures of health and well-being

Changes in body shape have a significant impact on the individual and those providing day-to-day care, as summarised within the NHS Purchasing and Supply Agency's *Buyers Guide: Night time positioning equipment for children* (Centre for Evidence-based Purchasing, 2009). Changes in body shape effect:

- *'The musculoskeletal system (contractures, loss of joint integrity e.g. hip dislocation, decreased bone density, reduced range of joint motion and deformity e.g. spinal scoliosis).*

- *The neurological system (spasticity/muscle tone, primitive reflexes, altered sensation and joint position sense, pain, weakness).*

- *Respiratory function.*

- *Digestion (including swallowing and choking, both of which are compromised by poor head to neck posture) and kidney/renal function.*

- *Personal hygiene, ease of toileting and changing.*

- *Functional ability (e.g. weight bearing, transfer and hand function).*

- *Environment interaction (sensory perception, body aesthetics, learning, communication).*

- *Sleep pattern and irritability.'*

(Centre for Evidence-based Purchasing, 2009)

Should an individual experience difficulties with these aspects of their health and well-being, or additional aspects such as pressure areas or increased pain, careful consideration should be given to the positioning strategies being used. Additional support can be sought from physiotherapy and occupational therapy teams, wheelchair services and community nursing teams.

Equipment provision

Specialist equipment is often needed in order to provide comfortable, safe and appropriate levels of support to individuals. There are three fundamental pieces of equipment that for most people will ensure they have support for the majority of the 24-hour period. A person's wheelchair, their alternative seating and their night time positioning need to be carefully assessed and monitored on a regular basis. If one of these pieces of equipment is not appropriate or even missing entirely it will have a negative impact on the person and those supporting them.

The Community Equipment Code of Practice Scheme (Donnelly, 2015) provides a quality framework for the procurement and provision of community equipment, including wheelchairs. There have been numerous reports, campaigns and pieces of research (available on the CECOPS website) that have highlighted the difficulties faced by people accessing community equipment.

In many parts of the UK, a physiotherapist or an occupational therapist will identify whether an individual needs a particular piece of equipment. The therapist will usually then arrange an appointment with a representative of the equipment provider for an assessment. Preparation for the assessment is vital if all those involved are to have a complete picture of the needs of the individual.

Preparing for an assessment – seating and lying

Key points to consider for any form of assessment include the following:

- Equipment provision should take place within a framework called a care pathway. A care pathway details the different stages of the provision including training, who should do what and how long the process should take.

- If the person is offered an assessment, ask for information about where this is to take place, how long the process will take and what to expect. Practical considerations such as the availability of a place to change, or whether to take food, drink or medication, may make the difference as to whether the experience is a positive one.

- If the person being supported is likely to be distressed by a change in environment or a novel experience ask whether the service can accommodate visits, provide social stories or if the assessment can take place in a more familiar environment such as within the person's own home.

- Consider carefully who should be present at the assessment. Ideally everyone there will bring valuable information, which could be in relation to the equipment or knowledge of the specific needs of the person. If the person does not communicate using words it is essential that someone is present to act as an advocate, ensuring that the person's views and responses are understood by all.

- Provide photographs of how the person currently sits and lies. It is important that both positions are taken into account as they impact on one another greatly.

- During the course of a seating assessment the practitioner will assess the person's range of movement and body shape, this part of the assessment should be conducted on a plinth with the person lying down. If this does not happen, be sure to ask why as valuable information will be missed.

- Provide as much information as you can in relation to the general health of the individual. Common difficulties associated with equipment for seating and lying may include pressure, temperature regulation, discomfort or pain.

- Ensure that everyone at the assessment is aware of any upcoming surgery or changes in circumstance that are likely to impact on the use of the equipment – it is reasonable to ask for the assessment to be delayed until after surgery.

- Consider carefully the clothes the person wears for the appointment – overly bulky or striped clothing will cause difficulty for the practitioner conducting the assessment.

- Take photographs during the assessment. This will help everyone to remember what was discussed and can be used to share information with people that are not present.

- Before leaving the assessment find out what happens next, the time frames that can be expected and who to contact in the event of any difficulty.

The assessment process for any piece of equipment is only the beginning. Following the assessment it is important to have a clear time frame for how long the equipment will take to be provided. This may include time for a decision to be made as to whether the equipment will be provided at all.

It is common practice for complex pieces of equipment such as wheelchairs or night time positioning to be officially handed over, this process involves training in the use of the equipment and an opportunity to ask any questions or address difficulties in its use. Ensure that the contact details are recorded in the event of difficulty with the equipment – it may be that any concerns need to be raised with the therapist that prescribed the equipment or you may need to work directly with the equipment manufacturer. Ensure that there are copies of any product warranty, complaints or support services in a safe and accessible place. Many equipment manufacturers are members of The British Health Trades Association (see resources) and as such should comply with their code of conduct which is enforced by Trading Standards.

Reviewing an individual's postural care

Change is a constant factor in everyone's lives; a particular piece of equipment or method of supporting an individual will change over time and as such regular reviews are vital. Weight loss and weight gain, pain, surgery and changes in medication and amongst many factors which may affect the use of existing equipment. Services differ in the way in which they are accessed and may be open to self-referral (meaning they can be contacted directly for support) or whether another health practitioner such as a GP has to refer the individual.

Conclusion

Postural care is becoming more widely understood, which will in time lead to reductions in the number of people that experience devastating changes in body shape. There are a number of potential barriers that seem to get in the way of this straight forward and highly effective intervention. These may be experienced by individuals accessing services, family carers and support workers as well as health and social care practitioners working hard to deliver services. They include: a lack of awareness of how to protect body shape, low expectations and a sense of inevitability that changes in body shape cannot be prevented, inadequate funding for both equipment and training, inadequate support to help people to undertake behavioural change at night time, and lack of standards for equipment services.

Individuals, families and health and social care practitioners working in partnership can make a difference and protect body shape in the future but we all need knowledge, support and equipment to make it happen.

Summary points

- Postural care is the provision of support in order to protect a person's body from the predictable effects of gravity.

- The less independent movement a person has, the greater their risk of developing changes in body shape.

- Changes in body shape happen slowly over time and so awareness and monitoring of the impact of positioning strategies is vital.

- Changes in body shape are avoidable if the correct positioning strategies are used by everyone involved in a person's care.

- A person's wheelchair, alternative seating and night time positioning provide the basis for good postural care. Additional equipment may also be required.

- Preparation for assessments is essential if the right equipment is to be obtained.

- Postural care is everyone's responsibility.

References

Centre for Evidence-based Purchasing (2009) *Buyers' Guide: Night time postural management equipment for children* [online]. London: NHS Purchasing and Supply Agency. Available at: https://dspace.lboro.ac.uk/dspace-jspui/bitstream/2134/7368/1/AR2616%20Buyers%20Guide%20Night%20Time%20Postural%20Management%20Equipment.pdf (accessed October 2016).

Clayton S (2000) The Mansfield Project: postural care at night within a community setting. *Physiotherapy* **86** (10) 528–534.

Clayton S & Goldsmith L (2008) Posture, mobility and comfort. In: S Carnaby & J Pawlyn (Eds) *Profound Intellectual and Multiple Disabilities: Nursing complex needs* (pp 328–347). Chichester: Wiley-Blackwell Publishing.

Clayton S & Goldsmith J (2010) Biomechanics and prevention of body shape distortion. *The Tizard Learning Disability Review* **15** (2) 15–29.

Donnelly B (2015) *Code of Practice for Disability Equipment, Wheelchair and Seating Services: A quality framework for procurement and provision of services*. Buckinghamshire: CECOPS.

Fulford GE & Brown JK (1976) Position as a cause of deformity in children with cerebral palsy. *Developental Medicine and Child Neurology* **18** (3) 305–314.

Goldsmith L, Golding RM, Garstang RA & Macrae AW (1992) A technique to measure windswept deformity. *Physiotherapy* **78** (4) 235–242.

Heslop P, Blair P, Fleming P, Hoghton M, Marriott A & Russ L (2013) *Confidential Inquiry into the Premature Death of People with Learning Disabilities: Final report* [online]. Bristol: Norah Fry Research Centre. Available at: http://www.bristol.ac.uk/media-library/sites/cipold/migrated/documents/fullfinalreport.pdf (accessed October 2016).

Hoghton MH & Royal College of General Practitioners Learning Disabilities Group (2010) *A Step by Step Guide for GP Practices: Annual health checks for people with a learning disability* [online]. London: General Practitioners Learning Disabilities Group. Available at: http://www.rcgp.org.uk/learningdisabilities (accessed October 2016).

Palisano R, Rosenbaum P, Walter S, Russell D, Wood E & Galuppi B (1997) Development and reliability of a system to classify gross motor function in children with cerebral palsy. *Developmental Medicine and Child Neurology* **39** (4) 214–223.

Resources

CECOPS: http://www.cecops.org.uk/publications/

British Health Trades Association: http://www.bhta.net

Part III

Service users, carers and family, and the hospital experience

Chapter 17: Meeting the health needs of people with learning disabilities: working together with families

Hayley Goleniowksa

Introduction

As John Donne stated, 'No man is an island,' and likewise a patient with a learning disability does not exist in isolation.

People with a learning disability are not simply a set of symptoms, a syndrome or co-morbidities, or the sum total of one particular behaviour pattern; they are one part of a family network and community, a complex and unique individual. They have their own likes and dislikes, friendships and relationships, with their own habits and ways of doing things. Patients with learning disabilities deserve the very best quality healthcare, delivered with respect and compassion, and one of the best ways to ensure this is to work closely with those who know them the best.

Carers, family members and support workers are in a privileged position to know and understand the person fully, and are therefore a medical professional's greatest resource; a resource that could prevent vital healthcare issues being missed or a diagnosis being delayed by making false assumptions about a person's typical behaviour (diagnostic overshadowing); a resource that can pinpoint the reasonable adjustments that must be made to ensure a positive outcome for the person.

Professionals and families: what are the possible hurdles?

As the mother of a girl who has Down's syndrome, I understand that families universally want the best possible care and support for their loved one, who they understand implicitly. They will have experienced many medical and healthcare appointments and procedures together, some of which may have been negative experiences or presented significant challenges.

Essentially, it's personal, and emotions can easily come to the fore in these situations. Even a relatively minor procedure can bring back memories of a major operation and the fear associated with it, for both the patient and those of us supporting them. It's even possible for high-profile negative media stories to prey on families' minds; phobias can develop and frustrations build.

Families can feel ignored, their concerns brushed aside, or they can feel a lack of respect for their loved one. Any kind of indication that their family member is not receiving equal respect and treatment to anyone else is bound to cause upset.

In worst case scenarios, when communication breaks down or when dangerous assumptions are made, lives can be needlessly lost, as people with a learning disability are misunderstood, diagnoses are missed or delayed, or essential care is not delivered in time or at all. The *Death by Indifference* report (Mencap, 2007) makes frightening reading for families, and it is up to us all to make sure that no one with a learning disability dies younger than they should.

It is therefore crucial that teams work together on building one another's trust, learning to communicate effectively and listen fully, exploring all possibilities and making reasonable adjustments in delivery of care that could make all the difference. Healthcare should not be about two opposing sides with communication breaking down, but about shared goals and aims.

The mother of the late poet Adam Bojelian, who died following sepsis, is keen to spread this message.

She aims to educate that:

- The NHS is available to all without discrimination.
- The NHS has a duty to promote equality and human rights.
- The NHS has a duty to diagnose, treat and improve mental and physical health.

Families and carers are at the heart of this, for 'together we are better.'
(Laverty, 2015)

Clear communication with the person with a learning disability and their family

What is most important for families when meeting the health needs of someone with a learning disability? Good communication and respect is what families like ours consider their main priority. They want to be truly listened to and taken seriously. Families and carers should be considered as 'lead professionals', since they are experts in the subtle cues that give an accurate picture of their loved one's health and play a vital role in ensuring that their healthcare needs are met. The family are your greatest resource and it is important to value this.

When asked, carers suggested the following ways of making communication simpler for all:

- **Create a hospital/health passport** – These can be completed at home by the person with learning disabilities and their family or support workers, and should be taken to all hospital or clinic appointments. Include information on whether the individual has communication difficulties, if they attend a mainstream or special school or support centre, who their key workers are, and what their likes and dislikes/fears are. This is also a place to note medication and vital health data. They can take any format but an example template of a hospital passport can be downloaded from the University of Bristol (visit http://www.uhbristol.nhs.uk/patients-and-visitors/information-for-patients/hospital-passport/).

- **Use Easy Read information** – Facts on healthcare should be accessible to all by being presented with few words, instead making use of pictures and symbols. These can help explain procedures or teach people how to lead a healthy lifestyle. The Clear Communication People provide a selection of Easy Read documents on common tests and hospital procedures and allow families to prepare for procedures together at home in their own time.

- **Do not make assumptions and listen to families** – Someone with a learning disability will need support with taking medication, attending appointments, participating in therapies and so on, so enlist the help of family members. Do not make assumptions and always check for understanding after giving explanations. It is also important not to attribute any symptoms to the person's learning disability alone. It is crucial to eliminate other conditions by listening to families when they pinpoint any changes in their loved one's mood or behaviour.

- **Learn some key Makaton signs** – Using sign, symbols or pictures can help reinforce a message visually and provides a focus for some. It is particularly valuable when communicating with someone who uses sign as their primary method of communication. Families will advise on which methods work best for their loved one.

- **Communicate with the person with learning disabilities** – Although families play a crucial role in communication, diagnosis and treatment, it is important that medical professionals talk to the patient directly, not assuming they need a spokesperson. Find out their needs and ask them how they feel before turning to those who support them. Simply looking at the person while talking is enough to make them feel valued. Respect their privacy and ways of doing things as much as for any other patient.

Actress Sarah Gordy, who has Down's syndrome, has created a useful video called *Wood for the Trees* (Gordy, 2015), in conjunction with the General Medical Council, outlining the dangers of making assumptions and ignoring vital signs in patients with learning disabilities. It provides a very good starting point for discussions on communication between families and medical professionals, and warns of the dangers when they aren't listened to. In one moving scene, where doctors finally grasp the severity of her character's situation, Sarah says, 'You weren't looking. I was here all the time' (Gordy, 2015).

Motivational public speaker James Hamilton, who also has Down's syndrome, speaks to all new employees at his local NHS trust university hospital. He talks about life with learning disabilities and how difficult it can be when being admitted to hospital.

'Doctors and nurses forget that we can't understand when they use a lot of medical terminology. Sometimes we need our families to help us settle and may need them to speak on our behalf, like an advocate. If we are rushed in with no time to prepare, our hospital uses a hospital passport so we don't need to be asked questions when we are least likely to understand and be in a position to reply calmly. Sometimes we want people to act out what they want without using words. I think all medical professionals need to think of us as people first and not just as a person with a learning disability who cannot or will not understand what they are saying.'
(Hamilton, 2015)

The family's role in ensuring that the healthcare needs of those with learning disability are met

In order to build understanding and trust between individuals receiving care, families and healthcare professionals, it is important to share medical information with family members as well as the individual who is being treated.

Consider using online access to medical records

Family and carers can also be granted permission to view this information which is vital to their loved one's well-being and ensuring they get the right treatment and support. This cutting-edge system was pioneered by Dr Amir Hannan of the Houghton Thornley Medical Centres.

Dr Hannan states that, so far, 20% of all his patients with learning disabilities are signed up to his GP Electronic Health Records:

'We know that patients and their families who access their records have a better understanding of their own health and are "ahead of the game". They know what is in their records and usually find it easy to see any recent letters, test results or scan results and what was discussed in previous consultations.'
(Hannan, 2015)

The aim is to see an increase in health literacy for many families/carers and people with learning disabilities, and to improve a family's understanding about a patient and be enabled to cater for their needs and access available services.

It is the professionals who are ultimately required to make decisions on the healthcare that is in someone's best interest if they lack capacity, but they are legally obliged to include the family in reaching this decision.

The family and carers will be aware of any past problems with procedures that could be avoided with some reasonable adjustments, and may be able to suggest solutions, for example, keeping a patient away from bright lights or noise, role playing procedures and visits in advance. So really listening to what they have to say is vital.

Invite families to ensure that regular health screening checks are made

'The annual health check should do a top to toe "MOT" of a person with learning disabilities. Enlist the support of family members to make sure this happens regularly.'
(Blair, 2016)

To get this right, health professionals must engage the person, their family, carers and supporters as well as community learning disabilities nurses. Only by doing this will a holistic picture emerge of what the person's health status is, and how a plan to address health needs can be formulated.

Encourage families to be organised

Encourage families to be organised and to keep medical information, letters, appointment details and the hospital/health passport in a file. The will save a lot of time and stress and help them keep track of healthcare needs.

Finding a solution together: what additional support is available for patients with learning disabilities and their families?

Learning disability nurses

These specialist nurses help liaise between the family and surgical teams and discuss the specific needs of patients. The result is a calmer, smoother and shorter period of time in hospital. They are worth their weight in gold, so put families in touch with this specialist team.

I became aware of learning disability nurses when our daughter went into hospital for a routine operation. The nurse was able to liaise with the anaesthetist to arrange skipping the pre-med and also advised surgical teams that she should go to theatre as early as possible on the day to avoid uncomfortable situations that she would not be able to deal with mentally and emotionally. I thought of her as a bridge between our family's concerns and the medical team's aims. She acted as a sort of medical translator.

Learning disability nurses play an invaluable role in hospitals. They remove fear and they make sure procedures and stays in hospital go as smoothly as possible. They mediate and translate between the families and the consultants, surgeons and managers, as well as being a vital mouthpiece to communicate the needs of those with learning disabilities. In the long run they save time and money.

The early days following our daughter's diagnosis at birth would have been so much easier with their calm, unbiased support on hand from day one. They are in a unique position to help break down the medical model of disability and bring us to a more realistic social model, that each individual is unique. This approach, and indeed the introduction of learning disability teams at antenatal consultations, is something that I believe would be beneficial to many new families.

Support groups and online forums

Online communities are becoming more and more popular. They bring together medical professionals, patients and their families and allow the sharing of information and advice, as well as a place to talk openly and freely about worries and concerns or ideas that worked. Try finding a specific group that deals with a relevant health issue or syndrome in order to connect with others going through similar experiences.

'Online communities that focus on a particular disease or condition and can include patients, carers, clinicians, researchers and industry. These communities are beginning to change how patients are perceived and how services are delivered.' (Hodgkin, 2015)

The following online groups and charities provide just this kind of support:

■ The British Institute of Learning Disabilities: http://www.bild.org.uk

■ Down's Syndrome Association: http://www.downs-syndrome.org.uk

■ Mencap: https://www.mencap.org.uk

■ Scope: http://www.scope.org.uk

■ Firefly Garden: http://community.fireflyfriends.com

■ Special Needs Jungle: http://www.specialneedsjungle.com

■ Makaton: https://www.makaton.org

■ Easy Read: http://www.easy-read-online.co.uk/

■ Foundation for People with Learning Disabilities: http://www.
learningdisabilities.org.uk

Conclusion

Healthcare professionals, patients, and their carers and support workers all want quality, family-centred healthcare, delivered with compassion.

'By working together with families, good practice can be shared to ensure the very best for patients who have a learning disability. It is this patient-centred, family-centred approach that is the way forward. We must value every patient equally as a unique individual in their own right.'
(Powell, 2015)

To arrange James Hamilton to be a motivational speaker in your organisations, contact his father, Philip, at philip.hamilton4@ntlworld.com.

Summary points

■ Value all patients equally and work with family units to get to get a full picture when working with a person with a learning disability.

■ Consult with patients and their families on which reasonable adjustments are needed to deliver the very best healthcare you can.

■ Signpost support and think of ways of organising and sharing information together.

■ Take full advantage of the support that learning disability nurses can provide at all stages of a patient's life.

References

Blair J (2015) *The Health Needs of People with Learning Disabilities: Issues and solutions* [online] https://www.bjfm.co.uk/the_health_needs_of_people_with_learning_disabilities_issues_and_solutions_25769832825.aspx (accessed October 2016).

Gordy S (2015) *Wood for the Trees* [online]. General Medical Council. Available at: http://www.gmc-uk.org/learningdisabilities/532.aspx (accessed October 2016).

Hamilton J (2015) Speech at North East London Trust (NELFT) day for professionals.

Hannan A (2015) *Surgery CARES: Implementing Instant Medical History™ in General Practice* [online]. Available at: http://www.htmc.co.uk/pages/pv.asp?p=htmc0473 (accessed October 2016).

Hodgkin P (2015) Private correspondence.

Laverty (2015) *Positive Choices* [online]. Available at: https://positive-choices.com (accessed October 2016).

Mencap (2007) *Death by Indifference* [online]. London. Available at: https://www.mencap.org.uk/get-involved/campaigning/our-reports (accessed October 2016).

Powell H (2015) Taken from LDAN Conference, January 2016.

Chapter 18: Through our eyes: what parents want for their children from health professionals

Jim Blair and parents

Jim Blair
Mary Busk Expert by Parental Experience
Hayley Goleniowska Expert by Parental Experience
Simon Hawtrey-Woore Expert by Parental Experience
Sue Morris Expert by Parental Experience
Yvonne Newbold Expert by Parental Experience
Stephanie Nimmo Expert by Parental Experience

Introduction

Who knows best? Families of people with learning disabilities, their carers or healthcare professionals? This is a difficult question to answer, but it is certainly true that health professionals as well as those working in social and education settings can only get care and support right when they involve those who have lived experience, namely people with learning disabilities and their families. This chapter focuses on family members, who present here, using their own words and their own names, their feelings about health services and what changes they would like to see. It is essential that all health professionals gain a clear, focused sense of what it is like to experience health services through the eyes of those who use them.

The challenges and difficulties families face when entering the world of hospitals and health service settings are captured in the following piece by Yvonne, a mother of a child with severe and profound learning disabilities and complex health needs.

What I would wish for

'Hospitals will always be a part of our family life – it goes with the territory when you have a child with complex needs. Even though I spend several hours, sometimes several days and nights, in hospital every month, I absolutely dread every minute we're there, and it gets harder with each passing year.

What one thing would make the whole experience more bearable? That's easy. I wish that every single hospital employee could learn how to truly listen.

Some health professionals barely listen at all. Others appear to listen, but you soon realise that it was only so they could formulate their reply. Occasionally, we meet someone very special who really listens, and with their whole selves, so they even hear what's left unsaid.

They're the ones who make magic happen. As well as absorbing our words, they gain a tangible sense of what our lives are really like in a way that parents like me seldom experience. Time stops still while compassionate kindness soothes suffering. In that moment, something profound happens; my sick child becomes the only thing that matters.

You hear and take my concerns seriously, somehow knowing this is my first adult conversation in days. You make me feel like an equal rather than someone less. You understand all I say even though I'm barely talking coherently. You help me make sense of all of my fears. You acknowledge the essence of who my broken, hurting little boy really is, barely noticing his disabilities and equipment. You make a holistic assessment based on quality of life rather than individual symptoms.

When my child doesn't co-operate with your examination, you ask for and accept my help. I suggest we turn it into a game, you play along enthusiastically.

You offer me a glimpse of the future when all health professionals are like you. When we will all pull together on the same side, working in partnership solely to enhance my child's life.

I can tell by your eyes that you know the things we haven't talked about. You recognise my exhaustion and notice how my hair hasn't seen a comb for a week, but you don't judge me or make me feel inadequate. You 'get' how my life is. A never-ending merry-go-round of sleep-deprivation, of coping with double incontinence, of tube-feeds, of nasal-cannulas, of oxygen-saturation monitors, and of the ever-present vomiting and chest physiotherapy in the middle of the night.

You know how my son's fragility terrifies me, frightened that his tenuous grip on life could snap at any moment. You feel my guilt that I can't stop his pain, and you sense how hard I work to keep him alive. You know better than to ask me how I'm coping because you know I'll always say 'I'm fine'. You understand that that's better than me starting to cry and never being able to stop, so we don't go there. We don't have to because for that moment, you were already there, with us and for us.'
(Yvonne Newbold is the author of *The Special Parent's Handbook*, published in 2014.)

This powerful piece clearly sets out the treadmill effect that is often felt by families when accessing healthcare. It also offers solutions, stating that in order to get it right all health professionals need to:

- take time to be with the person with a learning disability and their families to understand their lived experiences

- pick up not only on what is said, but also what is not said, and avoid hurrying the interaction.

Getting support and care right

Getting support and care right is not easy, and ensuring that health professionals effectively engage and interact with families and those who love and know the child/person with a learning disability is central to making sure the interaction and outcomes are helpful, accurate and appropriate. Hollins and Hollins (2005), both parents of an adult son who has a learning disability, highlight the need, as did Yvonne, to first of all listen to parents and other people who love the child or young person. It is vital to remember that doctors and nurses frequently see and get to know a child for a very small number of minutes or hours in any year. Compare that with the amount of time that family members spend together. Hollins and Hollins ask, who, then, are the experts? It cannot be the health professionals alone. Health professionals must therefore strive to create a strong trusting relationship with families. This requires health professionals to really adopt what Yvonne referred to earlier.

Sometimes families are considered difficult. A so-called 'difficult' family is one who doesn't yet trust health professionals, perhaps because they have had bad experiences with health professionals in the past.

More than a diagnosis

Another element that should be central for health professionals is to always be mindful that there is more to the child or young person than their medical diagnosis. Human development involves emotional adjustments for every child and every parent, whether a child is disabled or not. Every individual responds, reacts and interacts in a unique way to difference. Health professionals will be able to help with these adjustments by respecting and supporting the person with a learning disability and families to face any difficulties they are experiencing (Hollins & Hollins, 2005). They should make efforts to about find out about the person; who they are, what they like, what they can do and how they contribute to family and social life.

Learning to listen

Words such as 'respect' and 'empower' give some sense of what should be central to the relationship between healthcare professionals, people with learning disabilities and their families. One part of empowering people is to equip them with the tools to understand what is happening to them in 'this place, at this time, with these caregivers'. This might include information but, even more importantly, it includes helping them to share their hopes and their fears in whatever way they can. The Books Beyond Words series tell stories about many health and social care experiences and can be a powerful way of restoring confidence and hope for people who find pictures easier to understand than words.

In the beginning, the fight

At the start of life with a child with a learning disability it can feel like your life is no longer your own. Stephanie illustrates this clearly and explores a way through it here.

'In the early days I fought against the system, I fought against the fact that suddenly your life was not your own, that even 18-year-old student nurses could sit and read notes about your child that you were not allowed to look at. Lives on view for all to see, every emotion, every outburst.

The first lesson I learnt was that when your child is really complicated and has a really rare condition then medicine becomes no more than educated guesswork. The doctors don't have all the answers, the ones you respect are the ones who will admit that they don't know what to do and will work with you to find out.

The internet becomes your best friend and your enemy. You spend hours trawling through case studies, trying to find the answer that will help your child. Believe me, as time goes by you don't go to the internet anymore. It does not have all the answers; your child is unique and while the internet will give you pointers there are no guarantees that treatments that work for others will work for your child.

You do not have to be alone. It took me a long time to realise that. And by talking and opening up to other parents who have walked your path you can gain the benefit of their experience, what they did that worked, what they wished they had done.

I have learned time and time again that it is important to have a good relationship with the doctors treating your child. You don't have to like them, but you have to work with them. I have learned over the years that doctors really do care, even the ones that appear not to, some of them don't have the best bedside manner; some are very arrogant. Yes, they can go home and switch off, but they all have your child's best interests at heart and sometimes their views will clash with yours.

This is why taking another person along to meetings, involving a support group, an intermediary, the PALs [patient advice and liaison] *service is so important, because at the time in your life when you are dealing with the most extreme of emotions and are so terrified that you may lose your child, you also have to be calm, rational and efficient.'*
(Stephanie Nimmo)

Open partnerships

Sue, whose son, Darrell, is 18 years old with a great sense of humour, Down's syndrome, severe learning disabilities, physical disability, and a variety of complex health and behavioural issues, suggests that parents and health professionals should work in open partnership:

'As a parent, I would like to see health professionals who see their role as a joint partnership with the parent/carer, to be open when a parent suggests what they think is wrong with their child and looking into those concerns. All people are

different and react differently, so do people with learning disability, which is why we need staff in our NHS who can adapt to all our children: one may need space and another may need a lot of interaction. Understand we may have already had the biggest struggle just getting to the appointment, so go easy on us. I have already witnessed over the years how a little banter goes a long way and welcome this with open arms – sometimes we need to laugh to escape the harsh reality.'
(Sue Morris)

The need for confident parenting and confident staff

Many parents feel the key to good care and health outcomes is for them and staff to be confident. This is clearly set out in the following piece by Simon.

'Scarlett is now approaching her 11th birthday, and over those 11 years we have clocked up a whole range of experiences and emotions with the National Health Service. Human nature means that all the early trauma of a premature birth and emerging reality of our darling daughter having global development delay, a hole in her heart and hypothyroidism have faded, and we are able to, for the most part, stay in the present and not think too far ahead or reflect on the past. She's a very happy, confident little girl who loves people and we feel very blessed.

From our early experience of the medical world trying to support Scarlett, we realised the importance we as parents play in ensuring the quality of care she gets. We have found that we need to be on the front foot and asking the questions and making reasonable requests to ensure the often traumatic experience of hospital treatments goes as well as possible.

Confident parenting and confident staff can make a huge difference to the experience. Where we see the best experience is where Scarlett and I are known and staff communicate well in terms of what adjustments can be made, waiting time expectations and positively engaging with Scarlett rather than through me – taking the time to connect with Scarlett as an anxious little girl rather than as just the next patient. At times I have wondered if they even noticed her or her wheelchair. Eye contact even with me isn't guaranteed at 'check in'.

Our experiences have been very mixed and there has been very little if any 'flagging' [alerts denoting a person has a learning disability placed on the medical records of the person so that adjustments can be made] *to date, which I feel would make a huge difference to us.*

We've had to wait three hours in A&E when Scarlett can't sit still for two minutes; I've had my head x-rayed trying to hold Scarlett's leg still as she freaked out in a cold, dark room; we've had a nurse try to get her to read the board in an eye test when she can't speak or understand the task; and we've waited 90 minutes before the staff realised that her notes were still at the main reception. This was despite my regular request for an update.

But then we've had amazing experiences at hospital when she has her bloods taken – a procedure that could be hugely traumatic, but the nurses are amazing with Scarlett. Once we get into the system and are with consultants and nursing staff who are self-confident and take time to connect with Scarlett, things are 100 times better for all concerned.

One area the majority of clinical staff we have experienced seem to find it hard to relate to, no matter how experienced, is what it's like journeying through life with a child with physical and learning disabilities. It's exhausting. It challenges all relationships in the family unit. It's relentless. It can feel claustrophobic and it can feel very lonely as the rest of the world gets on regardless. Medical appointments often bring all these emotions together. Even after 11 years I still dread them and try my upmost for Scarlett not to pick up on this.'
(Simon Hawtrey-Woore)

What needs to change?

Simon has also identified what change is needed:

- *'More regular training to build confidence in, and improve awareness of learning disabilities – if in doubt ask, don't judge.*

- *More opportunities for those with learning disabilities to work in the organisation.*

- *More training around effective communication with patients and parents with learning disabilities.*

- *Allow more time in the process/system at key moments in the patient pathway – taking time to connect, build trust and work out the best way to communicate is key to successful experiences.*

- *Ask how best to communicate and check in at regular intervals to maintain the connection/trust.*

- *Flag the person's disability and individual needs ahead of time, all the time, and communicating the difference it makes to parents and patients – it is not just another process or form; it really does make a difference!*

■ *Think about the context / background of the individual, rather than just seeing the person as the next name on the list – for most patients and parents simply travelling to and from the hospital or GP surgery is a big ordeal.*

■ *Support parents with what questions to ask and what to look for / expect – never assume that because some guide has been issued it has reached the parents or patients, is in the right format or has been read.*

And finally …

■ *Encourage parent responsibility and support of the clinical staff to help them make connections and communicate effectively with the patient. Emotions run high but a quality care experience is a 'partnership' between staff, parent and patient – it's not an entitlement.'*

When health professionals get it right

Health professionals, as Simon and other parents have outlined, can get it right.

The following is Hayley's experience of being in hospital and the care and support provided by a learning disability nurse. This example illustrates what happens when health professionals get care right.

'Our youngest daughter, Natty, is eight and has Down's syndrome, and it was only through a chance meeting at a conference that I met and learned about the role of learning disability nurses. I immediately made the false assumption that these professionals were on standby to help adults in need of support, and it was only when our daughter was admitted for a routine tonsil and adenoid operation some months later, that I began to wonder if they might be able to help younger patients and their families too.

The team were only too pleased to help and I received a call at home to talk me through my concerns ahead of our daughter's surgery. I was able to explain my worries about the little patient's phobia of needles and numbing creams, and her lack of understanding about why she might have to wait long periods of time without eating on the day of her operation. The nurse was able to liaise with the anaesthetist to arrange skipping the pre-med and also advised surgical teams that our daughter should go to theatre as early as possible on the day to avoid uncomfortable situations that she would not be able to deal with mentally.

Not only were these practical matters addressed with ease, but I found someone who understood my fears and worries as a mum, who realised that even minor surgery conjures up memories of more serious surgery in the past, and that however many times our little ones battle on, it doesn't get any easier for parents. Even my emotional tears on the phone were accepted and eased. My fears were taken seriously and eased considerably, just by having someone with the right experience to lean on. A member of the team made sure to visit us while the surgery was taking place too and we chatted that awful time away.

Learning disability nurses play an invaluable role in hospitals. They remove fear and they make sure procedures and stays go as smoothly as possible. They translate between the families and the consultants, surgeons and managers, as well as being a vital mouthpiece to communicate the needs of those with learning disabilities.

(Hayley Goleniowska is the founder of Down Side Up and has authored many publications, including Fink Cards, which are discussed later)

Usual rules don't apply

Mary and her husband have three children, one of whom has severe learning disability, autism, behaviours that challenge, mobility difficulties and other health needs. Mary sets out why usual rules do not apply and that health professionals necessarily have to think differently when working with people with learning disabilities.

'Our disabled son, Alex, does not look disabled at first glance, but although he is now 15 years old, developmentally he is three, and his language and communication younger than that. He also weighs 15 stone and is nearly 5 feet 5 inches tall.

Health professionals need to understand children and young people like our son better, and what high quality integrated services should look like for them. Normal rules about diet, expectations of co-operation and so on do not apply. Their needs as a whole person have to be at the centre of planning and understanding. This has to include how they can access health services, including the need for a highly preventative approach, given the range of physical and other health challenges they face and will face in the future, including from obesity.

We first came to the children's hospital many years ago to seek help from the feeding team because a combination of health issues and autism meant Alex had developed extreme problems eating that were affecting him and our family greatly. The team were very understanding and supportive, and have worked with us to support Alex to widen his range of foods and support weight management. We feel very supported as a family because they care for all the family and they understand Alex very well.

We have recently met the learning disability nurse lead, to resolve practical problems about Alex getting a blood test. As he has got older, bigger and stronger, we are struggling more than ever to get support and understanding in local services for these basic needs. We do not have these problems for our other two non-disabled children. Working with the children's hospital has helped our family, as there is immediate understanding of the issues; we do not have to beg for help or explain Alex's needs because they are understood. This has helped us to have less stress and worry, and we can feel more confident about ensuring that basic health needs for Alex are addressed now and in the future.'
(Mary Busk)

Being confident and being less stressed are core central components of life for everyone, but for parents of a child with a learning disability, it can be very hard. Parents can help each other and can also guide health professionals as to how they too can have a positive impact when talking to new parents, such as those of children with Down's syndrome.

Talking about Down's syndrome: conversations for new parents

Fink Cards, cards that can be used to assist understanding and generate discussion, created by Hayley Goleniowska (2015) are a powerful way to initiate conversations that may be difficult to start. 'Congratulations on the birth of your new baby,' is the emphatic welcome message from Hayley to other parents of newly diagnosed babies with Down's syndrome. Sadly all too often these are not the words that health professionals utter when giving news to parents that their child has Down's syndrome. The reality is that it is only an extra chromosome, so keep calm and carry on; yet society still conjures up visions of a future with little or no hope, worth or purpose for those individuals with Down's syndrome. How very wrong this is.

How health professionals give news is vital, and all too often the news that a baby has Down's syndrome is not given in a positive, supportive, fact-based, humanitarian and focused manner. This is why the more that health professionals know about Down's syndrome the better. But it is also why a learning disability nurse, as numerous parents advocate, must be more involved in delivering this news, since they are best placed to give a fuller, reality-based account of what Down's syndrome means as a child grows up and evolves into an adult than other professionals who are not solely qualified to work with people with learning disabilities.

Having Down's syndrome does not define who Hayley's daughter Natty is; just in the same way that not having Down's syndrome does not define her other daughter, Mia. Bob's (Hayley's husband and the father of both children) matter of fact approach that all would be fine is not what is usually experienced or expressed by other parents.

These cards – along with the excellent website www.downssideup.com set up by Hayley to enable new parents to see that life will go on – provides vital tips, stories, inspiration and love from her family to others. The cards are separated out into sections:

- **Conversations for new parents** – containing tips about how to use the cards, their purpose and very personal supportive messages from Hayley from her own lived experiences.

- **Your baby** – offers questions for parents to consider, such as, 'Can you describe your baby in three words?' 'Does Down's syndrome define your baby?' And, 'Have you kept your baby's first outfit?' These questions, along with others, can be extremely helpful for new parents to make sense of the world they have entered, which is, for many, not the one they once contemplated. They could also enable health and social care professionals to gain a small insight into what is helpful support for parents of babies with Down's syndrome, since it was created by a parent for other parents.

- **Diagnosis and health** – with questions such as, 'Do other members of the family feel the same as you about your baby's diagnosis?' And, 'What were your first thoughts when you were told your baby has Down's syndrome?' These cards get to the point quickly and in a focused manner.

- **Support** – asks questions such as, 'Who do you talk to about your fears and worries?' And 'Have you been told about any support groups?' These illustrate how essential it is for new parents as well as health professionals to consider why sharing and support are so pivotal to the early (as well as all) stages of having a child with Down's syndrome.

- **Life and relationships** – asks, 'Have you discovered any new friends since your baby was born?' 'Do people sometimes say things that hurt your feelings?' And, 'How has your relationship with your partner changed since the birth of your baby?' These and other such searching questions get straight to the core of the issues facing new parents and these cards provide a thought-provoking but neutral way of creating a space for individual and familial thoughts.

The Fink Cards are an extremely refreshing way for professionals to ensure that they get it right when meeting with and interacting with parents who have a child with Down's syndrome. These cards acknowledge that each parent and family member will feel differently when they hear the diagnosis of Down's syndrome for the first time.

The cards would be very useful for health professionals during their training to assist them in enabling attitudinal change and positive practices to flourish that cherish each child, young person and adult. Books Beyond Words can also be very helpful, especially when preparing a person with a learning disability to go into hospital.

Preparing someone with a learning disability to go into hospital

Preparing people with learning disabilities and their families, carers and supporters to go to hospital is not easy, but there is a useful guide available on the NHS Choices website (see the Useful resources and websites section at the end of the chapter). The Books Beyond Words publication *Going into Hospital* (Hollins *et al*, 2015) also includes two stories of people with a learning disability going into hospital and their experiences of what happens. The stories are told through pictures, to enable people with a learning disability, who may read through pictures rather than words, to develop – with the help of a person who knows them well – their understanding of what is likely to happen in hospital. At the back of the book there are tips and guides to getting the right care in hospital, which will prove helpful to people with a learning disability as well as those supporting them. The Beyond Words website also provides a wealth of information about a variety of health issues in an accessible format (see www. booksbeyondwords.co.uk). These materials can assist in getting things right for people with a learning disability.

How healthcare and support workers can get things right for people with a learning disability accessing healthcare

- Beware of missing serious illness – don't ignore medical symptoms by assuming they are part of the person's disability. Act quickly!

- Find the best way to communicate – with the person, their families, carers, friends. Not everyone speaks, so use photos, signs, symbols, accessible publications such as the Books Beyond Words series, and pictures alongside speech.

- The person, their family and carers are experts – they can help interpret signs and behaviours that may show distress or pain.

- Read and act on the hospital or health passport – these provide vital information about a person's needs.

- Assessing someone's capacity to consent to treatment is dependent on time, decision and topic.

- Make reasonable adjustments – for example, by finding someone a quieter place to wait and to be seen in, or by minimising waiting times

(Blair, 2013)

In order to ensure care is adjusted to meet a person with learning disabilities' specific needs a TEACH approach, first developed in Hertfordshire by the Community Learning Disability Team, is required:

Time – take time to work with the person.

Environment – alter the environment to meet the person's needs, for example, by providing quieter areas, reducing lighting and minimising waiting times.

Attitude – have a positive, solutions-orientated focus.

Communication – find out the best way to communicate with the person and their family, carers and supporters, and also communicate this to colleagues.

Help – consider what help the person and their family, carers and supporters need, and how can you meet these needs.

Conclusion

We can never know what it is like to see through another person's eyes completely, but health professionals must seek to gain a clear picture of how it is for people with a learning disability, their families, carers and supporters. The most effective change and help is often created by those with lived experience. Too frequently health and social care professionals choose not to appreciate what a wealth of knowledge, understanding and expertise parents have. It is only through really engaging parents, families and people with learning disabilities in the education of health and social care professionals, service planning, design and evaluation will we truly experience services that are effective, responsive, well led, safe and caring.

Summary points

Every person is an individual and unique. Each interaction and contact has to count. Health professionals do need to think differently and act creatively together with the person with a learning disability and their families. In order to get care right, health professionals need to:

- Dedicate time to being with the person with a learning disability and their families to tune into their lived experiences.

- Take a whole person approach, not just looking at the diagnosis.

- Tap into how the person with a learning disability communicates, interacts and usually is.

- Listen to parents and other people who love the child, young person or adult.

- Invest time and energy, not just for the moment but for the future as well.

- Pick up on what is and is not said and avoid hurrying the interaction.

References

Blair J (2013) Everybody's life has worth: getting it right in hospital for people with an intellectual disability and reducing clinical risks. *Clinical Risk* **19** 58–63.

Goleniowska H (2015) *Talking about Down's Syndrome: Conversations for new parents by Fink Cards*.

Hollins S & Hollins M (2005) *You and your child: making sense of learning disabilities*. London: Karnac Books.

Hollins S, Avis A, Cheverton S & Blair J (2015) *Going into Hospital*. London: Books Beyond Words.

Newbold Y (2014) *The Special Parent's Handbook*. Poole: Amity Books by CMP (UK).

Useful websites and resources

British Institute of Learning Disabilities (BILD) www.bild.org.uk
The institute helps develop the organisations that provide services, and the people who give support.

Books Beyond Words www.booksbeyondwords.co.uk
Publishes accessible stories in pictures to help people with learning and communication disabilities explore and understand their own experiences.

Disability Matters www.disabilitymatters.org.uk
An e-learning resource to enhance understanding and skills of staff.

Down's Side Up www.downsideup.com
Gently changing perceptions of Down's Syndrome.

Easyhealth www.easyhealth.org.uk
Provides over 250 free accessible leaflets, health guides and videos.

Mencap http://www.bacdis.org.uk/policy/documents/Gettingitright.pdf
A group of organisations working towards better healthcare, well-being and quality of life for people with a learning disability.

NHS Choices, *Going into Hospital with a Learning Disability* http://www.nhs.uk/Livewell/Childrenwithalearningdisability/Pages/Going-into-hospital-with-learning-disability.aspx
Information on preparing a person with a learning disability for hospital.

University of Hertfordshire http://www.intellectualdisability.info/
Understanding learning disability and health

Other useful reading

Blair J (2015) *To Know or Not to Know: Being alert – why it helps to know in advance if your next patient has a learning disability.* Available at: http://theqni.tumblr.com/post/129772074291/to-know-or-not-to-know-being-alert-why-it-helps

Blair J (2015) *Changing Culture, Shaping Care: Getting care right for people with learning disabilities.* Available at: http://theqni.tumblr.com/post/126087501176/changing-culture-shaping-care-getting-care-right

Blair J (2012) Caring for people who have intellectual disabilities – in A and E. *Emergency Nurse* **20** (6) 15–19.

Goleniowska M & Goleniowska H (2014) *I Love You Natty: A sibling's uplifting introduction to Down's syndrome*. Cornwall: Down Side Up. Available at: www. downsideup.com

Disability Matters e-learning course 'Caring for Parent Carers Matters'
The session gives insight into better understanding the needs of parent carers and the importance of supporting parent carers, informally and formally via carers assessments.

Chapter 19: Improving hospital experiences: a case study

Marian Marsham and Jane Hart

Introduction

It is fair to say that a high percentage of us do not like hospitals. Some of us may find that even just the smell can make us feel unwell. We are faced with a strange environment, which is daunting. We may feel alone and nervous. We may find it difficult to take in what is being said to us, as we are probably more preoccupied with worrying about what will happen next. Added to this is the fact that we are not feeling very well or are in pain.

Some who may be struggling to cope independently, or who are socially isolated, may view hospital as a comparatively preferable environment which meets their psychological, social and emotional needs, as well as alleviating physical symptoms. This can result in reluctance to actively participate in treatment, or even to be discharged when well. For the majority, though it is a lonely, frightening experience, where that feeling of 'just wanting to go home' is very powerful.

Unplanned admissions to hospital are confusing for anyone, and even more so for those who lack knowledge about what is wrong with them. It is hard for anyone not to feel vulnerable in this complex, unfamiliar environment. For people with learning disabilities, making sense of this experience is even harder. Communication is key to making people feel less vulnerable, and having the support of a learning disability nurse can save time, facilitate better access to investigations and treatment, and help co-ordinate the care needed for each individual.

Part of the role of health professionals is to ensure that the care of the patient is holistic and person-centred, meaning that the individual's needs are considered as a whole and are the central focus of the caring relationship, which must be empathic and non-judgemental. In this chapter we will reflect on our work with local hospital staff to improve patient experiences, which has led to strategies to ensure good practice. The authors both work within the complex physical health nursing team, which is part of the community learning disability team. Over the past two years a collaborative pathway between the community learning disability team and the learning disability nurse in the local acute hospital has been developed (see Appendix 1 which shows the collaborative pathway and Initial CLDT assessment tool: urgent acute care admission).

The service is set up to respond to any person with a learning disability who has an unplanned admission to acute care with the aim of them being treated and discharged home as soon as possible. Reasonable adjustments are then made where needed to make their experience as nice as possible, ensure they receive the right treatment, ensure a safe discharge home with follow up in the community and avoid re-admission where possible.

We have heard in the previous chapters about the impact of health inequalities and the need for reasonable adjustment. There is a general vulnerability of people with learning disabilities who are admitted to hospital, and the specific risks that they may face (Heslop *et al*, 2013; Mencap, 2007; 2012; Michael, 2008; National Patient Safety Agency, 2004).

Research has highlighted the need to consider the following core themes:

- Difficulties in communication.

- Diagnostic overshadowing leading to delayed or inappropriate treatment (where the symptoms of ill-health are wrongly attributed to the person's learning disabilities).

- Assumptions about quality of life and resuscitation decisions.

- The Mental Capacity Act (2005) as there is still non-compliance in some institutions. One should always assume a person has capacity until proven otherwise. Following the act, a mental capacity assessment should be carried out and if the person is deemed to lack capacity then an agreement should be made in the person's best interests.

- The role of families and paid carers, and the working relationship with ward and medical staff.

In practical terms people attending hospital for a planned admission can be offered pre-assessments, time to discuss pre-admission preparation and planning (which is not possible in the case of emergency admission) as part of reasonable adjustment. The value of having an acute care liaison nurse based in every hospital, is an initiative not yet introduced at all hospitals or well-resourced in others. Therefore, it is important for anyone involved in caring for a person with learning disabilities to develop skills to support effective access to hospital care and that reasonable adjustment is made (see Appendix 2).

Reasonable adjustments

A national survey of reasonable adjustments made for people with learning disabilities reported that 55 acute trusts (95%) made use of liaison staff with a specific role in providing health facilitation (Hatton *et al*, 2011).

The proportion of admissions to general hospitals which happen as emergencies are substantially larger for people with learning disabilities than for those who do not have learning disabilities (Emerson *et al*, 2011). Having the early involvement of a learning disability nurse would help flag up this vulnerable group for adjustments to be made which can be written into a care plan in order to meet individual needs in a timely fashion.

Case Study: Rohan

Rohan was taken to hospital by ambulance with respiratory failure and was admitted to the ICU, the community learning disability nurse attended the same day and completed the initial CLDT assessment – the urgent acute care admission (this assessment tool can be found at the end of the chapter). The learning disability nurse was able to provide the ICU staff with all the relevant information about Rohan's history, his baseline, likes and dislikes. Rohan has a diagnosis of moderate learning disabilities with anxiety disorder. Following a risk and support assessment, familiar staff were funded to support him for an allocated number of hours where ward staff were unable to cover and manage risks, support staff talked to him and reassured him to alleviate his fears and anxiety as he was not able to communicate during the time he was intubated. A learning disability nurse worked with Rohan and nurses in intensive care during extubation and weaning him off the trachea and sedation. Over a period of six months staff supported him to access the therapy and rehabilitation he required to get him back to his baseline and eventually home. In some situations we have seen hospital staff struggle to deal with a person refusing treatment and unable to deal with increased anxiety and the person ends up being discharged prematurely as being non-compliant. On this occasion, joint working with hospital staff enabled Rohan to have the outcome he wanted, the opportunity to receive therapies to aid his rehabilitation, which enabled him to get back to his baseline and have a safe discharge home. He remained open to the CLDT to support him with follow up outpatient appointments and annual health check, and implementing a health action plan to avoid any further admissions to acute care.

Making decisions

Every person with a learning disability needs to be involved in decisions made about their life, which includes their health and management of treatment, as far as possible. All involved in their care have a responsibility to assess capacity when making decisions. The main carers are key individuals in the assessment process as they have knowledge of the person's abilities in order to assist the team in reaching decisions around capacity. In addition, they also have a key role in supporting the individual with the decisions they make, or to support their best interests. In the absence of a carer or family member advocating for the person with a learning disability it is a good idea to refer them for an Independent Mental Capacity Advocate (IMCA). An IMCA can help people with important decisions about serious medical treatment or moving to a hospital or care home, and may become involved in other types of decision such as care reviews and adult protection.

Another issue to consider is if the person has capacity to make informed decisions. The Mental Capacity Act (2005) is a law which offers protection to people who are unable to make decisions. Central to this act is that people are assumed to be able to make decisions for themselves unless it is proved otherwise.

Sadly, there are still those in health and social care who fail to understand and routinely adhere to the Mental Capacity Act (2005) (see chapter 5). A key role of the learning disabilities nurse is to help facilitate the mental capacity act (MCA) process and help to implement the act for people with learning disabilities who lack capacity. Not adhering to the act can have a detrimental impact on a person's care. People are still dying in avoidable circumstances due to institutional failings to properly investigate, diagnose and treat people with learning disabilities to the same extent as other people (Heslop *et al*, 2013).

Case study: Adam

Prior to his first admission to hospital with respiratory failure Adam was a fit and healthy individual who had a really good quality of life, enjoying meeting up with his family, horse riding, shopping and going out for meals. An x-ray revealed a blockage/swelling in the trachea. Initially Adam was not considered for further investigation or possible surgery as the consultant deemed he lacked capacity to consent. There was no MCA assessment and it was assumed Adam would not understand or tolerate the proposed investigations/operation and, once medically fit, was discharged home for follow up with GP. Unfortunately Adam had a further episode of respiratory failure and paramedics had to resuscitate him. During this admission the LD nurse facilitated a meeting to provide clarity for clinicians and other stakeholders to follow the MCA in order that a best interest's decision could be made on how to proceed with his current health needs and re-admissions. The ward had also placed a Do Not Attempt Resuscitation (DNAR) on his file. A meeting was held which included hospital staff, family and other professionals involved in Adams care (nursing, physiotherapy, speech and language therapy). The decision reached by all was that with the right support and adjustments Adam would be able to tolerate the investigations. The DNAR was also reconsidered and removed from his file and it was agreed that Adam would want full escalation of care. The investigations carried out were important for an early diagnosis of a rare condition, which resulted in Adam receiving the appropriate treatment from a specialist in the form of surgery to remove the growth blocking his airway. This proved to have a good outcome for Adam, reducing further admissions for a life threatening condition that could have otherwise gone untreated and put Adam at risk of death. He is now back to his usual self, home and enjoying his social life.

Working with hospital staff

Effective partnership working across agencies can often prove difficult. There is a need for more close collaborative working across agencies. For this to happen more needs to be done to identify and meet training needs (learning disabilities awareness training) in order to provide effective care and treatment and challenge institutional discriminatory views as set out in the 'Getting it Right' campaign (Mencap, 2010). There is a need to improve the way that services are delivered in order that a range of different needs can be met.

As part of the collaborative pathway mentioned earlier emergency department care plans for those people with learning disabilities who were frequent or complex attenders to acute care were developed and implemented within the service. These care plans helped to speed up the learning disabilities care pathway to reduce unnecessary delays in investigations and extended admissions. One patient who was a frequent attender had such a care plan put in place as he would often be admitted to a ward due to possible aspiration pneumonia, normally caused by his percutaneous endoscopic gastrostomy (PEG) becoming dislodged and wrongly positioned. His feed and medication would be stopped via PEG until further investigations had taken place. During the waiting time for results he would become hungry, agitated and seizure activity would take place causing him to be unwell and extend his stay. The emergency department care plan states that he is to be fast tracked to have x-rays to see if his chest is clear and whether the PEG is in place, in order to diagnose the underlying problem for his visit to acute care. If he had a chest infection this was treated with antibiotics and if the PEG was dislodged it was repositioned so that he could continue with his feed and medication and be discharged home without any admission to a ward. This plan gave the hospital and young man the outcome everyone wanted; a quick diagnosis and discharge home, avoiding admission to a ward.

Effective care co-ordination can involve large multidisciplinary teams, therefore it is paramount that one named person should have the responsibility of looking at the individual's health problems, health inequalities and any diagnostic overshadowing. We should listen to the family and carer who know the person better than anyone. In our experience, involving them and encouraging the medical team to actually meet the person and their support network has proved beneficial to all; allowing them to have some insight into the person's quality of life, the special personal qualities they have and an opportunity to develop a rapport.

Part of the assessment looks at the support a person will need during their stay. Sometimes family/carers can provide this but it should not be expected. A useful tool is the Risk, Dependency and Support Assessment for Patients with a Learning Disability by the HFT (2008). This will highlight if additional support, above and beyond the norm, is required. If it is, this will usually be funded by the hospital. The most appropriate person to provide this care can be identified to support the patient and their family when they are at their most vulnerable. In our experience, the biggest obstacle to working together well is the attitude of some staff and their lack of understanding learning disability. A parent once said 'my child's biggest handicap was the attitude of professionals around them'. Part of our role is to foster positive approaches to providing care and treatment, to help people work together. As healthcare professionals, communication is paramount, as set out in the 6 C's: Care, Compassion, Competence, Communication, Courage and Commitment (Cummings & Bennett 2012). Communication is central to successful caring relationships and to effective team working. Listening is as important as what we say and do. Communication is the key to a good workplace, with benefits for those in our care and staff alike.

Case study: Barbara

Barbara is a woman in her 30s with a severe learning disability living at home with her sister, who was referred to the CLDT for nursing intervention due to having had more than 30 hospital admissions in four years. Prior to this referral, Barbara had not been known to the team. Views of the ward staff were that the family were not coping with looking after Barbara at home. The families' views were Barbara's re-admissions were due to poor discharges home with no planning/communication from ward staff or recommended follow up in the community. The learning disabilities nurse found that

Barbara had had some bad experiences in hospital and with discharges home. The family were signposted to the Patient Advice and Liaison Service to avoid further distress. Over the past year the learning disabilities nurse has worked with Barbara, her family and day services, liaising with her GP, ward staff and matrons. The GP has had regular contact with Barbara and her family along with the CLDT and there are no concerns about the care being provided at home. The learning disabilities nurse influenced the team into not just treating the initial reason for admissions (UTI/dehydration/seizures) but also convinced medics to carry out further investigations to pursue the underlying problem. Barbara now has three new diagnoses; stage 3 kidney disease (fluids increased and being monitored), type 2 diabetes (attends diabetic clinic/medication reviews/blood glucose monitoring), myelodysplasia (attends OPA/Bloods to monitor low platelet levels/observation). Barbara's health is now being safely managed in the community. Barbara has not had an admission for some months and is not expected to be admitted in the near future. This could be attributed to considering the whole picture and overall pattern of a person's illnesses.

Below are examples of what can help make hospital experiences better for people with learning disabilities:

- The person having a completed a hospital passport/traffic light assessment (history, baseline, likes and dislikes).

- Health action plan which holds current information about the person's needs (in grab pack on arrival in emergency department).

- Making individualised reasonable adjustments to improve outcomes e.g. early diagnosis and treatment.

- Providing Easy Read information for person, carers and family to understand their experience. These may include information about procedures, medication, the ward etc.

- Liaising with ward staff/multidisciplinary team, holding reviews when needed.

- Listening to the person/family/carers.

- Recognising and utilising the knowledge and expertise of the person/family/carers.

- Every hospital to have a LD liaison nurse.

- Learning disability awareness training for all staff.

- Resource pack for Drs/medics.

- Understanding the Mental Care Act and process.

- Co-ordination of care and information sharing.
- Reducing multiple transitions between wards.

Getting extra help

There needs to be efforts to reduce the amount of incidents of poor practice reported and improve and enhance the quality of care received by people with learning disabilities. If a patient, carer, staff or a family member feels ignored, they should talk to a learning disabilities nurse and/or ward staff. If possible speak to the senior/named nurse and ask for feedback from the Dr's rounds, handovers and the rationale for any decisions made. Families and carers often find it difficult to challenge professionals. Do not be afraid to ask for extra help. There are always issues to iron out so talk to somebody; it will help in getting hospital care right for all people with learning disabilities. If this issue still cannot be resolved the PALS team based at the hospital can be contacted with any complaints/concerns or safeguarding issues.

Discharge planning

Holding a discharge planning meeting is essential and plays a major part in getting someone home safely with the follow up care needed. In a busy work environment meetings can be seen as time consuming, however if you make sure that all parties involved in that person's care are invited to contribute, it will save you time in the long run and hopefully avoid the person being re-admitted. If key people are unable to attend it is important their views are sought and they are asked to contribute. Experience has shown that planning helps in reducing re-admissions and ensures the person feels safe during the transition back home. If the person's needs change and their discharge is delayed, hold another meeting (this may not take as long as the first). You will be surprised how the plan may need to change to accommodate their new needs and to spot solutions not even considered before.

Discharge planning and follow up in community: Top tips from practice

- Involve multidisciplinary team (carers, physio, speech and language therapist, consultants, occupational therapy, care manager/social services care package) and the person who will be the initial main carer on arrival home to be present at the meeting, so they can handover to other staff.

- Discharge planning meeting/agenda/checklist.

- Good care planning and recording of decision making process and outcomes.

- Sharing information.

- Ensure all assessments required have been carried out e.g. physio, occupational therapy.

- Speech and language therapist report and copy of discharge report and action plan in place is forwarded to the community team for follow up once home.

- Identify additional needs as early as possible as the person may need an uplift in care package or help finding a home to meet additional needs.

- Evaluate the original plan to see if needs have changed, expect to repeat yourself; re-deliver message over and over.

- Palliative care: working with hospital and community for safe discharge with all equipment/medications needed.

- Obtain a copy of the discharge summary (copy to be given to person, family, carer, CLDT and GP).

- Follow up recommendations on discharge summary in the community.

- Attend out-patient appointments/annual health check-up.

- Inform the person of any medication changes, what it is for and possible side effects.

- Crisis/contingency plan, who to contact, relapse indicators.

Summary points

- Be prepared to repeat information to different ward staff, do not assume it has been handed over.

- Ask questions if unsure.

- Do not be afraid of asking for information in layman's terms.

- Take notes! (If possible take someone with you to take notes.)

- Get a copy of the discharge summary.

- Work to open lines of communication.

- Seek to understand the different points of view.

Conclusion

This chapter looked at how we are trying to improve hospital experiences for people with learning disabilities. One way of achieving this is to work with the staff on the wards to achieve better outcomes for the patient, along the collaborative care pathway, incorporating person-cantered care plans and following the Mental Capacity Act guidance. Communication is key to a positive experience and if it is not effective, it can have a detrimental impact on the patient, carers and families whole experience from arriving at the emergency department to discharge home. We strive to shorten and avoid admissions to acute care by educating and making reasonable adjustments. By continuing to liaise with professionals and assisting in developing their knowledge and confidence in working with people with learning disabilities, we will hopefully help with treating people right, strengthening the commitment and avoiding 'death by indifference' with this vulnerable group of adults.

References

Cummings J & Bennett V (2012) *Compassion in Practice: Nursing, midwifery and care staff – our strategy* [online]. Leeds: NHS Commissioning Board. Available at https://www.england.nhs.uk/wp-content/uploads/2012/12/compassion-in-practice.pdf (accessed October 2016).

Emerson E, Hatton C, Robertson J, Roberts H, Baines S, Evison F & Glover G (2011) *People with Learning Disabilities in England*. Lancaster: Improving Health and Lives/Department of Health.

Hatton C, Roberts H & Baines S (2011) *Reasonable Adjustments for People with Learning Disabilities in England 2010: A national survey of NHS trusts*. London: Improving Health and Lives.

Heslop P, Blair P, Fleming P, Hoghton M, Marriott A & Russ L (2013) *Confidential Inquiry into Premature Deaths of People with Learning Disabilities (CIPOLD): Final report* [online]. Bristol: Norah Fry. Available at: www.bris.ac.uk/media-library/sites/cipold/migrated/documents/fullfinalreport.pdf (accessed October 2016).

Home Farm Trust (2008) *Working Together: Easy steps to improving how people with a learning disability are supported when in hospital* [online]. Available at: http://www.heartofengland.nhs.uk/wp-content/uploads/WorkingTogether.pdf (accessed October 2016).

Mencap (2007) *Death by Indifference*. London: Mencap.

Mencap (2010) *Getting it Right Charter*. London: Mencap.

Mencap (2012) *Death by Indifference: 74 deaths and counting – a progress report 5 years on*. London: Mencap.

Michael J (2008) *Healthcare for All: Report of the Independent Inquiry into Access to Healthcare for People with Learning Disabilities*. London: Aldridge Press.

National Patient Safety Agency (2004) *Understanding the Patient Safety Issues for People with Learning Disabilities*. London: NPSA.

Useful resources

Communications Team
Mental Capacity Implementation Programme
5th Floor, Steel House
11 Tothill Street
London SW1H 9LH
Telephone: 0207 210 0037/0025
Email: makingdecisions@dca.gsi.gov.uk
Website: http://www.dca.gov.uk/legal-policy/mental-capacity/index.htm

Easyhealth.org.uk
73 Summerstown, Tooting London SW17 0BQ
Telephone: 0208 879 6333.
IHAL https://twitter.com/ihal_talk
The latest tweets from **IHAL** (@ihal_talk). Improving Health and Lives – the
Learning Disabilities Team in Public Health England. England.

Mencap
123 Golden Lane
London EC1Y 0RT
Telephone: 020 7454 0454
Fax: 020 7608 3254

Mencap Direct
Telephone: 0808 808 1111
Email: help@mencap.org.uk

Patient advice and liaison services (PALS)
http://www.nhs.uk/Service-Search/Patient-advice-and-liaison-services-(PALS)/
LocationSearch/363

Appendix 1

Collaborative pathway for community learning disability team (CLDT) & learning disability co-ordinator in acute hospital setting

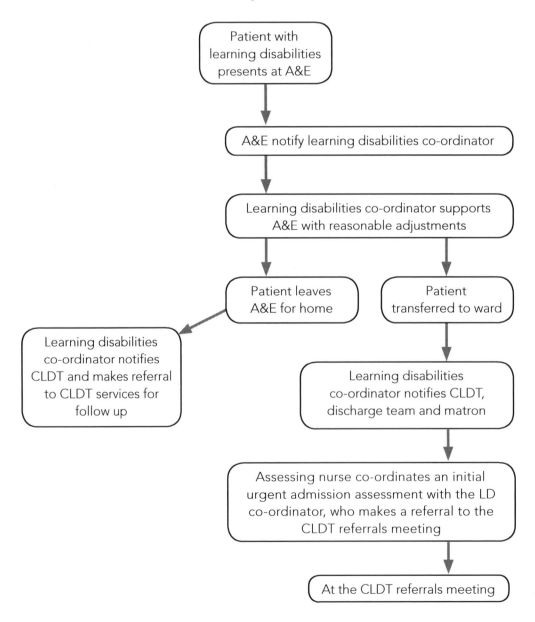

Appendix 1: Continued

Allocation and intervention by the CLDT nurse is decided:

- Reasonable adjustments.
- Liaison with matron/ward team.
- Co-ordinates CLDT involvement.
- Liaison with learning disabilities co-ordinator, provides support with risk assessment.
- Problem solves barriers to discharge.
- Discharge planning.
- Professional joint meeting protocols.
- Follow up and case management.
- Reporting progress to service referrals meeting.

Initial CLDT assessment tool: urgent acute care admission

The initial part of the assessment involves taking basic information, which includes personal details and information about the person's past medical history, looking at previous hospital admissions as well as the current situation, investigations and probable diagnosis. It also prompts people to ask questions about DNAR, continence, eating and drinking, carers support, communication, how the person expresses pain and so forth. The assessing nurse would then action any outcomes, for example updating people involved in the person's care, supporting the person, family, carers and ward staff, co-ordinating meetings, discharge planning and making new referrals.

Initial CLDT Assessment – Urgent Acute Care Admission

Patient:	Information to gain:
DOB:	
Patient's Address:	Date and time of admission:
Assessor:	Date and time of alert to CLDT:
Informant and role:	A&E escort name (if escorted):
Ward seen on:	Reason for admission:
Next of kin/ carer's contact details:	

Information to provide	
1 – ICD coding diagnosis (if known)	Ward(s) since A&E admission:
2 – My next patient series 'Caring for the Patient. Keele University.	Investigations and results:
3 – Traffic light form: Complete or give to carers to complete. To be kept by bedside and cross referenced in medical notes.	Probable diagnosis:
4 – NHS Leaflet: 'Your Next Patient'	Probable treatment:
5 – CLDT poster	Probable discharge:
6 – Write your contact details in medical notes.	Key contact on ward:
7 – Signpost to SLHT consent policy and MCA information.	

Good Practice Issues Checklist:

Ward staff aware of:

If answer no, provide information

Please tick as appropriate

Emotional needs:
- ☐ Person's specific fears, anxieties
- ☐ How to comfort

Communication:
- ☐ Aids used
- ☐ How patient asks for help

Pain:
- ☐ Diagnosis associated with chronic pain
- ☐ How patient expresses pain
- ☐ How patient is managed
- ☐ Need for Disdat 2/Abbey pain scale (if so provide)

DNAR:
- ☐ Decision made is recorded on form
- ☐ Decision fits with clinical presentation

Eating and drinking:
- ☐ Risk of choking
- ☐ Risk of malnutrition
- ☐ Dysphagia assessment required
- ☐ Dietetics assessment required
- ☐ Needs help with menu
- ☐ Needs help with eating and drinking

Toileting:
- ☐ Pads being provided
- ☐ Needs help to locate toilet
- ☐ Needs help to use toilet

CLDT observations:

Immediate actions:

- ☐ Note presentation

- ☐ Insights?

- ☐ Anxieties/fears?

- ☐ Previous hospital experiences

- ☐ Activities to prevent boredom

- ☐ Feel listened to?

- ☐ Recently known to paediatric ward? If so, contact for management advice.

NOTES:

Good Practice Issues Checklist:

Carers role:

- ☐ 1:1 supervision required
- ☐ Any 'working together' issues
- ☐ Carers/ family feel listened to
- ☐ Level of support provided at home
- ☐ Arrangements for breaks, refreshments
- ☐ Supervision and management if carers unavailable
- ☐ Funding issues
- ☐ Care management team informed of admission
- ☐ Patient wants carers to remain

Decision making:

- ☐ MCA consent policy compliance
- ☐ IMCA required
- ☐ Premorbid baseline ability and quality of life

Location:

- ☐ Person's view of ward/room
- ☐ Bed location appropriate
- ☐ Adequate space for mobility aids

CLDT observations:

Immediate actions:

- ☐ Note presentation

- ☐ Insights?

- ☐ Anxieties/fears?

- ☐ Previous hospital experiences

- ☐ Activities to prevent boredom

- ☐ Feel listened to?

- ☐ Recently known to paediatric ward? If so, contact for management advice.

NOTES:

Outcome: (tick)

- ☐ Inform clinical lead for health access
- ☐ Update current workers
- ☐ Other CLDT new referral
- ☐ Care management new referral
- ☐ Discharge coordinator alerted
- ☐ CPH nursing new referral
- ☐ No learning disability/signposted

Appendix 2

Reasonable adjustments

It is a legal requirement of the Equality Act (2010) for services to make reasonable adjustments for people with learning disabilities. This does not just mean hospitals putting in automatic doors and making it wheelchair accessible, it includes offering extended appointment times and looking at alternative strategies like desensitisation work around investigations, for example, needle-phobia. *Healthcare for All* (Michael, 2008) provides 10 recommendations for 'reasonable adjustments' that can be made so that people with learning disabilities are able to access the same healthcare services as the general population.

Recommendation 1

Those with responsibility for the provision and regulation of undergraduate and postgraduate clinical training must ensure that curricula include mandatory training in learning disabilities. It should be competency based and involve people with learning disabilities and their carers in providing training.

Recommendation 2

All healthcare organisations including the Department of Health should ensure that they collect the data and information necessary to allow people with learning disability to be identified by the health service and their pathways of care tracked.

Recommendation 3

Family and other carers should be involved as a matter of course as partners in the provision of treatment and care unless good reason is given, and trust boards should ensure that reasonable adjustments are made to enable and support carers to do this effectively. This will include the provision of information, but may also involve practical support and service co-ordination.

Recommendation 4

Primary care trusts should identify and assess the needs of people with learning disabilities and their carers as part of their Joint Strategic Needs Assessment. They should consult with their Local Strategic Partnership, their Learning Disability Partnership Boards and relevant voluntary user-led learning disability organisations, and use the information to inform the development of Local Area Agreements.

Recommendation 5

To raise awareness in the health service of the risk of premature and avoidable death, and to promote sustainable good practice in local assessment, management and evaluation of services, and the Department of Health should establish a learning disabilities Public Health Observatory. This should be supplemented by a time-limited confidential inquiry into premature deaths in people with learning difficulties to provide evidence for clinical and professional staff of the extent of the problem and guidance on prevention.

Recommendation 6

The Department of Health should immediately amend Core Standards for Better Health to include an explicit reference to the requirement to make 'reasonable adjustments' to the provision and delivery of services for vulnerable groups, in accordance with the disability equality legislation. The framework that is planned to replace these core standards in 2010 should also include a specific reference to this requirement.

Recommendation 7

Inspectors and regulators of the health service should develop and extend their monitoring of the standard of general health services provided for people with learning disabilities, in both the hospital sector and in the community where primary care providers are located. The aim is to support appropriate, reasonable adjustments to general health services for adults and children with learning disabilities and their families and to ensure compliance with and enforcement of all aspects of the Disability Discrimination Act (1995). Healthcare regulators and inspectors (and the Care Quality Commission, once established) should strengthen their work in partnership with each other and with the Commission for Equality and Human Rights, the National Patient Safety Agency and Office for Disability Issues.

Recommendation 8

The Department of Health should direct primary care trusts (PCTs) to secure general health services that make reasonable adjustments for people with learning disabilities through a Directed Enhanced Service. In particular, the Department should direct PCTs to commission enhanced primary care services which include regular health checks provided by GP practices and improve data, communication and cross-boundary partnership working. This should include liaison staff who work with primary care services to improve the overall quality of healthcare for people with learning disabilities across the spectrum of care.

Recommendation 9

Section 242 of the National Health Service Act (2006) requires NHS bodies to involve and consult patients and the public in the planning and development of services, and in decisions affecting the operation of services. All trust boards should ensure that the views and interests of people with learning disabilities and their carers are included.

Recommendation 10

All trust boards should demonstrate in routine public reports that they have effective systems in place to deliver effective, 'reasonably adjusted' health services. This should include arrangements to provide advocacy for all those who need it, and arrangements to secure effective representation on PALs from all client groups including people with learning disabilities.

Useful resources from Pavilion

An Introduction to Supporting the Mental Health of People with Intellectual Disabilities: A guide for professionals, support staff and families *by Eddie Chaplin, Karina Marshall-Tate & Steve Hardy.*
This booklet provides guidance on treating a person with intellectual disability for a mental health problem, adaptations to treatment that may have to be made, and how best to find the right services for an individual with intellectual disabilities and mental health problems.
Available at: https://www.pavpub.com/an-introduction-to-supporting-the-mental-health-of-people-with-intellectual-disabilities/

Taking Control of My Health: A training manual for health and social care staff to deliver a course for people with learning disabilities who have health conditions *by Mary Codling.*
A training manual and CD-rom that will equip workers with the guidance and tools required to deliver a programme for people with learning disabilities, designed to help people with learning disabilities to understand and talk about their health conditions.
Available at: https://www.pavpub.com/taking-control-of-my-health/

Successful Health Screening through Desensitisation for People with Learning Disabilities: A training and resource pack for healthcare professionals *by Lisa Harrington & Sarah Walker.*
This training resource is designed to help people with learning disabilities to successfully access health screening, by desensitising them to fears and anxieties they may have about the process.
Available soon at: https://www.pavpub.com/successful-health-screening-through-desensitisation-for-people-with-learning-disabilities/

How Safe is your Swallow: A practical guide and assessment tool for carers of adults with learning disabilities *by Pamela McIntosh & Lorraine Speirs.*
A practical guide and assessment tool that helps carers determine how safe an individual's swallow is and when to refer to a dietitian or speech and language therapist.
Available at: https://www.pavpub.com/how-safe-is-your-swallow/

The Mental Capacity Act and People with Learning Disabilities: A training pack to develop good practice in assessing capacity and making best interests decisions *by Steve Hardy & Theresa Joyce.*
This training pack introduces the Mental Capacity Act, its principles and associated issues to all staff working with people with learning disabilities.
Available at: https://www.pavpub.com/the-mental-capacity-act-and-people-with-learning-disabilities/

I Can Feel Good: Skills training for people with intellectual disabilities and problems managing emotions *by Bridget Ingamells & Catrin Morrissey.*
A training resource to empower people with mild intellectual disabilities to develop the skills they need to self-soothe and manage emotional distress.
Available at: https://www.pavpub.com/i-can-feel-good/

Guided Self-help for People with Intellectual Disabilities and Anxiety and Depression *edited by Eddie Chaplin.*
This manual can be used as a guided self-help resource for clinical use or to help promote positive mental health for people with intellectual disabilities.
Available at: https://www.pavpub.com/guided-self-help/

Mental Health in Intellectual Disabilities: A reader – fourth edition *by Geraldine Holt, Steve Hardy & Nick Bouras.*
This new and revised edition provides up-to-date information on mental health problems in people with intellectual disabilities and associated issues.
Available at: https://www.pavpub.com/mental-health-in-intellectual-disabilities/

Intellectual Disabilities and Personality Disorder: An integrated approach *by Zillah Webb.*
This handbook gives professionals a framework for understanding and approaching issues that arise when an individual has intellectual disabilities and a personality disorder.
Available at: https://www.pavpub.com/intellectual-disabilities-and-personality-disorder/